FLORIDA
FRUIT & VEGETABLE GARDENING

Plant, Grow, and Harvest
the Best Edibles

Quarto is the authority on a wide range of topics.

Quarto educates, entertains and enriches the lives of our readers—enthusiasts and lovers of hands-on living.

www.quartoknows.com

First published in 2015 by Cool Springs Press, an imprint of Quarto Publishing Group USA Inc., 400 First Avenue North, Suite 400, Minneapolis, MN 55401 USA. Telephone: (612) 344-8100 Fax: (612) 344-8692

quartoknows.com
Visit our blogs at quartoknows.com

Cool Springs Press titles are also available at discounts in bulk quantity for industrial or sales-promotional use. For details write to Special Sales Manager at Quarto Publishing Group USA Inc., 400 First Avenue North, Suite 400, Minneapolis, MN 55401 USA.

Library of Congress Cataloging-in-Publication Data

Bowden, Robert E., author.
  Florida fruit & vegetable gardening : plant, grow, and harvest the best edibles / Robert Bowden.
      pages cm
  Other title: Florida fruit and vegetable gardening
  Includes index.
  ISBN-13: 978-1-59186-614-5
  ISBN 978-1-59186-905-4 (sc)
  1. Gardening—Florida. 2. Fruit—Florida. 3. Vegetable gardening—Florida. I. Title. II. Title: Florida fruit and vegetable gardening.

  SB453.2.F6B68 2015
  635.09759—dc23

                          2014039034

Acquisitions Editor: Mark Johanson
Design Manager: Cindy Samargia Laun
Layout: S. E. Anglin

Printed in China

10 9 8 7 6 5 4 3

FLORIDA
FRUIT & VEGETABLE GARDENING

*Plant, Grow, and Harvest
the Best Edibles*

ROBERT BOWDEN

COOL
SPRINGS
PRESS

Home and Garden Experts

MINNEAPOLIS, MINNESOTA

PHOTO CREDITS

DEDICATION

To my thoughtful and loving wife, Gailann

CONTENTS

Bean	Eggplant	Radish
Beet	English Pea	Rutabaga
Broccoli	Garlic	Spinach
Brussels Sprouts	Kale	Squash
Cabbage	Kohlrabi	Strawberry
Cantaloupe	Lettuce	Summer Pea
Carrot	Mustard	Sweet Potato
Cauliflower	Okra	Swiss Chard
Celery	Onion	Tomato
Collards	Pepper	Turnip
Corn	Potato	Watermelon
Cucumber	Pumpkin	

WELCOME TO GARDENING IN FLORIDA

Growing plants in Florida can be a most rewarding experience. No, let me rephrase that, it's lots of fun. As gardeners, we can till the soil year-round, and the seemingly endless days of sunshine and pleasant weather are the envy of our northern gardening friends. Plant roots enjoy the warm soil throughout the year and their leaves

enjoy bountiful rain in all but a few months in late winter. For those interested in growing vegetables and fruits, Florida is paradise. Cool mornings, balmy days, rainy afternoons— what more could one ask for?

Despite the summer heat, Florida is a great place to learn all about gardening.

North Florida (the area from Pensacola to Jacksonville south to Ocala) experiences a true change of seasons when fall approaches, unlike the peninsula. Leaves turn brilliant shades of red, yellow, and orange, and nighttime temperatures have been known to reach single digits on occasion. The soil is often characterized as a sandy loam with clay in some places, and long-leaf pines and magnificent centurion live oaks dot the landscape. For those moving from more northern climes, areas of North Florida are the most like their former locations. Cold winters, cool springs, balmy summers, and pleasant autumns are the norm. The schedules of vegetable planting and harvesting are most like northern states, and pests and diseases are diminished as a result of winter's cold temperatures. Because of the soil's ability to retain moisture and nutrients, gardeners in North Florida can water less and apply fertilizer less often and in smaller amounts than their neighbors in Central and South Florida.

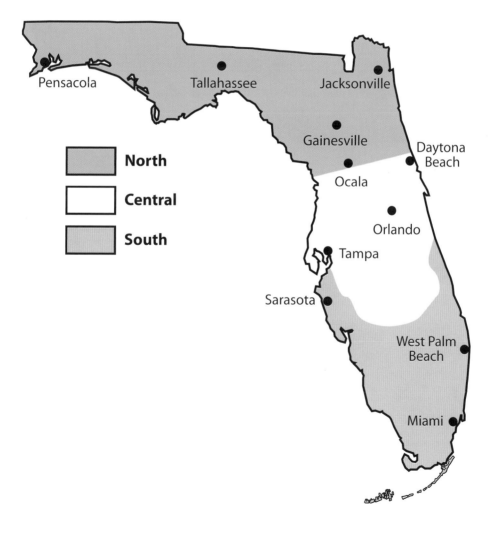

Florida leads the nation in commercial watermelon production. It's a good bet for home gardeners, too.

Determining the correct time to plant vegetables and fruit trees in North Florida is much less complicated than in other areas of the state. Unlike Central and South Florida, where the three and sometimes four seasons can be confusing, there are two seasons in North Florida: winter and summer. Nearly all the summer vegetables can be planted in the spring once the danger of frost has passed to be grown in the nearly ideal conditions of warm days and cool nights. But one crop of winter vegetables planted in the fall often must be protected from severe freezes.

Central Florida (the area from Ocala to Lake Wales) has the best features of both North and South Florida. The soils, although low in nutrients, are sandy and drain well. (There are pockets of muck soils, which are highly organic but poorly drained, but they are the exception.) In the summer, from May to October, daytime temperatures get very hot (95°F) every day and nighttime temperatures rarely drop below 75°F. Autumn is of short duration, from November through December; winter includes January and February; and spring in Central Florida consists of March and April. If you have moved here from a more northern climate, scheduling the planting and harvesting of vegetables will be very confusing. As an example, tomatoes can be planted in the fall and the spring, but they will succumb to winter cold and cannot grow in summer given our extreme summer heat. If you plant tomatoes too late in the fall, the occasional cold snap will kill them. If you plant too late in the spring, the summer heat will make them wish they were dead. That's why the planting table on pages 35 through 37 is so valuable. It takes all the guesswork out of the what, where, and when to plant.

The most difficult thing to get used to in Central Florida is the realization that you can't work outside all day like you can in North Florida. The older one gets, the less time one wants spend in the summer heat. In the summer, don't be surprised if you can't work past 11:00 a.m. I find that I often go outside after dinner to do a little gardening after the day has cooled just a bit. Wide-brim straw hats are essential and you must have copious amounts of water close at hand whenever you are outside performing your gardening chores in Central Florida.

Because the sandy soil in Central Florida drains so well there is nothing to keep organic matter, water, and fertilizer from percolating right past the root zones of plants. While in North Florida a regular fertilization program may require two applications, in Central Florida four or five fertilizer applications are not uncommon. A small amount of fertilizer applied often to the plants is the norm. Applying water, however, is a different story. If you water often in small amounts, the roots tend to migrate close to the surface, and with the onset of hot weather the roots will likely die or be injured because of the heat. It's important to water infrequently but deeply. By watering for longer periods, the sheer weight of

You can plant a small garden by filling a pallet with soil and planting between the boards.

additional water will force it deep into the soil. Plant roots will follow the water and, in turn, will grow deeper into the cooler soil. When hot weather returns, the roots will be growing in deep, cool soil—just the way they like it. I often see homeowners merely sprinkling their landscape plants and lawn with a water hose and the tip of a finger; then they wonder why their plants die when hot weather comes along. Water deep for the best plant growth and leave the fingertip water sprinkling for washing the car.

The first time I added good, rich compost to my untouched vegetable garden soil, I thought I was finished. Later that season, most of the compost had either burned away in the hot sun or seeped deep into the soil, far away from the roots of my vegetables and fruits. Given that I have added two to three inches of compost to my garden every year for decades, the best I can figure is that my gardening counterparts in China must have some really good soil by now. The point is, you must add compost or organic matter to the soil every year or, even better, several times a year. Adding compost to the garden is not a onetime deal. The more you add the better the soil's ability to retain water and the less fertilizer you will have to add. Another benefit of a good, organic, rich soil is that you will have fewer numbers of nematodes (see page 56 for "The Nematode Nemesis"). The sandy soils of Central Florida can be enriched with landfill compost (available free in most counties), homemade compost, oak leaves, peat moss—just about any natural material that will further decompose. In February and March, when the oak trees lose their leaves, I gather literally hundreds of bags from my neighboring street curbs and spread the contents over my entire garden. In the shrub borders I just let the leaves lie there as mulch; eventually they will break down and add organic matter to the soil. In the vegetable garden I use them as mulch to hold the weed barrier down. Later, I turn them into the soil with a rototiller or shovel after the growing season is over.

I have one last thing to share about growing veggies and fruits in Central Florida: everything you have heard about the bugs is true. They are everywhere and they come in nearly every shape, size, and color you can imagine. Some bite, most suck, and many chew, but they all enjoy the little seedlings and seeds you thoughtfully place in the ground for them to eat. Because Central Florida doesn't get much cold weather compared to North Florida, pests can be a real problem. But, as you will read in this book, bugs rarely adversely affect healthy plants. Keep the plants healthy—well fed, well

Gather up oak leaves when they fall in February and March and spread them on your garden to help inhibit weeds.

If you're just getting started with your vegetable garden, it's best to start small.

watered, and grown in adequate sunlight—and most will fare very well. There might be a need for an occasional "intervention" from time to time, but as long as the plants are growing well, bugs should not be a problem. Critters, such as slugs and nematodes, can be troublesome, but they can be managed, also.

If there is a heaven on earth it's South Florida (which includes the tip of the peninsula and the coastal areas to Cocoa Beach on the east coast and to Tampa on the west coast). The greatest thing about living in South Florida is that, with minor exceptions, you can grow fruit and vegetables year-round. Due to South Florida's moderate temperatures (Key West has never had frost), growing tropical fruit trees is a passion of many gardeners there. Many of the tropical fruits that most of the civilized world only dreams about, such as mango, lychee, and avocado, all grow in backyards like apples grow in upstate New York. Do you need a banana for your corn flakes or orange juice for breakfast? Go into your backyard and pick some fresh fruit! Do you need a little snack after dinner? Well, go pick a cluster of longans, and eat them as you watch a colorful sunset on the horizon. Mango and papaya smoothies are minutes away. Your fresh star fruit salad will be a big hit at the next plant society's potluck.

The soil is variable in these areas and commonly ranges from sand to organically rich muck to limestone-rich "marl." Sandy soil is great for gardens provided you enrich it with compost. Marl, though, is another story all together. Marl is made of clay and calcium carbonate and as such is extremely difficult to work with. As you read the fruit tree sections in this book, you will notice that in many cases, the planting instructions indicate to place a tree on top of the marl and place a large bed of composted soil around the rootball in a ten- to twelve-foot diameter, to a depth of two feet. The tree's roots will never penetrate the marl; they'll simply grow in the prepared soil *above* the native soil. I remember when I lived in the Florida Keys, contractors building houses would have to use dynamite to create a home's foundation; the backhoes couldn't budge the rock an inch. Of course, if you live in the muck-rich Homestead area, growing fruits and vegetables couldn't be easier.

That's the good news. If you thought bugs in North and Central Florida were bad, then take pity on the gardeners in South Florida. It rarely gets cold—we were looking for winter parkas when temperatures got down into the mid-sixties in the Keys. Apparently bugs and diseases enjoy the mild temperatures, too. Diseases of all kinds are common because of the daily 3:00 p.m. rainstorms. You can drench or spray with copper or sulfur only to have it wash off the next day in the rain. The same goes for insecticides. There are cultural practices that can be utilized to alleviate some of the troubles, such as planting resistant selections, choosing appropriate planting dates, and so forth. But my recommendation is to simply know what you are getting into. If you haven't grown vegetables or fruit trees before, start small—one or two trees and a small garden plot is fine. As you become more proficient and learn what performs well and what doesn't, your garden can become larger and more trees can be planted. Gardening in South Florida is not a onetime activity—it's a journey.

CHAPTER 1

GROWING YOUR OWN: THE GARDEN

Planning a garden, planting, and harvesting vegetables are rewarding life experiences. The satisfaction of being outside in the garden on a cool early morning while the dew still clings to the tomato leaves, the pleasure of digging for tiny red potatoes, and the taste of a fresh-picked strawberry planted just months ago can make for many wonderful memories. In the early morning hours as you cultivate the soil you can listen to the neighborhood wake up. In the balmy, after-dinner hours you can enjoy a cup of coffee as you stroll your garden paths. When you grow your own food you can proudly share the overflowing bounty of green peppers with neighbors and donate fresh-picked nectarines and mangoes to the local food bank.

There is no better place to enjoy the sunrise than in a Florida vegetable garden.

Make gardening a family affair by including your children and their friends in the work.

How to Get Started

Why Grow Your Own?

Library shelves are filled with books and magazines giving advice and instruction on growing food. One would think by the sheer number of available pages alone that it is a complicated and difficult task to master. It's not.

There are many reasons to grow your own food, but simply put vegetables and fruit fresh out of the garden just taste better. If you have ever eaten a plum right off the tree or munched on newly harvested snow peas you know what I mean. If you haven't, then you are about to set out on a great adventure filled with discovery.

Let's talk a bit about growing food. For those without much gardening experience, first and most important: you can do this. Once you learn a few basics, the rest is common sense. You will have some successes and you will have some failures. When you ultimately realize and understand that sometimes plants die due to no fault of your own you'll begin to feel a little better about gardening. Not everything grows perfectly all the time. Where should I place the garden? Do I have enough sun? What about my dirt; is it okay, and if it's not, what do I do about it? What do I grow? When do I grow it? How do I know when to pick it? Just remember it's okay to make mistakes, and, boy oh boy, will you make them over the next few years! I still laugh at the slip-ups that I made decades ago. (When you see me sometime, ask me about the mayonnaise on corn silks fiasco.) That's one thing we all have in common though; we are always willing to share successes and failures, more often than not with a chuckle. All of this should be fun and enjoyable. There are no plant police watching your every move. The minute it gets to be work, stop, and buy your food at the store.

Gardening is a good way for different generations to create memories.

I must say though, despite my many years of growing fruits and vegetables, I still learn something every year—a new staking technique, a new harvesting indicator, a new plant variety, or a new tool. Reading a new seed catalog is like reading a good book for the first time and not knowing the conclusion. Certainly with vegetables and fruit you know how it's supposed to end, but with plants, weather, and the revolving cast of pests, one never really knows how it will turn out. In every growing season there are more than a few surprises, a twist in the plot (pardon the pun).

As I said earlier, gardening often creates indelible memories. Someone in my office recently planted her very first vegetable garden. She invited her daughter and two-year-old granddaughter to join her, and together they planted a few tomatoes and beans. It may not seem like much now but all of them will remember sharing that experience. Come to think of it, some of my best memories of my father are in the backyard garden. We would plant (and later eat) carrots and beans as we talked about guy stuff. My brother and I would occasionally have a ripe tomato fight in the kitchen (we spent more than a few days cleaning up *those* messes), and my mother and I would preserve extra vegetables for people in town who couldn't afford to buy their own. I learned my ABCs by reading the plant descriptions in a Burpee Seed Company catalog, and I learned to write by oh-so-carefully printing my seed wish list on the order form. Life has become much more complicated since then, but the cycle of life in the garden remains simple and undemanding.

Especially now, growing your own fruit and vegetables is the right thing to do. Ever since I read Rachel Carson's book *Silent Spring* back in the sixties, I have believed we should all be on a neverending quest to make the planet we live on a better place, one small garden at a time. We all can do something to help the cause, and growing food without using harmful chemicals is my own way of effecting change. I'll be very honest: I have and still do, on occasion, use chemicals to slay a bug or disease, but I do everything else possible first and use them only as a last resort. There are many cultural growing techniques that will deter pests and diseases, and one of the purposes of this book is to share a few of those methods so that you will use them first and reach for the bug spray last. We can all play a part. The famous anthropologist Margaret Mead said, "Never underestimate the power of a few committed people to change the world. Indeed, it is the only thing that ever has."

When you grow vegetables and fruit you are sustaining yourself, if only partly, and for that reason growing food is a very personal thing as well. Certainly, as you increase your gardening knowledge, you'll feel more comfortable growing things, and the more you grow, the more you learn.

Children may be amazed at how large some vegetables will grow.

Getting Started

If you are new to gardening it can seem a bit intimidating at first. After all, there are countless Internet pages dedicated to the subject, thousands of books discuss the topic ad infinitum (or is that ad nauseum), and home improvement stores dedicate entire departments to gardening. Where do you start?

Whether you are a seasoned gardener or new to the whole idea of digging in the dirt, remember that a small, well-maintained garden is better than a large, messy one. Even those of us who have been gardening for decades forget that from time to time, and we often plant more than we can care for, use, or share. By season's end, believe me; you'll be cussin' that 20-foot row of yellow banana peppers when you only needed one plant. Small is sometimes better.

Remember, it's okay to make mistakes; just make certain you learn from them. That's where a garden journal helps. It doesn't have to be expensive or fancy; it can be a spiral-bound notebook. It's important to find ways to make your garden better year after year. For instance, if you planted tomatoes in November only to see them killed by an early frost, write that down in your journal. Next year as you plan you'll know to plant the tomatoes sooner. Maybe one fertilizer works better than another. You will find that certain varieties of vegetables work better than others in your garden. The journal will help you remember the varieties that work best and the ones that didn't perform as well. I know many gardeners who actually staple an empty seed pack or two into their journal to help jog their memories. Don't forget to review your notes from time to time, too. One of the trickiest parts of growing plants in Florida is knowing when to plant. If you have moved here from somewhere else or have never grown a food garden before, your journal will become your best friend and will remind you not only what to plant, but when.

Your neighbors and fellow gardeners are helpful sources of information. Watch the newspapers and the Internet for notices about classes at garden centers or local botanical gardens. Most often taught by seasoned gardeners in the area, the speakers provide current information to experienced and novice gardeners alike. Growing fruits and vegetables are always popular topics so be sure to sign up early. Classes will often be separated into beginner and expert levels, so there's no reason to be intimidated thinking

GROWING TIP

Place a birdbath in the garden to encourage birds to visit. Birds love to eat bugs and can help as automatic bug-eating machines.

that the class will be over your head. One more thing—because growing food is so popular, many botanical gardens have display gardens that demonstrate how and when to grow vegetables and fruit trees. Track down one of their gardeners and ask questions—after all, that's what they get paid for.

Planning the Garden
Site Placement

You have heard in real estate it's all about location, location, location. This is certainly true for growing fruits and vegetables. The biggest mistake new gardeners make is squeezing a vegetable garden or planting a fruit tree into a space where there isn't enough sun or water. A good example is the amount of sunlight a site receives; any amount over eight hours is fine, but don't think six hours or less will be enough—it won't be. Plants grown in too little sun will grow spindly and stressed, creating a perfect environment for insects and diseases. Plants grown in poor light won't be able to produce fruit.

In just about every gardening book I have read there is a chart that describes those vegetables and fruit trees that can be grown in less than six hours of full sun. Don't fall for it. Planting trees, bushes, seeds, or transplants where there isn't enough sun is asking for trouble. If you had planted your garden in the right spot to begin with, bugs and diseases wouldn't be a problem.

The same advice works for drainage. Have you ever heard the phrase "You can't make a silk purse from a sow's ear"? If the site you're contemplating is soggy and wet most of the year, you need to think about building raised gardens. Unless the site has a slight slope to it or can be drained, you will be fighting a lost cause. On the other hand, if you have clay, be thankful that you will fertilize and water less than those of us growing in sand. Adding compost and/or sand to the planting location will help.

Another thing to keep in mind: don't plant fruits and vegetables where there is competition for water and nutrients. Rototilling or using a shovel to turn the soil over is very difficult if nearby tree roots have extended into the place you have selected to plant your garden. If you think annuals and perennials are hungry wait to see how much water a tree can suck up out of the ground. Not long after you have watered your veggie garden soil, it will be bone dry because the tree has thirstier (and more) roots than your squash. Likewise, fertilizer is absorbed by neighboring tree roots, so although the tree will be happy, the vegetables and fruit trees might not get enough "groceries" despite your best efforts.

Remember that many of the fruit trees described in this book can grow very large. Mangoes, for instance, can grow to 30 feet tall and 30 feet wide.

Plant them where they have a chance to grow without heavy pruning. Many of the small trees, such as plums, nectarines, and peaches, can be planted fewer than 15 feet away from a house or other structure, while others, such as loquat and avocado, are going to need some room. The more you have to prune the fewer fruits you will have, so give them room to spread their branches.

Size Does Matter!

If you are new to growing vegetables, it may be difficult to judge how large or small your garden should be. Not to worry: start small and adjust as needed. I discovered that as

Grow tomatoes up a trellis to save garden space and keep plants healthier.

my family situation changed (departures, new arrivals, marriages), the garden changed, too. One of my children absolutely loved snow peas. He would come home after school and dash out into the garden to see if there were any to eat. Now that he is married no one else in the house likes them so we don't grow them anymore. And that is how it should be. Simply jot down in your garden journal the veggies that everyone enjoys and grow those. Take my word for it; there is nothing more frustrating than growing the "perfect 10" broccoli if no one eats it. That's wasted space that could have grown something someone would have enjoyed. This is not to say that you shouldn't experiment with a new vegetable or two every season. Just like Picasso had his blue period, one year I had my "purple period" and the new veggies were all purple—purple cauliflower, purple kale, and purple mustard. Who knew if anyone would eat them, but they sure looked pretty out there in the Florida sun!

A small, well-maintained garden is better than a large, unkempt one. Even experienced gardeners need to be reminded of that. There is no shame in growing one tomato plant or one cucumber plant. Try your luck, see how they taste, see if they are easy or difficult to grow on your site, and see if anyone eats them. Remember, the next season isn't that far away in Florida; you can adjust then. Unlike our northern gardening friends, if the one

It's best to start small; planting only one or two of the bigger vegetables such as tomatoes.

tomato plant worked well this fall, next spring when you plant the spring tomato crop you can grow more. That's one great thing about living in Florida: something is always growing in the garden.

What to Grow?

Grow what you and your family will eat. If you're not sure about what to grow, talk to you neighbors who grow food and ask them what grows best for them. Attend some classes at your local botanical garden and learn what others are growing. If you have a small garden or are just starting out, you may want to postpone growing things such as watermelon and cantaloupe because they require so much space. Some plants perform better than others depending on where you live in Florida. Many fruit trees, for instance, have been hybridized so heat tolerance is built into their genetic make-up. Others, such as mangoes and lychees, simply can't take cold weather and should only be planted where it stays warm most of the time. The plant profiles in this book describe different climate ranges and my recommended varieties. Unfortunately, there are some things that just won't grow in Florida. Although many have tried, we can't grow good, big, full, crunchy apples here. Yes, there are a few varieties that will survive, but surviving and thriving are two different things. We can't grow cherries here either. There is a long, long list of fruit trees and veggies that just won't take the heat and humidity. On the other hand, you just can't grow a good banana in Cleveland. Rather than obsess over the things you can't grow, think of all the amazing things you *can* grow here, and be thankful you don't have to shovel that white stuff anymore.

GROWING TIP

The Top Ten vegetables grown by gardeners are, in order of preference: Tomatoes, Cucumbers, Sweet Peppers, Beans, Carrots, Summer Squash, Onions, Hot Peppers, Lettuce, and Peas.

GROWING TIP

Do you usually have too much zucchini maturing at one time? Plant one hill or one plant in a row and, when that plant begins to bear fruit, plant another to spread out the harvest.

Plan It on Paper

You don't need to be a landscape designer, but creating a garden on paper is a good way to maximize your space. Prepare the plan by including dimensions of your garden plot, the list of veggies you want to grow, and the spacing needs of each. If you fly by the seat of your pants on this one you may plant a tomato in the front of lettuce, which won't get enough water or light. Or, you might plant the broccoli on 12-inch centers instead of 36-inch centers, resulting in a smaller harvest. Prepare the plan with all the information you can gather and then set it aside for a day or two. Look at it again, make any adjustments, and begin to plant. Just remember a few things:

- Plant in full sun (at least 6 hours).
- Site the garden where water is readily available.
- Plant away from tree roots.
- Think small.
- If you planted a garden in the same space last season, don't forget to rotate crops (place them in different places than the season before).

Do you want to start an animated discussion with other gardeners? Ask them this seemingly simple question: "Should I plant my rows north to south or east to west?" It's like asking them their thoughts on foreign policy or their political affiliation. Want some fun? Go on the Internet to read what the research says. It seems everyone has an opinion and the "data" to back it up. However, the truth is it really doesn't matter. Just be smart about it. Clearly, if you plant in an east-to-west orientation, you don't want to place taller plants on the south side of the garden because the tall plants will shade the smaller plants behind them. If you are planting east to west, plant the tall stuff in the back or on the north side of the garden. If you're planting in a north-to-south orientation, just make sure you plant the taller plants together and graduate to smaller plants on either side of them. Tall plants can be planted at either end or in the middle, provided shorter plants are planted on either side and even shorter plants next to them and so on. If you use an overhead irrigation system, be certain that it either is tall enough to spray the water out over the tall stuff to the smaller ones or locate the tall plants the farthest away from the sprinklers.

It's okay to make mistakes, so don't fret about the small stuff. All of this should be fun and enjoyable. One of the great things about gardening is sharing your horror stories with other gardeners, and believe me, there are some show stoppers out there. Once the garden is ripped up after the harvest, you can laugh about your bloopers and move on.

Growing More in Less Space
Cluster Gardening

For the life of me I have never been able to figure out why gardeners plant vegetables in single rows. Maybe it's the photos of corn in their long rows that we have seen in photographs, or maybe it's because "we have always done it that way." The plain truth is that planting in single rows is inefficient. I've used the term "cluster gardening" for many years to describe various methods of gardening that utilize available space. It maximizes yields over the entire growing season. Cluster gardening has many advantages:

Grow some flowers along the perimeter of your vegetable garden to encourage pollinators.

- When vegetables are grown close together, weed seeds don't have the necessary light to germinate, and as a result weeding is reduced to almost nothing. Weeds simply cannot compete with the vegetables.
- Because you reach in from the edges of a wide bed to plant seeds and harvest the fruit, the soil won't become compacted by anyone stepping on it. The soil in the bed will stay nice and fluffy—just like you want it.
- You'll use less water because of the small amount of space being used.
- Although the total number of fruit harvested per plant may be less, because of the increase in the number of plants, the total yield will be higher than single-row plantings.
- Less mulch is needed. With cluster gardening, the growing rows are wider and only the walking paths need mulch, instead of the entire garden.
- Heavy rain is less likely to splash dirt on your growing vegetables. If you have ever eaten grit-laden spinach that has been grown in straight rows, this advantage will really appeal to you.
- Even the most inhospitable of sites can be used to create areas that can produce food.
- Harvesting is easier; you can pick more vegetables from a single location.
- Less fertilizer is needed because all of the soil that has been prepared is used.

A combination of several techniques is often used for the best advantage in the vegetable garden. Even in small urban plots where space is limited, cluster gardening will yield more in less space per square foot than traditional methods.

Square Foot Gardening

One of the best-known forms of cluster gardening is the square foot gardening method created by Mel Bartholomew. The method uses soil plots, which are 4 feet × 4 feet square, and each plot is subdivided into 1-foot squares using twine or string. It's a really ingenious method of positioning plants close together as needed by the individual plants. Seeds are carefully placed into the soil with very exacting measurements as determined by the needs of the person or family growing the plants. The plots are small and can be reached from all sides, so maintenance is much easier. The number of individual plants depends on how many people will be eating the vegetables. For more information, refer to Mr. Bartholomew's book *All New Square Foot Gardening, 2nd Edition* (Cool Springs Press 2013).

By gardening in raised beds, you can grow more food in less space and more easily control the soil and growing conditions, while contending with fewer weed problems.

Raised Beds

Raised bed gardening is another form of cluster gardening. Because the prepared soil literally sits atop the native soil, raised beds offer a number of advantages:

- Even in areas where the soil is soggy from a high water table, you can grow food in raised beds.
- In urban areas, raised beds can be placed on top of old or abandoned pieces of property, such as old home sites that have since been torn down, old parking lots, and so forth.
- Even on rooftops, raised beds (containing a "light" soil) can be utilized to grow food.

Raised beds are traditionally made of 2 × 10-inch boards, 4 feet wide, and as long as the space will permit. I have seen raised beds that are 30 feet long. That's a bit too long for me—it takes time to walk all the way around to the other side if you need something; but two 2 × 10-inch × 14-foot boards can build one raised bed 4 × 10 feet. Materials other than boards can be used, too. Raised beds can be made of steppingstones, interlocking concrete wall stones, Florida limestone rock—anything that will keep the improved soil from spilling out will work fine. I have seen some pretty inventive ideas in urban gardens all over the country. I saw one in Sarasota County, Florida, that was edged with old, rusted metal Tonka trucks! We make the beds 4-feet wide so you can reach into the center without stepping on the new fluffy soil.

There are other good things about raised bed gardens. In cooler areas of the state, the soil in raised beds warms up faster than the surrounding native soil, and plants can be planted into the soil earlier than usual. Because you only want to place "good" soil in the bed, the new soil should have better drainage than the soil beneath the bed. Given that the raised bed is just that, the elevated planting, cultivating, and harvesting is easier on the back. This makes it a good choice to use in gardens designed for the physically impaired or older gardeners who have a difficult time bending over. The raised bed can be as high as you make it; I have seen raised beds in an assisted living facility that were three feet high and were maintained by seniors who were approaching their 100th birthdays!

Wide Row Planting

Second only to square foot gardening, wide row planting is the most popular alternative form of cluster farming. It is best suited to small plants, including lettuce, spinach, onions, carrots, beets, radishes, turnips, and bush beans. Instead of single rows of plants, a seedbed ranging from 24 to 48 inches wide is prepared for planting. The seeds of the chosen vegetable are then thinly sprinkled over the entire seedbed and tamped gently to provide good soil-seed contact. As the seedlings emerge from the soil they must be thinned to the distance recommended on the seed package.

Wide row planting is a very effective way to increase vegetable yields per square foot. You simply lean across the bed to pull weeds or harvest. Because of the beds and the corresponding lack of walking paths, wide row gardening yields four to six times more per square foot than traditional methods. Not all vegetables lend themselves to wide row planting, however. Corn and tomatoes, for instance, need plenty of space and sun to grow properly. Larger plants can be planted using the wide row method; they just need more space between each plant. Think of it this way: instead of planting a single row of beans, plant three to four rows of beans next to each other in a wide row (with proper spacing) and the yield increases exponentially over single row plantings. This works with cabbage, peppers, and English peas, too.

Many carrots can be planted in a small area.

My first experience in wide row planting happened purely by accident. I was determined to plant my vegetable garden one year despite twenty-mile-per-hour winds. As I sprinkled the seeds over the seedbed, the wind gusted and, well, the rest is history. I had inadvertently spread seeds 2 to 3 feet wide, but as it turned out, the carrots grew quite well, and I have been practicing wide row planting ever since.

Grow Up, Not Out

It seems that most yards that accompany new homes are getting smaller and smaller as the price of real estate soars. Gardeners need to be more creative regarding ways to grow plants in small spaces. (There are smaller bush forms of some traditional vegetables that I will talk about later.) Clearly, growing sprawling cantaloupe and watermelon in small gardens is out of the question, given the need for space. Impossible, that is, unless you grow vertically. Growing plants on trellises, teepees, cages, stakes, strings, or fences has many advantages over growing them on the ground. Cucumbers, cantaloupe, winter squash, and small gourmet watermelons can be grown vertically. The advantages are many: the fruit remains cleaner and virtually free of slugs and other ground-dwelling critters, the fruit can be seen more easily for harvesting, and during harvest you won't step on the vines, causing injury that promotes diseases. If you have limited space, look for vining varieties of the standard vegetables. Pole beans versus bush beans, for instance, will produce higher yields than bush forms. For large-fruited vegetables (melons, squash, and so forth), extra support will be needed to prevent the fruit from pulling the vine off the support structure. Companies make expandable plastic mesh, but recycled women's nylon stockings work very well. Just make sure that whatever you use, place a tall structure at the north side of the garden so the structure will not shade out the vegetables behind it.

Interplanting

Interplanting is another way to maximize yield in limited spaces, and many gardeners think that by placing certain vegetables together they seem to grow better (although there is no hard data to support it). Interplanting involves planting two or more different crops together in the same wide row or single row without overfilling the space. When young peppers are planted in the garden, there are lots of spaces between the individual plants until they grow larger. By interplanting other vegetables that mature at a faster rate (and are harvested earlier than the peppers), the space is better utilized and the "quick" crops are gone before the peppers reach their full size. Quick crops in this case could include radishes, lettuce, or even spinach. Longer season crops that can be used in this way include Brussels sprouts, cabbage, and tomatoes. I have seen gardeners interplant flowers and herbs with vegetables. They swear it reduces the number of pests in the garden, but even if that weren't the case, it sure makes a dull, ordinary vegetable garden look impressive.

With the declining population of honeybees over the last ten years, many vegetables (especially squash) don't get pollinated properly. The result is a premature fruit drop or no fruit production at all. To ensure proper bee activity for pollination, plant annuals and perennials to attract bees. Good plants to attract pollinators include agastache (hyssop), African blue basil, penta, cosmos, marigold, verbena and coreopsis.

Varieties That Save Space: Dwarf Plants

Although technically not a form of cluster gardening, planting bush forms of vegetables that normally take up lots of space is particularly valuable to gardeners who have small gardens. Not everyone has space to grow vegetables, so growing up is one alternative; the other is to grow special varieties of vegetables that have been hybridized to grow fully formed fruit on smaller or bush-type plants. Even if you only have a patio or terrace, you can easily grow dwarf varieties in large containers. For example, bush forms of cucumbers grow fully formed 6- to 7-inch cukes but on vines that only grow 2 feet long. Vining forms of beans instead of bush forms are fun to grow, and even various melons have been bred to grow smaller vines and full-size fruit. It may take some hunting, but they are out there. Even corn has a dwarf selection; 'Chires' only grows 3 feet tall and produces the little ears of corn used in Asian stir-fry recipes.

OTHER VARIETIES OF DWARF PLANTS

Bean, French	'Golden Child', 'Allicante'
Beet	'Baby Ball'
Cabbage	'Baby Pixie'
Carrot	'Little Finger', 'Parisian', 'Round Romeo', 'Atlas'
Cauliflower	'Snowball'
Cucumber	'Very Kuhl', 'Spacemaster', 'Bush Champion'
Eggplant	'Bambino', 'Pot Black'
Kale	'Dwarf Blue Curled'
Lettuce	'Tom Thumb', 'Little Gem', 'Bambi', Claremont'
Pak choy	'Extra Dwarf'
Pea, English	'Little Marvel', 'Half Pint'
Pumpkin	'Jack Be Little', 'Small Sugar', 'Baby Boo'
Tomato	'Patio', 'Small Fry', 'Tiny Tim'

Hot peppers grow well in containers.

Container Growing

No discussion about growing fruit trees or vegetables would be complete without talking about growing them in containers. Gardeners with large yards can spread out and grow lots of fun things. Despite the perception, those with smaller yards or no yards living in apartments, condos, and zero lot lines can grow many fruits and vegetables even though they may not have any land at all. It just takes a little ingenuity. All of the guidelines to growing vegetables and fruit trees in the ground are true for those growing in containers. You need full sun (at least six hours), plenty of water, and good soil. Growing in containers has the advantage over growing in the ground—the modification or addition of soil amendments is much easier in containers because of the size of the container. It's one thing to change the mix of garden soil; it's much easier to do the same in containers. Are you tired of the soil in the eggplant pot? Just throw it in the compost pile and start fresh! Do you need to change the pH? Just add a tiny bit of sulfur and you're done. This isn't so in a bigger garden.

I enjoy gardening in containers because they are mobile. If you're like me, you like to change things up a bit, and what better way to do that than to move pots around. Today I like the arrangement that way, tomorrow I may not. Learn to play with textures, heights, and colors of the fruits and vegetables for unique combinations. You can even plant vegetables and fruits with annual and perennial flowers in very attractive combinations. The containers themselves are a fun part of the container growing experience. You are only limited by your imagination. I have seen the theme parks use horse troughs, galvanized trash cans, and even metal pails hung from chains to grow vegetables.

It seems everyone has gotten the container bug because everywhere I go, I see someone selling pots. Not only do they have beautiful colors, they also have amazing designs. The materials have changed a great deal over the last several years too. We used to be able to get pots in terracotta clay. That was it. Now, of course, they come in plastic, urethane foam, and fiberglass. Hauling heavy clay pots from place to place is a thing of the past. I use plastic or foam pots almost exclusively nowadays because in the Florida heat, a clay container pulls any available water out of the potting soil through evaporation. As a result we may have to water every day or twice a day depending on the location. Many of the plastic and foam pots are so well designed you can't tell the clay from the foam, anyway. An expensive clay pot can crack and break apart while the foam and plastic will seemingly last a lifetime. For containers larger than 24 inches in diameter, you might want to think about putting the pot on casters to make moving easier.

Timing

They say timing is everything, and that's especially true in Florida gardening. With fruit trees, the plants are usually grown in plastic nursery containers and can be planted anytime. I like fall planting best, however, because although the air begins to cool down in the fall, the soil is still warm and the roots continue to grow until the soil cools down. When spring arrives, the roots have established themselves and are ready to supply the leaves and branches with all the water and nutrients they need as the air warms up. If trees are planted in the spring, or worse yet, in the heat of the summer, the roots are asked to perform a Herculean task with just the roots they came with. It's not uncommon to see fruit trees die because of a lack of water several months after they have been planted.

With vegetables it's a different story. Many of the things we grow are sensitive either to heat or cold, so they have to be planted at the time of the year that they grow best. If you plant a tomato too late in fall, just as the tomato plant begins to produce nice red fruits, a frost will hit and there goes the tomato plant. If you plant too late in spring, just as the tomato begins to set fruit, hot weather arrives and the plant will die because of the heat and humidity. That's why timing is so important. The planting chart found on pages 34 to 37 may become your second-best gardening friend (after your garden journal). The correct planting season is absolutely critical to Florida gardening. Even after planting vegetables in all three growing zones for thirty years, I still get it wrong. During the growing season it's best to stagger the planting of some crops to harvest at the peak of nutrition and flavor. Vegetables such as beans, radishes, and lettuce should be planted in small quantities every two to three weeks to harvest them when they taste best. Others, such as carrots and potatoes, can be harvested at various stages in their development and you will still get the same nutritional value.

Pay special attention to the insect and disease charts in Chapter 8 of this book. You will notice a few descriptions cautioning against the use of pesticides when the flowers are in bloom. Fortunately, vegetables are always in bloom—that's where the fruit comes from. To get around this it's recommended that gardeners spray in the evening after the bees have flown back to their hives.

RECOMMENDED VARIETIES

Vegetable	North Zone	Central Zone	South Zone	Recommended Varieties	Plant Spacing (inches)	Row Spacing (inches)	Direct Sow or Transplant (D/T)	Planting Depth (inches)
Bean								
Bush	Mar-Nov	Oct-Apr	Oct-Apr	Blue Lake 274, Cherokee Wax, Commodore Improved, Contender Flaco, Goldrush, Greencrop, Improved Golden Wax, Jade II, Pike, Strike, Tiger Eye	6	18	D	1
French	Mar-Nov	Oct-Apr	Oct-Apr	Golden Child, Allicante	6	18	D	1
Italian	Mar-Nov	Oct-Apr	Oct-Apr	Roma II, Romano Gold	6	18	D	1
Lima	Mar-Nov	Oct-Apr	Oct-Apr	Burpee Improved, Christmas Pole, Dixie Butterpea Speckled, Fordhook 242, Speckled Calico, Big Mama, Willow Leaf	6	18	D	1
Pole	Mar-Nov	Oct-Apr	Oct-Apr	Asparagus Yard Long Red Noodle & Thai #3, Blue Lake, Cherokee Trail of Tears, Christmas, Florida Buttered Speckled, Half White Runner, Kentucky Wonder, Kentucky Wonder Wax, Purple Podded, Purple Trionofo Violetto, Rattlesnake, Romano	6	18	D	1
Shell	Mar-Nov	Oct-Apr	Oct-Apr	French Horticultural, Jacob's Cattle, Painted Pony, Tiger Eye, Vermont Appaloosa	6	18	D	1
Beet	Sep-Mar	Oct-Mar	Oct-Mar	Baby Ball, Bull's Blood, Chioggia, Cylindrica, Detroit Dark Red, Detroit Golden, Long Season Lutz, Piatta D'Egitto, Seven Top	2-3	12-18	D	¼
Broccoli	Sep-Jan	Sep-Jan	Sep-Jan	Emerald Jewel, Green Comet, Green Goliath, Lieutenant, Packman	36	36	D/T	¼-½
Brussels sprouts	Sep-Jan	Sep-Jan	Sep-Jan	Jade Cross II, Long Island Improved	24	24	D/T	¼-½
Cabbage	Sep-Jan	Sep-Jan	Sep-Jan	Baby Pixie, New Jersey Wakefield, Copenhagen Market, Bonnie Hybrid, Samantha, Savoy Ace, Savoy Deadon, Savoy Chieftain	18	24	D/T	¼
Cantaloupe	Mar-Apr	Feb-Apr	Aug-Sep & Feb-Mar	Ambrosia, Bush Star, Honey Rock, Planter's Jumbo	24	48	D/T	½-1
Carrot	Sep-Mar	Oct-Mar	Oct-Feb	Baltimore, Chatenay Royal, Imperator 58, Ingot, Little Finger, Lunar White, Nantes Half Long, Tendersweet	2	12-18	D	1/16

RECOMMENDED VARIETIES

Vegetable	North Zone	Central Zone	South Zone	Recommended Varieties	Plant Spacing (inches)	Row Spacing (inches)	Direct Sow or Transplant (D/T)	Planting Depth (inches)
Cauliflower	Sep-Jan	Sep-Jan	Sep-Jan	Artica, Brocoverde, Cheddar, Minuteman, Snowball, Verdi, Violet Queen	6	18	D/T	¼-½
Celery	Jul-Sep	Jul-Sep	Jul-Sep	Giant Pascal, Red Venture, Stoke's Golden Plume	12	24	T	$1/16$
Collard	Jan-Dec	Jan-Dec	Jan-Dec	Georgian Southern, Morris Heading, Yates	36	36	T	½
Corn	Feb-Apr	Jan-Apr	Oct-Mar	Golden Cross Bantam, Early Sunglow, Sweet Riser, Kandy King, Silver Queen, How Sweet It Is, Sweet Ice, Peaches and Cream, Seneca Dancer	8	30	D	1
Cucumber								
Fall Garden	Aug-Sep	Sep	Sep-Oct	**Garden Straight:** Cherokee, Cucina, Dasher II, Indio, Indy	10	36-48	D/T	½
Winter Garden	too cold	too cold	Nov-Dec	**Pickling:** Adam, Eureka				
Spring Garden	Feb-Apr	Jan-Mar	Jan-Mar	**Bush:** Burpee's Bushmaster, Bush Slicer				
Summer Garden	too hot	too hot	too hot	**Greenhouse:** Toska, Fabulous, Sweet Success				
Eggplant	Jun-Sep	Jun-Sep	Jun-Sep	Astrakom, Bambino, Bangladeshi Long, Black Beauty, Casper, Green Goddess, Fengyuon Purple, Green Goddess, Kermit, Louisiana Long Green, Ping Tung Long, Rosita, Traviata	30	30-36	T	¼
Kale	Sep-Mar	Sep-Mar	Sep-Mar	Lacinato, Nero de Toscana, Red Russian, Yates Blue Curled, Winterbor	18	24	D/T	¼
Kohlrabi	Sep-Mar	Sep-Mar	Sep-Mar	Early White Vienna, Eder, Early Purple Vienna, Kosak, Quickstar	6	18	D	¼
Lettuce	Sep-Oct & Feb-Mar	Sep-Mar	Sep-Jan	**Bibb:** Australe, Buttercrunch, Deer Tongue, Merveille des Quartre Saisons **Romaine:** Bambi, Garden Babies, Freckles, Parris Island, Winter Density **Leaf:** Black Seeded Simpson, Red Sails, Oak Leaf, Ruby Red, Green Salad Bowl	6	12-18	D/T	¼

RECOMMENDED VARIETIES

Vegetable	North Zone	Central Zone	South Zone	Recommended Varieties	Plant Spacing (inches)	Row Spacing (inches)	Direct Sow or Transplant (D/T)	Planting Depth (inches)
Mustard	Sep-May	Sep-Mar	Sep-Mar	Garnet Giant, Florida Broad Leaf, Misuna, Savanna, Southern Giant Curled, Tah Tsai, Tatsoi	12	18-24	D	¼
Okra	Mar-Aug	Mar-Aug	Aug-Sep	Candelabra, Cherokee Longpod, Clemson Spineless, Cow Horn, Little Lucy, Red Spray, Silver Queen	24	36	D/T	½
Onion	Sep-Mar	Sep-Mar	Sep-Mar	Chippolini White, Granex White, Granex Yellow, White Lisbon Bunching, Matador Shallot, Shimonita	4	18-24	D/T	¼
Pea, English	Jan-Mar	Sep-Feb	Sep-Feb	Little Marvel, Super Sugar Snap, Wando, Oregon Sugarpod II, Green Arrow	2	30	D	1
Pea, Southern	Mar-Aug	Mar-Aug	Aug-Apr	Brown Crowder, Calico Crowder, California Blackeye, Iron and Clay, Knucklehull Purplehull, Mississippi Silverskin, Rouge de Noir, White Acre, Zipper Cream	4	30	D	1
Peanut	Jun	Jul	Aug	Valencia	8	24	D	1 ½
Pepper	Feb-Mar & July-Sep	Feb-Mar & July-Sep	Aug-Sep	**Standard Sweet:** California Wonder, Cubanelle, Jalapeño Fooled You, Orange Blaze, Pimento, Sweet Banana, Yolo Wonder **Hybrid Sweet:** Big Bertha, Gypsy **Standard Hot:** Ancho, Bhut Jolokia (Ghost Pepper), Cajun Bell, Caribbean Red, Chili Jalapeño, Habanero, Hungarian Yellow Wax, Long Thin Cayenne, Tampiquero, Trinidad Scorpion, Scotch Bonnet **Hybrid Hot:** Super Chili	18	24	T	1/8
Potato	Jan-Mar	Jan-Mar	Sep-Jan	French Fingerlings, Kennebec, Onaway, Red Pontiac, Russian Banana, Yukon Gold	8	36	D	6
Spinach	Oct-Nov	Oct-Nov	Oct-Jan	Bloomsdale Long Standing, Malabar Red Stem	6	24	D/T	½

RECOMMENDED VARIETIES

Vegetable	North Zone	Central Zone	South Zone	Recommended Varieties	Plant Spacing (inches)	Row Spacing (inches)	Direct Sow or Transplant (D/T)	Planting Depth (inches)
Squash	Mar-Apr & Aug-Sep	Feb-Mar & Aug-Sep	Jan-Feb & Sep	**Summer Squash:** Cheetah, Early White Scallop, Peter Pan, (scallop), Lioness, Zephyr **Winter Squash:** Spaghetti, Table King, Table Queen, Table Ace, Waltham, Early Butternut **Zucchini:** Cocozelle, Eight Ball, Reward	36	36-48	D/T	1
Sweet potato	Mar-Jun	Feb-Jun	Dec-Sep	Beauregard	12	48	T	6
Swiss chard	Sep-Mar	Oct-Mar	Oct-Mar	Bright Lights, Fordhook Giant, Italian White Ribbed, Peppermint Stick, Rhubarb	12	18-24	D/T	½
Tomato	Feb-Mar & Aug	Mar 1 & Aug 1	Aug-Mar	**Indeterminate (large fruit):** Better Boy, Bonnie's Best, Striped Cavern **Indeterminate (small fruit):** Everglades, Husky Cherry, Sweet 100, Sweet Chelsea, Solid Gold **Determinate (large fruit):** Celebrity, Tasti-Lee **Determinate (small fruit):** Floragold	36	30-36	T	½
Turnip	Jan-Apr & Aug-Oct	Jan-Mar & Sep-Nov	Oct-Feb	**Greens only:** Seven Top, Southern Green **Roots and greens:** Golden Ball, Lunga Bianca A Colletto Viola, Purple Top White Globe, Round Red, Scarlet Queen Red Stems, Snowball, Tokyo Cross	3	12-18	D	½
Watermelon	Mar-Apr & Jul-Aug	Jan-Mar & Aug	Jan-Mar & Aug-Sep	Jubilee (Florida Giant), Crimson Sweet, Charleston Grey 133, Sugar Baby, Mickeylee	36	84	D/T	1 ½

CHAPTER 2

STARTING AT THE BEGINNING WITH SEEDS

There are many reasons why gardeners grow plants from seed. Seed companies provide greater diversity than grocers. Perhaps you don't want to grow the standard zucchini squash but instead want the golden-yellow variety. You would be hard pressed to find anyone in a nursery growing that one for sale. However, on the Internet you'll probably locate ten sources.

Perhaps most important to many, however, is that starting vegetables from seed is more cost effective than buying plants from a garden center or produce from the store. Depending on the vegetable variety, a packet of 100 seeds may cost $2.50. Recently, when I went to the garden center, the individual plants of the same variety cost $4.50 *each*. If you were planting a garden for a small family you would need a second mortgage.

If you grow your own plants and later collect seeds from those plants, you know how they have been grown. Nearly everyone would agree that growing food without the use of chemicals is a good idea, but if you buy seedlings from a store you really don't know what they have been sprayed with at the nursery. I'm a firm believer in the "less is better" theory, and I want to know

Sow bean seeds directly into the soil.

that the food I feed my family is safe. You have taken the time to select the right container, the correct soil, plant the seed at the correct depth, and water the seeds carefully for proper germination. When the little seedlings push their way up out of the soil, it is a proud moment. And when you harvest in a few months, you will know that you really accomplished something. With the exception of F^1 hybrid seed (which won't grow like the parent plant) you can also collect your own seed for the next season. Simply let one or two plants go to seed, collect the seeds when they have matured (you will see several pods begin to open), save them in a plastic bag, and place them in the bottom of the refrigerator.

Direct Sow vs. Transplants

In the vegetable charts on pages 34 to 37, there is a column titled "Direct Sow or Transplant" to guide your planting efforts. For the most part, when

---

GROWING TIP

If you want to start seeds in egg cartons, be sure to use the styrofoam type, *not* the paper type. By the time the seeds are large enough to transplant, a paper carton will have fallen apart.

Plants grown in peat cups can be planted directly into the garden without removing the peat cup.

Beans are one of the earliest plants to pop up in the garden.

possible, planting directly into the soil is better than planting transplants because the plant roots are not disturbed during the transplanting procedure. When seeds come up through the soil their roots and stems are at the correct height and they seem to grow better than transplants. There are some plants, including beans, peas, and squash, for instance, that just don't like to be moved once they're planted. If you must plant seedlings, grow them in peat cups and plant them gently into the garden when it's time.

Many vegetables, such as broccoli, cabbage, and tomatoes, can also be grown as transplants in peat cups or recycled cell-packs and moved to the garden later. (Usually transplants are moved when the seedling has three to four pairs of "true" leaves.) When pulling them out of the cell packs make sure you get all of the roots—sometimes pushing up from the bottom helps. Be certain that the young seedlings are planted a little high in the soil to prevent stem diseases that could kill the plant.

Root crops, including potatoes, carrots, and rutabagas, must be planted directly into the garden. Onions can vary in their planting requirements. For example, Lisbon bunching onions are best planted directly into the soil from seed. Others, such as the variety 'Granex' and shallots, should be planted into the garden as "sets" (or individual bulbs) so that one-half of the onion bulb can be seen above the soil.

Sowing Seeds Indoors: Getting a Head Start

Nearly all vegetable seeds can be planted directly into the garden, sometimes referred to as "direct sown," and others can be planted earlier indoors to get a head start. Because of their fleshy taproots, a few vegetables cannot tolerate being transplanted. (Refer to the chart on pages 34 to 37 for a list of those that must be direct sown.) Many gardeners plant seeds in some type of container with good potting soil several weeks before they are to be planted out into the garden to get that jump on the season. If you don't have the inclination or simply don't have room to start seeds indoors, don't fret; just wait until the temperature is right and plant them in the ground at the right time.

If you want to get that head start, though, you can do so without fancy equipment or greenhouses. A container, potting soil, water, and sun are all you need. Generally, you will plant seeds indoors several weeks before they are to be planted into the garden. In the northern areas of Florida if you plant seedlings outside too soon, they could be killed by frost. Likewise, in the fall if you plant them outside too soon, they could shrivel up and die due to the heat. Every vegetable has a different length of time to maturity, so study the chart on pages 34 to 37 before you get started. Once you spend a few minutes reviewing it, you'll have a better sense of when to plant.

Malabar spinach

WORKING WITH SEED PACKETS

Once you have selected the seeds, it's time to plant them. Begin by tapping the packet, forcing the seeds to the top. Carefully open the seed packet by tearing the bottom of the package. Gently sprinkle the seeds over the soil leaving a few seeds in the packet. Cover with fine soil to the depth recommended on the seed packet. In case all of the seeds don't germinate, you will have a few extra seeds to fill in the seed tray or complete a row in the garden. The seed package can be folded tightly from the bottom, held closed with a paper clip, with the full variety name intact at the top. Store leftover seeds in an airtight container in the bottom of the refrigerator. Many seeds (beans, corn, broccoli, and cucumbers, for instance) can be stored this way for several years. I find it's helpful to mark the opening date on each packet with an indelible marker for quick reference.

GROWING TIP

When transplanting seedlings grown in peat pots, remove the upper 1 inch of the cup. If this is left, the remaining peat pot "rim" will act like a wick to draw water out of the ground causing the soil in the peat pot to dry out more quickly.

Let's talk dirt. When seedlings are small and just beginning to grow, they are very vulnerable to a variety of maladies, such as root rots, stem rots, and leaf spots. For that reason it is important to get the seeds off to a good start by growing them in soil that is free of diseases. You can dig some soil out of your yard and sow the seeds in it, but you would be amazed to know of all the bad things in there: fungi, bacteria, viruses, microscopic worms—the list is endless. It's a wonder that anything can grow in it. Because growing seeds indoors is a modification of a seed's normal outdoor environment with its good air circulation, predatory insects, and such, it's important that the transplant potting soil be as critter free as possible. Yes, you can sterilize garden soil in small amounts by heating it to 180 degrees Fahrenheit for one hour. I tried it once in the kitchen oven using my wife's best roasting pan but the odor was pretty bad. Later, I tried the barbeque grill and it worked okay, but I find that it's much easier to buy a good quality potting soil at a garden center instead. (By the way, ever since I used that roasting pan, the Thanksgiving turkey has never been quite the same.) Potting soil in bags is usually clean enough to start seeds without any worry.

Selecting the right container to grow the seeds in couldn't be easier provided you remember a few things. First, the soil needs to have good drainage. Anything less and the seeds will become waterlogged and die. Water them from the top or bottom using a saucer; it doesn't make any difference as long as the seeds are not washed away with a heavy stream when they are watered. When I can find them, I like to use peat cups or expandable peat pellets to start seeds. Peat cups can be filled with potting soil and the seeds planted as usual. The peat pellets need to be expanded first (hot water works well to hasten this process), and the seed is inserted at the proper depth into the sterile medium. When the seedlings are ready and the planting time is right, the peat pot or peat pellet can be planted directly into the garden. Just about anything else can be used, too. Egg cartons, the bottoms of milk cartons, and even newspaper folded into cups will work. Reusing old plastic trays from last season's flowering annuals work very well, and it beats throwing them into the landfill.

GROWING TIP

Cut seed potatoes three or four days before planting, dust liberally with sulfur, and allow them to air dry before planting.

Seeds may also be broadcast over a soil-filled seed tray or "flat," and covered with the correct amount of soil. Unlike seeds grown in individual containers, the seedlings must be gently lifted from a tray and later placed into individual containers for planting into the garden. Lifting or "pricking out" the seeds can be done once the seedlings have produced two to three sets of leaves that look like the plant's mature leaves. An old dinner fork (or a new one, if no one is looking) works fine for this purpose. Just stick the fork into the soil, gently lift the seedling and its roots from the tray, and place the seedling into its new pot of sterile potting soil. Water gently and grow as you would other plants until the seedling is ready to plant outdoors. When sowing seeds in trays, be careful not to plant the seeds too closely together. If there is limited air circulation, seedlings often succumb to a variety of diseases.

When sowing seed read the instructions on the packet, or, if you buy in bulk from a feed store, ask the salesperson how deep the seeds should be planted. As a general rule, seeds are usually planted twice as deep as their diameter. Place the soil into the container, plant the seeds at their proper depth, cover, and water gently. Once a seed has been watered, it's important to keep watering often until the seedling emerges from the soil. As long as the soil is well drained, watering every day will be sufficient. Once a dry, newly planted seed becomes wet, it begins to expand and it is at this stage when a seed is most vulnerable. Be careful not to let the soil dry out.

Finally, once the seeds have been sown in a pot or flat, place the seeds in a warm location. Until the seedlings emerge from the soil, sunlight is not necessary. Once the seeds sprout, move them to a sunny location, and water as needed to keep the soil moist. After a few weeks, check the holes in the bottom of the pot for evidence of root growth. Once the roots have become well established in the pot (every plant will grow at different rates), it's time to plant them out into the garden.

Moving Outdoors

Once indoor-grown seedlings have emerged from the soil, it's important that they be acclimated to the outdoors gradually. Otherwise, they will resemble a Yankee on a Florida beach in August. Plants, especially seedlings, can get sunburned, too. After the seedlings emerge, they need to be toughened up. Take them outside for an hour or so every day, increasing the length of

Harden off plants by setting them on your porch or patio during the day and bringing them in at night until they are acclimated to outside conditions.

exposure until they can be in the sun all day. This process is called "hardening off." If the transplants are being planted in a cooler time of the year, be careful of freezing temperatures, and protect the new plants with row cloth available at most garden centers or with lightweight, old blankets.

To prepare your garden space for planting, follow these simple tips. For single row planting, after digging and turning the soil with a shovel or rototiller, rake the seedbed smooth, especially when sowing small seeds. Straight rows will help distinguish weed seedlings from vegetable seedlings later on. To prevent compacting the soil with your feet, start at one end of the garden and work backwards. Many people place a 1 × 10-inch board between the rows to help distribute the gardener's weight and to avoid leaving deep footprints in the new fluffy soil. Pound a stake into the ground at either end of the seedbed and stretch a string between the two.

For small seeds (carrot, cabbage, radish, and mustard) make a shallow impression using the entire handle of a hoe or rake laid down in the loamy soil and gently press the handle with your foot. Sow the seeds according to the recommendations on their individual packages. Gently tap the seeds out of the package—not too many—or place the fine seeds in your hand and gently sow them into the newly made furrow using a rubbing motion between your thumb and index finger. Don't worry whether the seeds are right side up or not. They will figure that out for themselves. Go back over the slight soil impression with extra seeds to make certain there are no gaps. Larger seeds (squash, bean, and pea) need to be planted deeply; the sharp edge of a hoe can be used to make a furrow (1 to 2 inches deep). In either case, gently cover the seeds with your hands or feet and *gently* tamp the seeds to obtain a good seed-soil contact. Immediately mark the rows by placing a plant label at the end of each; plastic labels available at garden centers work fine but the wooden types deteriorate too quickly in Florida. Use a china marker or grease pencil to write the name and variety of the seed planted and place the marker at the end of each row. Water gently every day using a watering can or a garden hose (or any device that will create a gentle flow of water) until the seeds sprout. Always leave a few seeds in the package to sow a few weeks later to fill in any gaps where the seeds didn't germinate.

One more thing: plants grown too closely together will not grow properly. The carrots will be tiny, the cauliflower won't grow a curd, and the tomatoes will be small. The tendency is to sow seeds too close together. The seeds are so small it is almost impossible to sow them evenly with proper spacing. It happens to everyone, so don't feel bad. Unfortunately, the excess seedlings must be removed or "thinned." Trust me on this: *you must thin seedlings to get good production.* Thinning should be done in either of two ways. Using scissors, snip off all but one stem, leaving the largest and

Radishes and other plants with tiny seeds will need to be thinned.

sturdiest seedling. To thin in the garden, this means getting "up close and personal" (on your hands and knees) and clipping all but the one at the correct spot in the row. Seedlings can also be removed by pulling the seedling to the side when the soil is moist. This method lessens the damage to those plant roots remaining in the ground. Once the process is completed, water the remaining seedlings with a gentle spray.

Saving Seeds

One of the questions most asked of gardeners is, "Can I save the seed from my vegetables and fruit trees and grow new plants?" As you would expect, the answer is "yes" and "no"—nothing is easy in this line of work. I am not a geneticist, but let me explain the best I can.

First, the question begs to be asked, why bother? After all, it's much easier to simply go to the local feed store, garden center, or nursery and buy them either in bulk or in seed packs right off the shelf. But there are some good reasons. It's important to remember that when seed companies collect

GROWING TIP

Station lifelike fake lizards and snakes in your garden to help keep birds away from your beans and squash as the seedlings emerge.

seed to sell the following year, they collect all the seed of a given plant on their farm. That includes seeds which are both the very largest and the runts of the pack, and the seeds are mixed together. When you collect seeds in your garden you will collect seeds from only from the largest and healthiest plants. Assuming Mendel was right about genetics, many of the positive traits that you selected the seeds for—resistance to disease, vigor, height, and so forth—will pass down to most of the next generation in the seed. True, not all will be the best and the greatest, but hopefully many will be. With some plants, saving seed will take some sacrifice. After all, let's say you have selected a specific plant because of certain qualities; maybe it's spineless or has good insect or disease resistance. To collect the seed from a plant with unique characteristics means you will have to let that plant go to seed, and that means you won't be able to eat it. It will be difficult to watch a perfectly good plant go to seed and not be able to taste it, but that's the name of the game.

Crossing specific parent plants produces a hybrid seed (plant) by means of controlled pollination. These hybrid seeds are often called "F^1" or "F^1 hybrids." Hybridized plants require the cross breeding of carefully chosen parent plants and the resulting seed will produce plants with very specific characteristics. The primary disadvantage of hybrids is the seeds cannot be saved from year to year. Seeds saved from hybrid plants usually will not produce the same plant the following year because most varieties are not self-sustaining. Offspring of hybrids usually show an unpredictable mixture of characteristics from the grandparent plants instead of being similar to the parent. So the bottom line is if you select F^1 hybrid seed, you cannot collect seed from the mature plant to use next year.

I save seeds for one simple reason: I know what has been sprayed on the parents. Many commercial companies' seeds are sprayed with insecticides and/or fungicides to prevent pests from eating them or to prevent them from going bad during storage. If you collect your seeds from your plants that have not been sprayed and then store them in your refrigerator, you're safe on both counts.

One more thing about saving seeds: You can save a ton of money. I bought several packages of vegetable seeds recently. Not only were there very few seeds in each package (there seem to be fewer and fewer every year) but a small package of seed cost more than $2.50. If you multiply that cost times the number of different vegetables on your planting list, you'll see that you can spend a small fortune. Even worse, most fruit trees are not sold as seed but as fairly expensive saplings that must be purchased in nursery containers. Granted, many must be grafted onto hardy, resistant rootstock, but for those that can be grown from seed, the savings can be tremendous. (Of course, what you trade is the time already spent growing the tree to sapling stage; sometimes, it's worth the investment to obtain a plant that's already started.)

One common mistake many gardeners make is collecting the seed too soon. The fruit of vegetables and fruit trees should be mature, maybe even a little past ripeness. Collect the seed from the fruit, gently wash the seeds with plain water to remove any pulp or flesh, and air dry the seeds in a cool, dry location. A shady spot, using newspaper as the drying material, in a well-ventilated space works best. In Central and South Florida where the humidity is very high, gardeners can also dry seeds by placing them in silica gel for a period of time (small seeds take only four to five days while large seeds can take up to ten days). Tomatoes are the exception to the rule. I usually mash the fruit and let it ferment for a few days outside until it starts to look nasty. The fermented pulp, often two to three days old, is then placed in a glass or jar filled with water. After stirring the fruit pulp for a few minutes I let the entire concoction rest. The seeds that sink to the bottom are viable and those that float on top can be thrown out with the pulp. Dry the "good" seeds like other seeds described and store in a location that has low humidity and cool temperatures.

Remember that seeds are living things and need to be treated as such. First, to prevent mold on stored seeds make sure they are dried thoroughly before they are stored. Often it looks like the seed is dry, but it may not be. Change the drying papers often during the process and turn the seeds over

Store leftover seeds in a clear jar or plastic bag. A cool, dark space is best.

a few times to make certain that all sides are dried equally. The storage containers can make a difference, too. Metal-capped glass jars work well, but they are clumsy to work with if you only have a few seeds. My favorite is a simple plastic sandwich bag with a top that can be sealed. With the clear plastic bag, the seeds can be observed often and moldy seeds can be removed quickly. Bags store flat and many can be stored together. Make sure you label any storage container well with an indelible marker or inexpensive labeling machine available from the local office supply store. A grease pencil or china marker works equally well and can be purchased at an art or craft store.

Seeds need to be stored in a cool, dark place to arrest the diseases and bacteria that could harm them and to keep the seeds in a suspended state until they are asked to sprout in the garden. There are many photographs in books that show handsome garden sheds with jars of seeds on a shelf just waiting to be planted. Nothing could be worse for the seed. My shed is always twenty degrees warmer than it is outside and as for air circulation, well, there is none. That's where the refrigerator comes in. Claim a vegetable crisper drawer as your space. Just take it, and don't relinquish it to anyone. It fulfills all the requirements: good air circulation, cool temperatures, and low humidity. Seeds stored in this environment can last for several years. Finally, don't share the space with any ripening fruit, especially apples. The ethylene gas that apples emit could have a negative impact on the viability of the seeds.

When you get ready to use the seeds, spread ten or so evenly on a damp paper towel. Cover the seeds with another damp paper towel or simply roll up the single thickness. Place the seeds in a warm location, and check them periodically over the next several days to see if the seeds have germinated. If many seeds have sprouted, fewer seeds will be needed to grow the fruit. If just a few have sprouted, you know that more seeds will have to be sown to get the same number of plants from the same given space.

Test the germination rate of your seeds by spreading a few on a damp paper towel and monitoring their progress.

CREATING THE PERFECT SOIL

If you live in an area of Florida with good, rich soil, thank your lucky stars because you have a leg up on everyone else. Throughout the Sunshine State many of our soils consist of those with high clay content, sandy loam, deep sugar sand, muck, peat, or limestone rock covered by marl or sand. The "soil" in which we are expected to grow plants often needs serious attention.

Use material from your compost pile to improve your soil.

If you look at sandy soil under a microscope you will see what appear to be small rocks. There is nothing there to hold water or nutrients. In some areas of the state there is red clay that requires a pick-axe to plant anything, and in other areas you'd need dynamite to blast a planting hole in the marl. It's a crazy place to try to grow anything, let alone food for your family. Make no mistake, however, everyone who lives here can grow fruits and vegetables; it just may be a little harder in some places than others. But first, let's talk a bit about what makes a great garden soil.

Loose is Best

When someone describes soil as "loose," what they mean is that it crumbles in the hand. That's the ideal soil, but few people have such

Squeeze a ball of soil; if it breaks apart in your hand, it should be workable.

naturally. If you do not, it can be attained by adding organic matter, including leaves, peat moss, animal manure, and compost. Clay soil feels slick and slippery to the touch and forms a ball when squeezed in the hand. Sandy soil, in contrast, flows through the fingers like . . . sand. There are variations throughout the spectrum but simply stated vegetables and fruit trees like soil that lets their roots move through the soil without difficulty or obstructions. Imagine tiny, tender roots as they meander through the soil in search of nutrients and water. Clay is made up of very tiny soil particles that obstruct fragile root hairs from wandering their way through the dirt. As a result, water has a tough time draining through clay soil and it becomes waterlogged. In clay soils, adding organic matter creates spaces in the soil that allow water and nutrients to move around. In sandy soils, organic matter absorbs and "grips" water and nutrients to keep them around for the plant to use. Otherwise, plant roots would have to grab what they could as any water passes by.

GROWING TIP

To improve fruit set on tomatoes, shake the tomato stake or hit the top of the stake a few times every day.

Conversely, if soil is "waterlogged" it means that the pockets of air in the root zone are filled with water. If the soil stays wet for too long the plant will drown. In areas that typical soil is deep clay or where limestone rock is close to the surface, getting soil to drain well may be difficult. Mechanical means, such as installing plastic drain lines such as those used in septic tanks, may be the only alternative. If the clay in your proposed garden spot isn't too deep, the addition of organic matter and coarse sand may help. In other locations where the clay is never ending or where the rock is just below the surface (as it is in South Florida), raised bed gardening or container gardening may be the only answer. For fruit trees, a large bed (the size depends a great deal on the strength of your back) several feet in diameter and 18 inches deep of good soil brought in from elsewhere will create an artificial, above ground root zone. For vegetable gardens, smaller beds 4 feet wide work best. You should be able to reach into the center of the bed to plant seeds and pull weeds without stepping onto the soil. Raised boxes can be made of any number of things, including 2- × 10-inch boards nailed together, landscape timbers, rocks, and even concrete blocks or seawall stones. Anything that will hold soil in the box is fine.

Good Ol' Dirt

When a gardener speaks of the soil being "neutral," they're not referring to its political affiliations. Instead, they are talking about the relative acidity or alkalinity of the soil. Soils in areas with low rainfall tend to be alkaline and where rainfall is high, soils tend to be more acidic. You may also have heard of "pH," which refers to acidity or alkalinity on a scale from 1 to 14, with 7 being neutral (neither acid nor alkaline). Each individual plant has an ideal pH range. For instance, lemon juice and battery acid are acidic and fall in the 0 to 7 range; whereas seawater and bleach are alkaline and fall in the 7

Periodically gather a soil sample and test with a pH testing kit.

to 14 pH range. Pure water is neutral, or 7 on the pH scale. Some plants have an ideal pH range that falls on the acid side, while others grow well in soils that range from slightly alkaline to slightly acid. The pH of your garden soil is important because the soil holds nutrients that allow the plant to grow and fight off diseases. As the pH increases or decreases, certain nutrients become more or less available for the plant to use.

The soil in a garden should be periodically tested and adjusted for optimum performance. If you have soil with a very high or low pH, you can alter it. A simple pH test kit, available at any garden center, can be used to see how the existing garden soil registers on the scale. The kit will also have instructions on how to change the pH of your soil for optimum growth. You can also test the soil by using litmus papers, available at many local drug stores. Mix a little of the soil with distilled water, and let it settle for a few minutes. Dip the litmus paper in the water and let it rest for one minute. The chart that comes with the litmus papers can be compared to the test paper, and the correct pH can be determined.

Most vegetables and fruit trees like soil that is slightly acidic—6.0 to 7.0. To make the soil more alkaline, add dolomitic lime powder according the package instructions. To increase the acidity in the soil by 0.5, add 2.75 pounds of elemental sulfur granules (available at garden centers) to a 100-square-foot site. Remember to change the pH only one point at a time. Changing pH should be considered a long-term project, so pH alterations should occur little by little. If the soil is too alkaline, consider creating a raised bed with good garden soil instead.

The Roots Run Deep

Deep, loamy soil is a wonderful thing. Often, however, a solid layer of clay is lurking just inches below the surface. In urban settings, buried construction debris or demolition rubble is lying in wait making it difficult for roots, nutrients, and water to move easily. All vegetables enjoy soil rich in nutrients and with good drainage. Additionally, many root vegetables such as potatoes and carrots require deep soils for their roots to develop properly. Other plants such as fruit trees depend on deep soils to anchor themselves and avoid being blown over in the wind. If your garden site has clay or rock hardpan, achieving deep soil may take many years to accomplish, but don't

GROWING TIP

Rather than use hay or straw as a mulch around your veggies, use oak leaves. Apparently slugs don't like the bitter taste of the leaves and will stay away.

give up hope. Even if raised beds are an option, bringing up a little of the native soil every time you prepare for the next crop will help create a good, deep soil over time.

The Nematode Nemesis

Organic matter is a gardener's best friend. It loosens the soil, it helps sandy soils retain water, and it helps clay soils drain better. It also does many other good things.

For instance, throughout the warm areas of the world, microscopic parasitic worms called "nematodes" hide in the soil looking for tender little roots to bite. They live on the sap inside the roots and prevent the plant from getting all the nutrients and water it needs to flourish. Now, mind you, we are not talking one or two worms. In one cubic foot of soil, there could be hundreds of thousands of these worms. They are microscopic, eel-like roundworms. The most troublesome species in the garden are those that live and feed within plant roots most of their lives. Although Florida has many different species of root-feeding nematodes, the most damaging ones to gardens are the root knot nematodes. They attack a wide range of plants, including many common vegetables, fruit trees, and ornamentals. As a defensive mechanism the plant's roots will form a scab (called a gall) around each nematode, and the roots become knobby in appearance. Above ground symptoms of a root knot nematode infestation include wilting during the

Nematode damage on tomato roots

hottest part of the day even with adequate soil moisture, loss of vigor, and yellowing leaves. Infested fruit trees and vegetable plants grow more slowly than neighboring, healthy plants and produce fewer and smaller leaves and fruits, and ones heavily infested early in the season can die. Damage is most serious in warm, irrigated, sandy soils. No matter how much water you provide, no matter how much fertilizer you add, no matter how much you talk to it, the plant will die.

All plants growing in warm climate areas of the world have to put up with nematodes. Not all plants, however, are overwhelmed by them; some survive until adulthood. Many, however, have abbreviated life spans because of the significant root damage. *There are NO pesticides to provide quick fixes either for nematode problems of existing vegetable and fruit plantings or to get rid of nematode threats before planting.* Managing nematodes may involve using one or more techniques that have proven to reduce populations.

One method of reducing the damage is to create an inhospitable environment for them. Soil solarization involves covering soil to be treated with clear polyethylene for an extended period in the summer. Solarization of field planting sites in Florida may be disappointing because it rarely heats soil sufficiently at the recommended depth (5 to 6 inches is common) to provide adequate control for the entire root zone area (usually at least 1 foot). This method doesn't kill the nematodes but rather forces them down into cooler soil. It takes several months for them to crawl back to the surface. This method also means that you can't grow vegetables on the site until after the procedure is complete— generally about 45 to 60 days. That's why most everyone does it in summer (June and July) when the sun can heat the dirt and fewer vegetables are typically grown.

Most of the problems with nematodes occur because vulnerable crops are grown in the same area each year. Gardeners need to consider rotating crops within the garden, and never plant very susceptible crops in the same place. Tomatoes, okra, cucumbers, squash, and melons are particularly susceptible so it's important to change their location at the beginning of each new growing cycle. Several vegetables have root-knot resistance. Some tomato varieties ('Celebrity', for instance), have been specifically bred to resist the pest. Some southern pea varieties such as 'Magnolia', 'Mississippi Silver', and 'Mississippi Purple' are also very resistant to the root-knot nematode. Plant any of these resistant varieties in areas where root-knot nematodes have begun building up or prior to planting a very susceptible crop. Most peaches, nectarines, and plums grown in Florida gardens utilize the Flordaguard rootstock that provides protection against root knot and other nematodes. Flordaguard replaces the better known but susceptible Nemaguard rootstock that has been used for decades. Barbados cherries and figs seem to be particularly susceptible to nematodes and are considered by many growers to be short-lived fruit trees. Carambola, sapodilla, avocado, macadamia, and muscadine grapes seem to be resistant. Adding organic amendments to the soil is an effective method of reducing damage by nematodes. These amendments may have an effect on the nematode population or plants in several ways. They may stimulate microorganisms in the soil that attack nematodes. Adding organic matter also improves soil structure and water-holding capacity, which makes for better growing conditions.

Add kitchen scraps and garden waste to your compost pile to create garden "food."

Feed the Soil

Last year when talking to a fellow gardener, I heard him say that he was going home to put some "groceries" on his garden. After that visual faded, the more I thought about what he had said, the more sense it made. As you plan the garden, think about feeding the hungry plants and their needs. Some people place fertilizer around the plants after they are planted; others place fertilizer in the soil and turn it under before planting. Either makes sense, but in either case the soil needs to be checked first to see what nutrients are present to start with. Apply fertilizer to fruit trees only two months after they have been planted. Any garden center has soil-testing kits of test tubes and color charts that can be used to check the fertility and pH of the soil. Every kit is different, but usually a little soil is placed into the test tube, the tube is then filled with water, and a capsule of powder is opened and placed in the tube. The whole thing is shaken for a few seconds and allowed to rest for an hour or so. In that time the soil will settle to the bottom and the water will change color. The colored water is then compared to the color charts in the accompanying booklet that came with the kit. Depending on the color, the booklet will provide recommendations on how

---

GROWING TIP

Most vegetables don't like deep cultivation because it breaks off their tender roots. Instead, cultivate to a depth of 1 inch to prevent bringing weed seeds to the surface.

---

much of specific fertilizers to apply for optimum plant growth. It's so simple my eight-year-old daughter used it.

Fertilizers can get a little complicated; just go to a nursery and try to figure out all those numbers on the different fertilizer bags. But, with a little knowledge, it's actually very simple. The three compounds that are used the most by plants, nitrogen, phosphorus, and potassium, are indicated by the three numbers on the bag in that order. The higher the number means more of that compound is in the bag. Nitrogen makes the plants grow. Phosphorous produces flowers and fruit, and potassium creates strong roots and provides resistance to disease. Once the soil tests are complete, apply the recommended amount to the entire garden area. Later as the plants grow you can add fertilizers in the amounts recommended in each of the plant profiles. If you want to be very specific, individual types and amounts of fertilizer can be

Organic material is good for the soil.

added by applying the fertilizer alongside of each plant, called side dressing, and scratching it into the soil.

Whether you apply synthetic fertilizer or organic fertilizer is up to you. Add no more than the recommended amount, and water it in well after application. If you add more than the recommended amount, then all your hard work would be for naught when the plants die from too much fertilizer. Plus, excess fertilizer will wash into and accumulate in bodies of water and even the aquifer, polluting them.

The next thing is to add organic matter. We know for certain that the addition of organic matter, regardless of the soil type, helps plants grow better. Any amount is better than none, but a 2- to 3-inch layer of compost spread over the entire space and turned into the soil either by a shovel or rototiller will work just fine.

When fertilizing fruit trees, make sure you put the fertilizer where the roots are. I've seen people in my neighborhood toss a coffee can or two full of fertilizer around the base of a tree. Unfortunately, that's not where the roots are. Fertilizer is wasted, or worse it causes damage to the trunk of the tree. Think of the fertilized area around the tree as a doughnut. Measure from the trunk of the tree halfway to the very edge of the foliage (called the "drip line"), add that measurement to the drip line circle, and fertilize that area. For example, let's say the distance from a tree trunk to the drip line is six feet. Beginning from a three-foot circle away from the trunk, add the recommended amount of fertilizer to an additional three feet beyond the drip line of the tree. Granted, there are many more roots growing beyond the drip line, but the tree will utilize what is applied in the doughnut area.

Many years ago when I was growing vegetables in a community garden at my alma mater, Florida A&M University, the gardener next to me had a garden spot that produced more vegetables and fruits than any garden I have seen since. My garden, on the other hand, produced what I thought was a pitiful amount. He started working in the garden at the same time that I did, and he even used the same varieties. One day I asked him how he did it and his response was simple: "Take care of the soil and the plants will take care of themselves." I listened to what he had to say, but quite frankly I didn't believe it. Surely nothing could be that simple. But over the years, as I added compost and oak leaves, my garden began to improve. It never has looked as good as his (after all, he had a good head start), but I always remember what he had to say and I've taken his advice to heart. What I learned more than thirty years ago still holds true today, and with every wheelbarrow full of compost I add to the soil I remember his words. Don't expect wonders overnight, but with the more good things you add to bare ground, the better it will be for growing food.

Improve your soil before you begin, and you'll be pleasantly surprised at how well your vegetables grow.

CHAPTER 4

WATERING THE GARDEN

Water is Florida's most precious resource and it's important that we use it to full advantage and not waste it. When providing water for a thriving vegetable garden or for fruit trees, there are many ways to be water smart.

Watering 1–2–3

Grow plants in the correct season. Squash grown in the heat of summer in Central and South Florida will always be asking for more water; it's just the wrong season to try to grow it. Plant summer vegetables (sweet potatoes, black-eyed peas, okra) when it's hot and plant cool-weather crops when things begin to cool down a bit. It may seem obvious, but many gardeners try to "stretch" a season and the end result can be a big mistake.

Make use of mulch. In addition to suppressing weeds and eventually adding organic matter to the soil as it breaks down, mulch does a great job of moderating soil temperatures and reducing evaporation. Mulch applied at a depth of 2 to 3 inches does a fine job, but too much may prevent water from reaching the soil. Oak leaves or straw will work just fine. A 2- to 3-inch circle of mulch around the base of a fruit tree will not only conserve water, it will prevent lawn mower damage to the bottom of the stem.

Watch indicator plants in the garden. Because fruit trees have deep roots it is sometimes difficult to tell when they need water. In the vegetable garden, it's hard to tell when plants need water until it's too late. There are, however, always one or two plants in the garden that display signs of water distress (wilting) before any other. Those can be your "indicator plants"; just hold off on the watering

Watering by hand with a watering can will allow you to direct the water to the base of the plants.

until your indicator plants begin to droop. When they begin to wilt, water everything in the garden nice and deep. Using indicator plants will allow you to water only when needed, which will force the plant roots to grow deep into the soil.

Maximizing Water Efficiency

Vegetable plants and fruit trees need three things to grow properly: water, sunlight, and nutritionally rich soil. Of the three, we have plenty of sunlight, and soil can be fairly easily amended to "create" the desired result. Water, however, is quickly becoming an issue. Unfortunately, water in Florida is in high demand and its availability in quantities we have utilized in the past is becoming smaller. North Florida gardeners are lucky to have some clay in their soil, which holds onto both water and nutrients. It's Central and South Florida where watering the garden often equates to real work. All three zones can need vast amounts of water in drought conditions; it's just that water in North Florida tends to hang around a bit longer. In the other two zones, water slips through the sandy soil as though it were a sieve, and more frequent watering may be necessary to grow trouble-free vegetables and fruit. Unfortunately, the commonest method of water application, aboveground sprinklers, is the most inefficient. In some studies it was discovered that

GROWING TIP

Submerge pots with a hole in the bottom adjacent to squash and melons to serve as a water reservoir. Fill the pots with water often to prevent the melons and squash from drying out in the sun.

more than 40 percent of the water applied using this method evaporates before it even hits the ground. We all need to learn how to use water in a more environmentally sensitive manner.

Let's talk about the water itself and where it comes from. Most of the water used by Florida homeowners comes from the ground. It's pumped up from layers of water in the ground called aquifers. It's from these aquifers that we obtain most of the water we drink and the water we use to irrigate our plants. Many people seem to like our weather and have moved here, and as a result, demand has exceeded available resources; some water now comes from desalination plants along either coast. In some areas of the state there is talk of pumping water from local rivers. Whether you get your water from municipally owned water agencies or from wells on your own property, many think there is not enough water to go around. Reclaimed water (treated water from wastewater treatment plants, also called "grey water"), is being introduced to communities throughout the Sunshine State, and it is being used to irrigate landscaped areas but it *is not recommended for food crops.*

Whether you agree or disagree about whether there is enough water to go around (some people think there may be enough water but that it just isn't being distributed properly), I think everyone will agree that water conservation is in everyone's best interest. The secret to watering a garden that produces food is to use whatever water you have available, municipal water or well or lake water, at its greatest efficiency. Not only is it wise to save water but it's wise to save money; the water coming out of your faucet is only going to get more expensive in the years ahead.

Rain Barrels, Drip Irrigation, and You

The simplest method for watering plants is to collect rainwater in a rain barrel. Unfortunately, water collected in a rain barrel that comes off the roof is not considered drinkable or "potable." Birds and other animals have been on the roof and when it rains, the contaminated water flows down the roof, into the gutter, down the downspout, and ultimately into the rain barrel. There it begins to cook an unhealthy concoction of E. coli, Salmonella, and upwards of fifteen to twenty other dangerous bacteria. Rain barrel water is

If you spread mulch such as oak leaves or straw around your plants, you'll get less soil splatter when you water.

fine if used on non-edible plants such as flowers or lawns but not on edible plants at any stage of growth.

In overhead irrigation, water is applied to a garden space via a variety of sprinklers. It is a very inefficient system, and any water lingering on the plants creates a great habitat for the growth of disease organisms. If you must use overhead irrigation make certain that you water deeply and as infrequently as possible while still maintaining adequate soil moisture for fruit production. It is generally accepted that watering in the morning before 10 a.m. works best; this gives the plants a chance to dry off during the day, reducing the chance of diseases. While overhead irrigation is easy (all you need is a hose and sprinkler), it is clearly the most ineffective way to disperse water.

The best watering system would be one that doesn't get the plant leaves and stems wet, and distributes water at the root zone. Such systems include drip systems, micro jet irrigation, and soaker hoses. The former utilize a series of supply hoses, generally ½ to ⅝ inch in diameter under low pressure, with many smaller tubes emanating from the supply tube to individual plants. All three types of "soakers" can be placed above or below newspaper mulch, and soaker types should be placed beneath the black plastic mulch when growing melons and pumpkins. All drip systems need a valve to control the dispensing of water at the proper time and a back flow preventer to prevent irrigation water from backing up into the drinking water system.

A drip irrigation system is best for both conserving water and watering at the base of plants.

Battery-operated control valves or electrically operated solenoids can turn the water on and off to individual areas of the garden or to individual trees. Trees need more emitters than vegetables due to their size. Your system can be engineered to fit the specific needs of your vegetable garden or the number and size of the trees you are growing. Older trees have more roots than young ones and consequently need more emitters as time goes on. If you have sandy soil, the emitters will have to be closer together because water doesn't travel far horizontally in sand. If you have clay soil the emitters can be spaced farther apart. Drip systems can also reduce soil erosion and nutrient leaching.

As its name implies, the drip method utilizes a small head that slowly drips a predetermined amount of water into the soil around the plants' roots below. Drippers can be purchased that distribute different amounts of water depending on your specific needs. Clearly, lettuce requires less water than a tomato plant, and the drip heads can be adjusted to water only what's needed, in the right amount, to the right plant, to the right place (the root zone).

Micro jets also utilize the same large and small supply tubes, but rather than emitting a drip of water, it utilizes a small spray head. The head sprays a predetermined amount of water to a wide area of the root zone, unlike the drip method, which delivers water to a smaller area and works primarily through capillary action. Both systems work extremely well but are initially more expensive than a simple hose and sprinkler setup. Depending on the design of the garden each year, the supply lines may have to be repositioned for proper spacing. Although it takes more time initially to set up, both the drip and the micro jets are the most efficient watering systems on the market today.

One last thought about watering. Soaker hoses work very well and provide water to the immediate root zone where it's needed. Many are very inexpensive and many brand names of hoses are recycled from old tires. A soaker hose connects to a standard garden hose, is very economical, and puts the water where it's required. That sounds like a pretty good system for someone just starting out. It's important to note, however, with the cheaper system comes less efficiency. The hose at the point closest to the water source will have more pressure than the hose farther away from the source. That means that the plants closest to the water source will get more water over time than those further down the line. Netafim™ is a soaker hose with engineered internal emitters will give you an even pressure across the entire length of the tube regardless of how long and how far away from the source it is. It's more expensive but well worth it, and can be placed underground or on top of the ground. Netafim™ is readily available at garden centers and home improvement stores (www.Netafim.com).

CHAPTER 5

GARDEN TOOLS

Entire books have been written about gardening tools. If you visit any home improvement store, you will see rows of tools of every description and for every purpose and for every price. For the first-time gardener it can be a little overwhelming. For us old timers the current price of a good shovel or rake can give us sticker shock—good tools cost money.

Tools are most often advertised as a help to make gardening easier. Who doesn't want a little help? Gardening of any kind in Florida, whether it's growing roses or fruit trees, is hard work. If I remember one thing my father said about gardening, it's that there are no short cuts. You have to put in the work to get anything worthwhile in return. By 10 a.m. the sun is beating down on your head, and the humidity from the previous afternoon's rain is oppressive. That's why many gardeners will hang up their gloves until after dinner when temperatures return to a bearable level. But to get started, these are all the tools you will need:

Hats

Let's start with the basics. Dorky as they may be, if you don't want sunburn (and the health problems that come with it) you'll need a hat with a wide brim. I've seen a few in mail order catalogs that would require a small loan to buy. Save your money. An eight dollar hat works just as well as a forty dollar hat. You may even have to replace it

Wide-brimmed hat

midseason, but it's only going to cost another $8 instead of $40. Remember, one of the reasons we are growing our own food is to save money. Your neighbors may think the hat looks funny but it may save you a trip to the dermatologist down the road. Cloth hats with wide brims are equally good and can be washed. You'll pay more, but they will last a long time.

Gloves

A good pair of gloves is another basic tool. But, confession time; I have never been a fan (primarily because I can never keep track of them). If you decide to wear them, spend the money. Inexpensive gloves won't last as long as those that cost a little more, and cheap gloves aren't designed as well. Sometimes a cheap glove will give you a blister before a hoe handle does. Good gloves will prevent blisters, dirty fingernails and hands, and will protect your hands from scratches. Good goatskin gloves are worth their weight in gold and are tough enough to prevent most prickles from gouging your hand.

Shovels

Picking the right shovel is critical. Like selecting a watering can, you need to take time to decide which type is best for you. Remember, your shovel will be your best gardening friend for a long time (perhaps even decades) and selecting the right one is a significant decision. It may seem I am giving the selection of a tool too much weight but a shovel can make you or break you when it comes to gardening in Florida's climate.

Shovels come in two basic types: one has a somewhat rounded steel blade (round shovel) and the other has a flat blade (spade). Each one works well but you will need to decide which performs best for you. Both are used to dig holes and turn soil over in preparation for planting. Likewise, shovel handles come in two "varieties" as well; one is a straight handle and the other has a T- or D-shaped handle. Both round shovels and spades can be manufactured with either a straight or a T-shaped handle. The straight-handled round shovel is the most commonplace. However, the spade with a T- or D-shaped handle is the most versatile. This type of handle gives the shovel some turning leverage and can be used for longer periods with less hand strain.

Round shovel

Again, don't try to save money on a shovel. Buy a good one. Either type of shovel should have two heavy "lips" at the very top of the blade on either side of the handle. These lips will permit you to place greater force on the blade when you step on it without hurting the

arch in your foot. The bigger the lip, the greater the force that can be applied to the shovel blade.

The manufacturers in the United Kingdom really know how to make a worthwhile shovel, and the expense will certainly be worth it. Several good dealers of steel T- or D-shaped handled spades can be found on the Internet and at local specialty stores. And remember, the shiny stainless steel and expensive shovels aren't any better than regular steel models.

A few things about shovel maintenance are important to know. First, make certain the shovel blade is sharpened regularly. There is nothing more discouraging than trying to cut through sod or a root with a dull blade. An inexpensive steel file can sharpen the blade before you place it back into the garden shed at the end of the day. This brings up the next point: clean the blade and handle before you put it away. A light spray of WD-40˚ on the blade before you hang the shovel up will help keep the shovel in good shape for a long time. When you need it, it will be ready to go. And one last thing—an old-time gardener taught me this fact about shovels many years ago. As he was watching me replace a broken shovel handle, he simply said, "A broken shovel handle is a sign of a lazy man." It made me pause. Sure enough, I had forced the shovel handle down with most of my weight while trying to remove a tree root. Had I spent more time digging and less time trying the force the shovel to do something it wasn't designed to do, I would still have that shovel with its original handle today.

Flat-tipped spade

Trowels

A trowel is basically a small shovel. I can say with great certainty that I have spent more money buying trowels to replace broken ones than I have for any other tool. Most trowels on the market have wooden handles with a bar attached to a blade with rivets. When you apply any pressure at all, the rivets break off, making the tool unusable. Ask any professional gardener and they will tell you, hands down, the best trowels are made from one piece of aluminum and have a comfortable foam handle. A $2 trowel is worth just that. Get the good kind.

All-metal trowel

Hoes

Pick up a hoe and you know hard work is just around the corner. Hoes are used to remove weeds around cultivated plants and to help make furrows

Grubbing hoe

when planting seeds. There are two basic types and, after a time, you will have both in your arsenal. The most common is often called a grubbing hoe; it has a wide steel blade at the end of a long handle. It is used to dig deep into the soil, removing weeds by their roots. A newer and somewhat easier version is called an oscillating, pass-through, or scuffle hoe. There are several versions of it. Most have a steel loop, flat on one side, at the end of a long handle, and they can be pushed or pulled. Rather than digging the entire root, a scuffle hoe passes ½ to 1 inch below the soil surface cutting the roots off. Other designs of scuffle hoes have heart-shaped steel. Other types of hoes include the collinear, swan neck, Reisch hoe, and onion hoe.

The advantage to a grubbing hoe (sometimes called an "eye" hoe) is that, in addition to pulling out the roots, you are cultivating soil at the same time, allowing good nutrient and water penetration into the soil. A scuffle hoe does cultivate but because many plants don't like their surface roots to be disturbed, a grubbing hoe is a good choice. You will have to decide which hoe is best for you in your particular situation.

Pitchforks

A pitchfork can be a versatile tool in the garden. You can use it backwards (tines down and drawing the pitchfork towards you) to rake up weeds and to scoop up the debris into the compost pile. A pitchfork can also be used to break up soil clumps in the garden prior to sowing seeds, and the handle can be used to create a shallow seed furrow.

Pitchfork

Lifting or Turning Forks

Perhaps one of the most misunderstood, and most underutilized, tools in the gardener's collection is the lifting fork. Unlike the pitchfork, which has four to seven round tines, a lifting or turning fork has four to five flat, pointed bars with a "T" handle. The turning fork, as its name implies, is used to dig and turn soil over, instead of using a shovel. After the soil is lifted and turned the fork can be used to break up any clods of soil. The turning fork can also be used to harvest root crops (such as potatoes, turnips, and peanuts) without harming the crop. The lifting fork is inserted into the soil, and, in several swift, lifting motions, it lifts the roots out of the soil. There is very little bruising to the roots while the soil sifts through the fork. To divide overgrown perennials, two forks are placed

Lifting or turning fork

71

back-to-back into a large clump of daylilies, liriope, or so forth; the clump can be gently pulled apart causing little, if any, injury to the plant roots.

Pruners, Loppers, and Saws

To complete any gardener's tool chest, you need something to cut branches and harvest fruit. Hand pruners come in a variety of styles, and it seems that someone is always trying to improve on the time-tested standards. Pruners are available in just two basic styles: the anvil or pinching style and the scissors style. The anvil type has a single blade and a flat surface that cuts a branch off. If someone gives you these pruners as a gift, immediately re-gift them. The

Scissors-style pruner

blade on this style become dull very quickly and is virtually impossible to sharpen. After time, the blade becomes so dull that rather than cutting the branch off, the anvil pruner simply pinches the branch off, causing damage to the remaining part of the branch. The scissors type, as its name implies, has two bypassing blades that create a nice, sharp cut. The blade can easily be sharpened after a day's work, and good models even have replaceable blades. Hand pruners should only be used when the branches to be pruned are less than ½ inch in diameter. For branches ½ to ¾ inches in diameter, use loppers. These long-handled pruners have scissor type blades also, and because the long handles can provide the needed leverage to cut larger pieces of wood, they are a useful tool. Anything more than ¾ inch in diameter requires a saw. The most common type of saw is a folding handsaw. The blades are very sharp and folding the blade into the handle when the job is finished will protect the blade and the gardener.

Loppers

Miscellaneous Tools

There are few other things you need as time goes on. A good garden hose is worth the money. Do not try to save money on a hose. Inexpensive hoses will kink (why spend all your time in the garden trying to unravel the hose?); the brass connectors at either end will bend or, worse, separate from the hose altogether; and a cheap hose will spring leaks. Start with at least a ⅝-inch hose made of good rubber that has some heft to it. Later, you may buy a ¾-inch hose with heavy brass connectors, but at first, buy what you can afford. Please, when you buy your hose also buy a water breaker designed to water plants, and a hose-end water valve. Water straight out of the hose will wash small seeds and seedlings away. Most breakers come attached to a long, aluminum watering wand that will help to reach those hard-to-get spots. Keep your car wash water nozzle in the garage where it belongs.

Folding saw

Watering cans, like shovels, are something you have for a long time so make sure you get one that works just like you want it to. You can pay a good sum for one, but the plastic versions can work just as well. (Put the expensive galvanized or copper versions on your birthday wish list.) The ideal watering can will have a good detachable "rose" (the device where the water comes out), the front half of the top opening should be covered (to prevent water from gushing out over the top when you tip the can), and it should have measurements marked on the side.

Garden hose with sprayer

At first, I thought gardening boots were a luxury, but after wearing out several pairs of tennis shoes, I learned otherwise. Good garden boots have a stiff, steel arch that helps immeasurably when you use your foot against the shovel to dig holes. Believe me; your arches will thank you at day's end. Good boots will also have reinforcement rubber along the outside of the arch and at the protruding ankle bone location on the inside of your foot. Finally, if you spray chemicals of any kind, rubber boots protect your feet and legs from chemical contact and can be cleaned with soap and water. (Chemicals are absorbed and their toxicity is intensified when you use leather shoes or boots.)

Rubber garden boots

CHAPTER 6

VEGETABLES & FRUITS

Growing food in Florida may be one of the most gratifying and satisfying accomplishments in your gardening saga. Eating fresh food that you have grown, often from seed, and nurtured to maturity is a remarkable voyage. The best news is that *you* did it. You know what has (or has not) been sprayed on the fruit and vegetables you are about to eat. You know the work involved in bringing food to the table (if you didn't eat all the peas out in the garden first). You saved your family's hard-earned money by growing food at home. And when you go inside after a long day in the garden and look in the mirror at your smudged face and dirty fingernails, you can be proud. Fellow gardeners, I salute you!

Planting and growing your own food can bring immense satisfaction to the whole family.

Bean 'Red Noodle'

BEAN

If you have a vegetable garden in Florida you have to have beans. Bush beans, pole beans, French filet beans, shelling beans, lima beans—all perform well in Florida gardens. Beans are a great way to introduce children to gardening because they may be the easiest of vegetables to grow. In my family, we often grow pole beans on bamboo poles, creating a little teepee "hideaway" for the younger folks. It's not unusual to find children tucked inside reading a book. Snap beans used to be called "string" beans because of the tough fibrous string on the back of the pod that had to be removed before cooking. Newer varieties don't have the "string."

■ When to Plant

In North Florida beans are best grown from March through November. In Central and South Florida plant beans beginning in February through May and again from August through October, thus escaping frosts and the hottest months. Plant a new row of seeds every ten to fourteen days to have a fresh supply of beans every week.

■ Where to Plant

Plant beans in a location that receives at least eight hours of full sun a day. Beans will provide a virtually limitless bounty if you take the time to prepare a good, compost-rich seedbed. And, if they are grown in good soil and receive ample water, beans can be pest free. Beans are a good candidate for growing in containers provided they get adequate light and plenty of water.

■ How to Plant

As with any legume with a deep taproot, beans do not like to be transplanted. Direct sow them in the soil where you plan to grow them. If you insist on growing them in pots first, use biodegradable pots that can be planted directly in the soil without disturbing the roots. Plant individual seeds every 5 to 6 inches in rows that are 18 inches apart. When the new growth emerges from the soil (three to five days after they're planted), the bean seedlings are often the favorite food of birds, especially brown thrashers. They will break off the tender seed that emerges with the new leaves, which will kill the new sprout. My daughter's 30-inch-long lifelike plastic lizard will scare them off most years but whirling shiny aluminum pie pans attached to strings on sticks will work too. If neither appeals to you, simply plant a few more seeds in the empty spots after the remaining seedlings get a little taller. Go easy on the fertilizer—more beans are killed by too much fertilizer than too little. Too much fertilizer also produces more leaves and fewer beans.

A tripod made from poles or canes lashed at the top is an easy trellis option for pole beans.

▮ Care and Maintenance

If you are searching for a carefree plant, look no further. If beans are prone to any disease it would be rust disease; tiny orange pustules that appear on the undersides of the leaves causing the leaves to drop off prematurely. The best way to prevent rust is to make it a habit to avoid walking through or handling bean plants while they are wet. Handling them will transfer the disease from one plant to another via water droplets. Wait until the leaves and stems are dry before handling them.

Fertilize every four weeks with a general-purpose fertilizer or one specific to your particular soil as determined by a soil analysis. Bean beetles and bean leaf rollers are the most common pests, both of which can be controlled using soap, spinosad, or pyrethrins. The leaf roller can also be controlled by *B.t.*

■ Additional Information

Bush beans are harvested while the bean pods are still tender and the beans have not fully formed inside. For bush beans, French filet beans, and pole beans, pull the beans gently from the plant being careful not to damage the stems and leaves. It's not uncommon to get three to four crops from each plant. The many varieties of bush beans are harvested while they are tender and no more than 6 to 7 inches long. Good varieties include 'Bush Blue Lake 274', 'Commodore Improved', 'Contender', 'Flaco', 'Greencrop', 'Pike', and 'Roma II' (Italian flat). The best yellow beans are 'Goldrush', 'Improved Golden Wax', and 'Cherokee Wax'. 'Royal Burgundy' is the best purple variety (burgundy colored beans will change to green when cooked).

French green bean 'Alicante'

Pole beans also produce many crops in one season, and they are easier to harvest than bush beans. Pole beans can grow to 8 feet tall and need some sort of support to grow on. Most often, two poles are placed at either end of a row and wire is stretched across the top. Strings are then gently and loosely attached to bean stems below the lowest leaves and then tied to the overhead wire. The beans will naturally climb up the string. A section of welded wire fencing (with 2 × 4-inch spaces) supported by posts at either end works well too and will last a lifetime. Good varieties of pole beans include 'Kentucky Wonder', 'Blue Lake', 'Christmas', 'Florida Butter Speckled', 'Yard Long Green and Red Noodle', 'Rattlesnake', 'Purple Trionofo Violetto', 'Romano Italian', and 'Big Mama'.

GROWING TIP

Once bush beans are planted they don't need any additional fertilizer. Pole beans and lima beans enjoy a little more "juice" after the blossoms begin to appear.

French filet beans have pods that are smaller in size but big on taste. Reported to be the most flavorful bean in the world, French filet beans are popular with professional chefs because of the tender pods and mild flavor. 'Allicante' and 'Golden Child' are the best varieties for Florida.

Shell beans can be harvested while the pods are still tender but more often are allowed to dry in the pod before harvesting for soups or dry bean storage. Good shell beans for Florida include 'Tiger Eye', 'Painted Pony', and 'Jacob's Cattle'.

Don't forget lima beans! They can be eaten fresh, canned, dried, or frozen. Use 'Dixie Butterpea Speckled', 'King of the Garden', 'Fordhook 242', 'Burpee Improved', 'Speckled Calico', and 'Big Mama'.

'Painted Lady' and 'Sunset' are climbing beans that will produce pods but are generally grown as a decorative variety for covering gazebos or arbors.

Lima bean 'King of the Garden'

Beet 'Detroit Dark Red'

BEET

Before you say it, I know not everyone likes beets. Their deep, earthy flavor may be an acquired taste but they are a very versatile vegetable when cooked in soups, served warm with a little raspberry vinaigrette and goat cheese, or used fresh in a cold salad. If you have only eaten beets from a jar or can then perhaps growing your own beets might change your mind. Their colors run the gamut from deep "church pew" red to yellow, white, and even striped red and white. Don't forget the beet leaves can be eaten in salads or cooked like spinach. Beets are high in a wide array of vitamins and minerals.

When to Plant

Beets are a cool-season crop and should be planted from September through March in North Florida and from October through March in Central and South Florida. They are tolerant of a little frost (short of hard freezes) and can also withstand a few warm days, making them a very long-season crop.

Where to Plant

Plant beets in full sun, in a well-tilled, well-drained soil free of rocks and stones. Beets can sometimes look stunted, which is often caused by soil pH outside the beet's comfort range of 6.2 to 6.7.

How to Plant

Each little beet seed actually contains the beginnings of three to four seedlings so don't be surprised if three little plants sprout from the ground where you only planted one seed. To prevent crowding, it is essential that you remove all but one seedling every 3 inches. Otherwise, the roots will be small and deformed. Soak the seeds overnight in warm water (I use an insulated thermos bottle or a foam cup) and sow the next day. Plant individual seeds ¼ inch deep and expect to see sprouts in seven to ten days. To prevent root maggots, sprinkle the row with a small amount of wood ash (½ cup for every 10 feet of row) from a fireplace. Space the rows anywhere from 12 to 18 inches apart.

■ Care and Maintenance

Beets are particularly sensitive to a lack of water. If you want big healthy roots, make sure they get plenty, especially during dry spells. Follow the directions based upon a soil analysis, but a general rule of thumb is fertilize the seedbed before the seeds are planted and again after the beets reach a height of 3 to 4 inches. Flea beetles are a problem from time to time but can be controlled with pyrethrins, spinosad, or pyrethrum.

■ Additional Information

Beet greens are best harvested when they are 5 to 6 inches tall. The roots can be harvested any time during the growing season, but they are best when they are less than 2 inches in diameter. If they are any larger than that they can get pithy and are difficult to eat. Hands down, 'Detroit Dark Red' is the best deep red variety. 'Burpee's Golden' is just that—a beautiful, deep-golden color. For a little novelty try the heirloom variety 'Chioggia'; when it's cut across the root, it has alternating red and white stripes (great for salads) and turns solid red when cooked. Other good varieties include 'Cylindrica', 'Piatta D'Egitto', and 'Yellow Detroit'. 'Baby Ball' is the preferred small beet for container growing and 'Blankoma' has a white root but the same beet taste. 'Bull's Blood' as the name infers has beautiful deep red leaves that are often used in salads, and 'Long Season Lutz' is grown primarily for its tall, luscious, bright green foliage that equals the leaf size of large Swiss chard.

GROWING TIP

Although beets come in several different colors, if they are cooked with red beets they will all turn red during the cooking process. If you want the orange beet to stay orange and the white beet to remain white, cook them in different pots and mix just prior to presentation.

Broccoli 'Veronica'

BROCCOLI

Despite being disparaged by a certain past president, broccoli, when prepared properly, is a delicious vegetable. Unfortunately, some people cook the pure life out of it by covering it with water and cooking it until it leaves the saucepan limp and lifeless. It is the unopened flower head that we eat, and a well-grown broccoli "head" can easily reach 6 to 7 inches in diameter. When the primary head is removed, smaller florets appear in the lower leaf nodes and can continue to produce for another 30 to 45 days.

■ When to Plant

Make no mistake—broccoli is a cool-weather crop. If an early-maturing variety is planted at the onset of cooler weather, a second crop can be planted and will grow until warm weather returns. (Be sure to rotate to another location within the garden if you plant a second crop.) But if it gets too much heat the plants will begin to flower and set seed (called "bolting") and it will be unusable.

■ Where to Plant

Plant broccoli in full sun and well-drained, moist soil with added organic matter (compost, leaves, peat moss, and so forth). Soil acidity in the range of 6 to 7 is best to prevent root diseases.

■ How to Plant

Broccoli is very easy to grow from seed. Place one or two seeds in a small flowerpot or seedling tray with good potting soil ¼ inch deep and cover with fine soil. To prevent seeds from washing away while watering, place the container inside a larger one containing shallow water and water from the bottom up, removing the pot when the soil becomes saturated. Seedlings will appear in four to seven days. If more than one seed sprouts, thin to one seedling per container. Keep the seedlings in full sun and prevent the soil from drying out. Once the seedling has developed three new leaves that look like the mature leaves, plant the seedling directly into prepared garden soil. Broccoli needs plenty of room to grow properly, so don't try to squeeze many plants into a small space. Space plants 24 inches apart in the row and place each row 24 inches apart.

■ Care and Maintenance

Once planted, broccoli is easy to grow. Give it plenty of water, and feed it every three to four weeks with a general-purpose fertilizer of 5-0-5 or 8-0-8. It is a shallow-rooted plant, so be very careful about deep cultivation. Once the heads have matured, but before the individual flowers begin to expand, cut the center head about 6 inches below the flower head. If you continue to feed and water as before, small flower shoots (florets) will begin to sprout and can supply more broccoli, albeit smaller, for four to five more weeks. Watch for aphids on the undersides of the leaves that often migrate to the central head. To remove the small insects before cooking simply soak the flower head in cold salted water for several minutes. The dead aphids can be washed off with a kitchen sink sprayer. Watch for armyworms when seedlings are first set out into the garden. A simple 3-inch collar of heavy paper secured with a paper clip and pushed partially into the ground around each transplant will keep the worms away from the stems.

■ Additional Information

Several varieties of broccoli are available, but some of the best include 'Packman' (an early season selection), 'High Dividend', and 'Green Comet.' 'Goliath' produces very large heads (8 to 9-inch diameter) and after the central head is harvested it produces very large florets (3-inch diameter) for another 5 to 6 weeks.

Harvest broccoli by slicing at the stem before the florets start to yellow.

BRUSSELS SPROUTS

When I first saw Brussels sprouts when I was eight years old, I thought they were tiny cabbages growing on a stalk. As it turns out, I wasn't far off. As a member of the same family, the taste is similar to that of cabbage and some even say, of broccoli. A planting of ten to twelve individual seedlings is usually enough for a family of four. Getting them to a size large enough to produce harvestable quantities may take a little longer than some gardeners have patience for, however; from seed planting to final harvest can be as long as 140 days

■ When to Plant

This is a cold-season crop and should be planted from October through February. Seeds should be started indoors or under cover forty-five days prior to transplanting into the garden soil; by then, the seedlings should have three to four pairs of true leaves.

■ Where to Plant

Plant Brussels sprouts where they will get plenty of sunshine (a minimum of eight hours), in enriched, well-drained soil. Give them room to grow, although the stalk where the little buds grow is only 1½ inches in diameter. It's the leaves at the top that are the plant's power supply, and they need plenty of space. Too little sun will cause the plants to stretch and the sprouts will be small, if any are produced at all.

■ How to Plant

Plant as seedlings 24 inches apart, in rows 24 inches apart. Don't worry if the seedlings fall over once they are planted. Brussels

Brussels sprouts

GROWING TIP

Many gardeners will pinch out the very top central shoot when the lower sprouts begin to mature. This encourages many sprouts to ripen along the stem.

sprouts are famous for lying down before they decide to grow upright. Staking is not necessary even though each plant can reach a height of 36 inches.

Care and Maintenance

Brussels sprouts are carefree plants. The sprouts and new growth at the top may attract aphids, but a simple spray of water from the garden hose usually takes care of that situation. If they persist, a light spray of spinosad, Neem, pyrethroids, oil, or soap will solve the problem. Growing plants in full sun with adequate moisture and regular feedings will allow the plant to defend itself. Keep the pH in the neighborhood of 6.0 to 6.8. Brussels sprouts are heavy nitrogen feeders so add additional nitrogen to your standard fertilizer application every three weeks to keep them going strong. If your fertilizer contains a few minor elements, especially boron, so much the better. You will get stronger buds and the stem won't get hollow. Brussels sprouts are shallow rooted so be careful when cultivating.

Additional Information

Before you plant, make certain you are committed to growing Brussels sprouts for the long term. Of all the vegetables, they can take the longest to produce a harvest and they need plenty of room to grow properly. The little sprouts mature from the bottom of the stalk up. To harvest, simply twist the individual sprouts off the stalk when they are about ¾ inch in diameter and firm. Small sprouts can be eaten but it takes more of them to make a meal. When they grow too large, they get fibrous and woody and their flavor is much stronger. Remove the lower leaves and buds, leaving a rosette at the top, to encourage more sprouts and leaves. Try 'Jade Cross', 'Trafalgar' and 'Long Island Improved' for best production in Florida. For an unusual heirloom variety, 'Rubine' produces colorful purple-red sprouts.

CABBAGE

Of all the members of the Brassica family, which includes Brussels sprouts, cauliflower, and broccoli, cabbage may be the least finicky of the cool-season crops to grow in the home garden. It's a great plant to include in a beginner's garden because it is so easy to grow, and there are numerous unique cabbage varieties to keep the more advanced gardener intrigued. Other than needing a frequent application of nitrogen fertilizer, cabbages can be grown just about anywhere and harvested at any stage.

■ When to Plant

Cabbage hates warm weather and will "bolt" (begin flowering) when temperatures get too warm. (They can also bolt when it gets too cold, but that's rarely a problem in Florida.) Plant one crop in late fall and another 30 to 45 days later to stagger the harvest. Trust me; one family does not need ten cabbages at the same time! Stop planting in March.

■ Where to Plant

Plant in full sun, in average, well-drained soil.

■ How to Plant

There are two schools of thought on how to plant cabbages. I once read that to grow cabbages properly you mustn't till the soil prior to planting. The advice was to simply remove the weeds and transplant seedlings into hard, unimproved garden soil. Another time, I read that you must till the soil deeply, add organic matter to a depth of 6 to 8 inches, and plant the seedlings in the prepared soil. After planting cabbages utilizing both methods, I didn't notice any difference. Lucky for me, cabbages don't know how to read. However, you must anticipate the eventual size of the plant (read the seed package or label when buying transplants) because different types of cabbages need different spacing. Cabbage can be direct sown into the ground but must be thinned to proper spacing to achieve proper growth. Spacing seeds or transplants too close together will yield small, weak plants.

■ Care and Maintenance

Well-drained soil, lots of water, and regular applications every three weeks of fertilizers high in nitrogen is the prescription for healthy cabbage. Keep the weeds away because they compete for

Savoy cabbage 'Deadon'

the water and nutrients. Occasionally after planting, armyworms will cut the tender stems of the new sprouts or newly planted transplants during the night, making them look as though a tiny lumberjack sawed his way through the garden. A 3 × 5-inch index card cut in half lengthwise, attached end to end with a paper clip or staple, and then pushed halfway into the ground will create enough of a barrier to prevent damage from the worms. Once the seedlings get a little older (and a little tougher), the collars can be removed.

■ Additional Information

Many different types of cabbages are available and some of the best information about which cabbage does best in your area may come from your fellow neighborhood gardeners. Ask around for their ideas; you'll be surprised how helpful that neighbor you never talked to before can be. Select early and late cabbage varieties for a constant supply. Other than asking a neighbor, try 'New Jersey Wakefield' (whose head grows to a point), 'Bonnie's Hybrid', and 'Copenhagen Market' to start. For a red cabbage variety, try 'Mammoth Red Rock'; and for a curled cabbage, plant 'Savoy Chieftain' or 'Deadon'. Both 'Baby Pixie' and 'Bobcat' are good varieties for growing in raised beds or containers.

Chinese cabbages are the "pretty boys" of the cabbage world, and many can even be used in ornamental plantings instead of bedding plants. 'Michihili' is without a doubt the best, followed closely by 'Jade Pagoda', 'Mei Oing Choi', and 'Rubicon'.

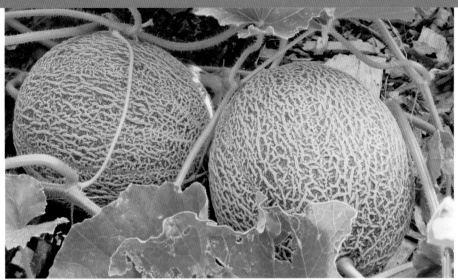

Cantaloupe

CANTALOUPE

Is there anything in the world more refreshing on a hot, Florida summer day than eating an ice-cold cantaloupe? Only a big scoop of vanilla ice cream dropped in the center could make it better. I am often asked why I got into gardening and it may very well be that eating a cantaloupe freshly picked off the vine is what demonstrated the difference between home grown versus store-bought. If you haven't attempted to grow cantaloupe because you don't have the space, believe me, it's worth the effort. However, given their nomadic nature, this plant really should not be considered for small gardens.

■ *When to Plant*

Plant seedlings or seeds in mid- to late February or after the danger of frost has passed. The earlier you can get them in the ground (but avoiding any chance of frost), the better your chances of growing ample-sized fruit before the bugs invade with warmer weather. Start seeds indoors three weeks before the last anticipated frost in spring.

■ *Where to Plant*

Plant in full sun, in well-drained, organically enriched soil. Depending on the variety, cantaloupes take up lots of room. For gardeners with small spaces, try the bush forms. Good air circulation is a must to fend off pesky disease organisms.

How to Plant

Given that weeds often grow faster and better than the vegetable you're trying plant, applying a weed barrier of some sort is helpful when growing melons. Seeds or seedlings can be planted either in rows 48 inches apart, with individual plants set 24 inches apart, or in hills 48 to 60 inches apart, with four to five seeds per hill. Place black plastic or landscape fabric over the entire area in which you want the vines to grow, or place a single layer of newspaper covered with coastal hay immediately next to the plants and wherever the vines are expected to grow. The vines will grow over the weed barrier without weed competition. If you use plastic or landscape fabric, cut a slit in the plastic and plant the seedlings or seeds as described. Give the seedlings at least 1 inch of water per week.

Care and Maintenance

Sometimes, cantaloupes will be visited by slugs and bugs that bore into the fruit. Much of their damage can be reduced, if not eliminated, by placing any half-grown fruit on a board or atop a recycled tin can. In addition, cantaloupe can be grown on a vertical support system similar to that of pole beans and the fruit supported by recycled nylon stockings or panty hose. Using this method, slugs are almost never a problem, and the fruit stays clean and easy to monitor for picking at the right time. One last thing, as the fruit begins to ripen, hold off on watering a little. The fruit tastes better if cantaloupes don't get too much water late in the game. Cantaloupes are ready to harvest when the fruit separates easily from its stem and/or the netting on the outside of the fruit turns from green to tan. Cantaloupes are heavy feeders and need plenty of soil moisture to perform well. Give each plant ½ cup of a 5-0-5 fertilizer ratio or fish emulsion three weeks after planting and again after the flowers appear.

Additional Information

The hybridizers have been busy with cantaloupes, but despite their best efforts I still think 'Ambrosia' is the best; the flavor is intense and the vines are resistant to diseases. Once you have conquered the standard varieties consider other members of the melon family, including banana melons, Crenshaw, French hybrids, casaba, Jenny Lind muskmelons, yellow canary melons, and Ogen melons. For small areas, try 'Minnesota Midget' cantaloupes—they have 3-foot-long vines.

CARROT

Carrot 'Atlas'

If you have ever pulled a carrot out of the ground, washed it off with water from a garden hose, and munched on it, you know how sweet and crisp homegrown carrots are compared to store-bought. After tasting their first garden carrot my children later would routinely run out into the garden after school to graze on the myriad fresh vegetables. Come to think of it, I used to do the same after my father introduced me to freshly picked peas. With our four children, carrots were the breakthrough veggie, followed by beans, peas, lettuce, and broccoli.

When to Plant

Carrots can be planted any time between September and mid-March. Two to three sowings during that period will provide roots that are tender and sweet.

Where to Plant

Plant carrots where they will receive at least eight hours of full sun, in a well-drained soil that is free from any rocks, stones, and roots.

How to Plant

A carrot is one of those vegetables that require just a little bit of extra care for good production. First, carrot roots tend to fork rather than have that straight, store-bought look when they reach any sort of obstacle such as roots of neighboring trees or shrubs, rocks, pebbles, and even irrigation pipes. It's important that you enrich the soil the best you can, fluff it up with a spading fork or rototiller to a depth of at least 12 inches, and remove any of these obstacles. Next, lay the handle of a rake or hoe in the prepared space and gently press it into the fresh soil to create a shallow furrow ¼ inch deep. Carrots often take two to three weeks to germinate, and it's difficult to remember where you planted them. To get around that, simply plant radish seeds 12 inches apart and ½ inch deep in the furrow. The radish seeds will germinate in two days and act as living "markers" for the carrot seeds. Plus, the radishes can be harvested in thirty days without harming the newly sprouted carrot seed. After planting the radish seeds carefully sprinkle a small amount of carrot seed into the furrow every 2 to 3 inches. *Do not cover the seed.* Gently water the seed with a watering can, which will cover the seed just enough to make them happy without burying them too deep. To make things easy, many seed companies are selling pelleted seeds—regular seeds covered with an inert substance that makes it easier to handle and space properly. I am convinced that this is the best way to sow small seeds.

■ Care and Maintenance

Unless you used pelleted seeds and regardless of how careful you were, you probably sowed too many seeds. To grow properly, the carrot seedlings must be thinned to one plant every 2 to 3 inches. Trust me, this is probably the hardest thing to do in vegetable gardening but is absolutely critical if you want fully and properly formed roots. You can gently pull the seedlings sideways or simply snip the extra seedlings off at ground level with a pair of scissors; both methods reduce root damage to the remaining seedlings. Plant three crops during the cooler months, four weeks apart. Carrots that grow too long past their prime will become woody and are inedible even in soups. At the end of their growing season, carrots require less water, and too much water can cause the roots to crack.

■ Additional Information

It's essential to rotate the location of your carrot crops in the garden every year. Carrots planted every year in the same location will encourage an infestation of wire worms, a tough-skinned maggot that bores into the root. Just to be on the safe side, when you till the soil in preparation for sowing seed, sprinkle a fair amount (½ cup to every 10 feet of row length) of wood ashes from your fireplace onto the soil and incorporate it into the mix. The ashes will repel root worms.

'Nantes Half Long' carrots perform well in Florida, as do 'Chantenay Royal', 'Imperator 58', and 'Tendersweet'. If you like the unusual, try 'Cosmic Purple' and 'Snow White' or 'Lunar White'. 'Atlas' and 'Parisian' are good varieties for containers.

CAULIFLOWER

Gardening is often about the little miracles that happen when you work in the dirt. One day you plant a tiny, vulnerable seedling a mere 2 inches tall, and after only six to eight weeks you can harvest a snowy white head of cauliflower that's more than 8 inches in diameter, weighing in at more than 3 pounds. Eat cauliflower raw with salad dressings, steam it with a little butter, and use it in casseroles—you decide! It's one of the most versatile vegetables you can grow and also one of the easiest.

When to Plant

Direct sow cauliflower seeds or transplant seedlings any time between September and January. Cauliflower, unlike many of its cabbage relatives, can take moderate frost but not hard freezes, so protect it from extreme temperatures.

Where to Plant

Plant cauliflower seeds or seedlings in well-prepared and composted soil with high water-holding capacity and a pH of 6.0 to 6.5. Site in locations where they will get at least 8 hours of full sun. Adding a little magnesium sulfate, either by itself or as part of the general fertilizer, will produce bigger yields. Follow the fertilizer container's instructions for the correct amounts.

How to Plant

Direct sow seeds ½ inch deep or plant seedlings. Space in rows 18 inches apart and individual plants 18 inches apart for proper air circulation and to prevent overcrowding. To grow cauliflower to its best ultimate size, the leaves must have plenty of room to manufacture energy, so the more room you give them, the better. Plants grown too closely together will be small and will produce small heads called "buttons."

Care and Maintenance

Cauliflower is grown much like one grows cabbage: lots of water, plenty of sun, and high-nitrogen fertilizer every three weeks. Weeds compete for nutrients and water so keep the rows as weed free as possible. For many years it was said that you must gather the leaves when the curd is about the size of a softball and secure with a rubber band. The reason was to keep sunlight off the curd to help keep the curds white (a process called "blanching"). With newer varieties like 'Snowball', the growers have developed leaves that naturally cover the head and blanching is not necessary. Unlike its broccoli relative, once the main head has been harvested, a cauliflower plant will not produce side shoots so the entire plant can be pulled up and added to the compost pile. Cauliflower rarely has any pest problems. A few holes chewed in the leaves by worms usually aren't of sufficient quantity to impact production. Regular additions of fertilizer are important to maintain good plant quality. Adequate soil moisture must be maintained to produce good flower heads. Inconsistent watering regimens will reduce overall curd quality and size.

■ *Additional Information*

Because of its self-blanching attribute, 'Snowball' and 'Minuteman' are at the top of my list. The heads are uniform and tightly grown. On the less traditional side, 'Brocoverde' is a broccoli/cauliflower cross and its light-green flower head is spiky with individual florets. 'Cheddar', as the name implies, is a yellow form of cauliflower, and 'Graffiti' displays a rich, deep-purple color. "Verdi" has an apple green color. All make wonderful additions to salads or dips. Purple heads turn green when they're cooked (as do purple beans).

Cauliflower 'Snowball'

CELERY

Celery

Unfortunately, most home gardens don't include celery. It's a shame because the flavor and texture of homegrown is far superior to store bought. Plus, the sheer joy of growing your own and later adding it to soups, stews, and salads is very gratifying! If you are looking for a vegetable that's easy to grow put this on the top ten easiest to grow list. Plant seed in a pot and transplant 45 days later into the garden. This is a vegetable that can be grown twelve months a year in the garden. The individual stalks can be harvested as you need them by pulling the stalks that are located on the outside of the bunch. An ice-cold gazpacho soup on a Florida summer day just wouldn't be the same without it.

When to Plant

Plant celery any time of the year. Celery can be harvested year round.

Where to Plant

Plant celery in well-prepared, composted soil with a pH of 5.8 to 6.8 in a spot that receives at least 8 hours of full sun. Wherever you plant celery, make certain that plenty of water will be available throughout the growing season. Celery needs highly fertile, well-enriched soil, ideally amended with lots of peat moss and well-rotted manure.

■ How to Plant

Celery seeds are so tiny that planting them outside is almost futile. Instead, plant two to three seeds in a container and barely cover them with soil. Mixing seeds with sand and sprinkling the seed/sand mixture on top of potting soil works well, too. Watering from the bottom usually works best so you don't wash the seeds away. When the seedlings are about 2 inches tall or have three pairs of true leaves, thin each pot to only one plant. Continue to grow the seedlings indoors until they are ready to plant in the garden. Generally, this is when they are about 6 inches tall. Transplant the individual seedlings into the garden 10 to 12 inches apart and in rows 18 inches apart.

■ Care and Maintenance

Water, water, water, and then water some more, especially during the hot summer months. Celery plants that are allowed to go dry develop dry, stringy, and tough stalks suitable only for stews and soups—not for eating raw. With the amount of water necessary to grow celery, that inevitable wet-weather pest, slugs, can sometimes be problem. They won't kill a plant but they will devour the leaves and make the plant look unsightly. Because I prefer to avoid using chemicals around vegetables, I use beer traps instead (which gives me an excuse to drink whatever is left). Celery stalks can be harvested at any time, and if you want white, tender stalks, tie them up with twine and harvest as needed. Blanched stalks will be less bitter. Celery doesn't like the cold so protect it when the weather gets chilly. Even if cold weather damages a few of the outside stalks, the interior stalks will be fine.

■ Additional Information

Plant six to eight plants of 'Conquistador' and you have plenty for a family of four. Try 'Giant Pascal', 'Stokes Golden Plume', and 'Giant Red' too. After you have used most of your store bought celery remove all but the tender blanched stems and place the remaining "heel" into a pot with potting soil. Place in part sun until roots form (usually about four weeks) and plant into the garden.

Collards

COLLARDS

Mention Florida gardening and my mind flashes to swept front yards, rickety white picket fences, and collards in the vegetable garden. The ever-present collard plant standing tall in the Florida sun is a symbol of self-sufficiency, strength, and southern pride. Once, an older friend of ours invited us to her house for some "sun tea" (although it turned out there was very little tea and quite a bit of Wild Turkey whiskey). When we were ready to leave, she gave us a bunch of collards from her garden. She was so proud of the greens, and I was proud to accept her homegrown gift.

■ *When to Plant*

Collards can withstand both heat and all but the most severe cold weather, so feel free to plant them whenever you have the notion.

■ *Where to Plant*

Like their cabbage relatives, collard seedlings need full sun and well-drained soil with a pH of 6.0 to 6.8. Give them plenty of room; plant individual seedlings 36 inches apart, in rows 36 inches apart.

■ *How to Plant*

Collards can be direct sown in the garden ½ inch deep utilizing the proper spacing or by planting transplants. If you're planting in the middle of summer, make certain the seedlings or transplants don't get a chance to wilt from a lack of water.

■ *Care and Maintenance*

Collards don't require much care. Occasionally, aphids will try to eat the new growth, but a strong stream of water will wash them away. Cabbage butterfly larvae will often eat holes in the leaves. They can be removed manually, or a light dusting of Dipel® (*Bacillus thuringiensis* or *B.T.*) will do the job. During the summer it's important not to water too much. The center of new growth at the very top can turn mushy under such conditions and ultimately the plant will die.

■ *Additional Information*

The best varieties for Florida include 'Yates Strain', a very large but low-growing variety with broad, thick, heavy leaves; and 'Georgia Southern', a variety that grows to 36 inches tall and can withstand a variety of soil conditions. A high-yielding variety of excellent quality when cooked, 'Georgia Southern' is the old standard for Florida. Collard leaves, known as collard greens, grow along a tall, inedible stem. The leaves are picked from the bottom up and should be selected before the leaves get large and tough. The leaves should then be chopped up into tiny pieces (every part of the leaf is used) and cooked for an hour or more with a ham hock, or any other smoked, inexpensive meat, for the best flavor. If collards are grown without a straw weed barrier, make certain you wash the leaves thoroughly three or four times to remove the grit and dirt. Collards are best eaten fresh but they can also be frozen after blanching for a short time (three to four minutes per pound).

CORN

Corn

When you think of summer, you think of growing corn—that is, everywhere but in Florida. Given the summer heat in Florida, sweet corn should be planted from October until April (depending where on the peninsula your garden is located) when the nighttime temperatures are cooler and the daytime temperatures aren't oppressive. To be quite honest, given the sheer number and kinds of bugs that attack corn foliage, tassels, and fruit (if they get that far), most gardeners decide after one growing attempt that it's easier to just buy a few ears at the local market. Make no mistake; growing corn is not easy in most areas of Florida. Another problem when planting corn is deciding which variety to grow. There are many, many varieties of sweet corn that can be grown in Florida, and they come in three basic types: super sweet (which has the longest storage time); normal sugary (which has the shortest storage time); and sugary enhancer (medium storage time). Corn can also be divided by color in each of these three types.

When to Plant

In North Florida plant sweet corn from February to April, in Central Florida plant from January to April, and in South Florida plant from October to March.

Where to Plant

Plant sweet corn in full sun in well-drained soil with a pH of 6.0 to 6.5. In the absence of a soil test, apply 3 to 4 pounds of 12-0-12 or similar analysis fertilizer per 100 square feet to establish a basic fertility level. Side dressing with a high-nitrogen fertilizer late in the growing season is also advisable. Soil temperature for normal sugary can be in the 60 degree Fahrenheit range (plus or minus), while the sugary enhanced and the super sweet will not germinate until the soil is much warmer. When growing super sweet corn it is important that there be no other corn plants close by (300 feet away is the minimum). Super sweet corn cross-pollinates readily through the air and if the super sweet corn is contaminated by pollen from normal sugary or sugary enhancer varieties, the super sweet won't taste as good. Start with fresh seed every year; even under the best storage conditions, corn seeds will only last two years. With the super sweet corn seeds, reports indicate that the extended storage can actually alter the corn's ultimate quality.

How to Plant

Did you ever shuck an ear of corn only to find that the kernels weren't fully formed or they were formed sporadically on the cob? Corn is pollinated by the wind so it's important that corn be planted in "blocks" rather than in long rows to increase the opportunities for pollination. Blocks of corn help ensure that pollen will fall directly below to the silks of the ears. With long row planting, any pollen hitting the ear silk is a hit-or-miss proposition, and proper pollination might not take place. Plant sweet corn 1 inch deep, 6 to 8 inches apart, and in rows that are 30 inches apart. When the new growth emerges from the soil (three to five days after planting) the corn seedlings often are

Grow corn in blocks rather than long, single rows.

the favorite food of birds (especially brown thrashers). They will break off the tender seed that emerges with the new leaves, killing the new sprout. My daughter's 30-inch-long, lifelike plastic monitor lizard will scare them off in most years, but aluminum pie pans attached to strings and allowed to twirl in the air will work, too. If neither appeals to you, simply plant a few more seeds to fill in the blank spots after the remaining seedlings get a little taller.

■ Care and Maintenance

Let me make it known: corn requires babysitting. Large quantities of both water (1½ inches per week) and fertilizer are required to produce full, healthy ears. Make sure weeds are removed as soon as possible so they don't compete for water or nutrition. The tassel is the part that emerges from the top center of a corn plant and contains the pollen. The tiny "hairs" that emerge from the top of each ear of corn are called silks and each strand of silk is connected to a single kernel of corn. It is the silk that accepts the pollen grains from the tassel above to fertilize the corn kernels. To enhance the chances of the pollen reaching the silks, try shaking the entire corn plant several times a day when the pollen first appears. That will increase the chances.

Not only do weeds compete for water and nutrients, they harbor a wide selection of pests. Fall armyworms are a corn plant's worst enemy. They get into the new expanding foliage at the top of the plant (whorl), often eating the leaves before the plant has a chance to produce a tassel. They also burrow into the ears and eat the kernels. Another important pest is the corn earworm. An adult female lays an egg on the newly emerged corn silk and the worm burrows into the ear, eating the kernels. Dipel® or spinosad lightly sprinkled or sprayed on the plant whorl or on the ear silk once per week will lessen the problem. Both products are organic. Spinosad is a newer, highly effective organic insecticide against caterpillars that does not harm beneficial insects. Once a worm burrows into an ear of corn, however, the home gardener can do very little, although some have had luck squirting mineral oil down into the silks after the worms have been discovered. Genetically altered corn has been developed that is resistant to both armyworms and corn earworms, but it has not been approved for organic gardens. If you are not growing many plants, a little sandy soil sprinkled on every ear as it begins to produce silk will prevent *some* caterpillar damage too. Apparently, a little of the grit gets into the top of the ear and prevents the worm from eating. It's recommended that the grit be reapplied after heavy rains. Raccoons somehow know that you plan to pick the corn the next day and will take a bite of nearly every ear the night before. Of all the methods to repel them, raccoons are immune to almost every one except an electric fence.

There are two ways to check for ripeness. When the silks of an ear of corn turn from a "blonde" color to brown all the way to the husk, the ear is ready to pick. Just to be sure, though, pull the husk back a bit to make sure that the kernels are fully formed at the top of the ear. Also, a kernel should squirt "milk" when you press it with your thumbnail. Sweet corn remains in the milk stage for a relatively short period; check the ears frequently. Corn that is too immature will ooze a watery material, while ears that are too old will have a tough, doughy kernel. To lengthen corn's shelf life, immerse the ears in ice-cold water to slow the breakdown of the sugar to starch. The old-timers will tell you that water should be boiling on the stove when you pick corn and that you should run back to the stove to cook it. Seriously, more than half of the sugar is converted to starch in the first twelve hours after picking.

Corn 'Blonde Stage'

■ *Additional Information*

Recommended yellow corn varieties include 'Golden Cross Bantam', 'Early Sunglow', 'Sweet Riser', and 'Kandy King'. The best white varieties for Florida are 'Silver Queen', 'How Sweet It Is', and 'Sweet Ice'. Of the bicolor varieties, 'Peaches and Cream' and 'Seneca Dancer' perform the best.

Cucumber 'Indio'

CUCUMBER

Growing cucumbers in Florida is all about timing and disease resistance. Cucumbers like it warm, but not too hot and humid, and they'll stop producing when it gets too cold. Given the heavy disease pressure in Florida it is important to find selections of cucumbers that have a built-in resistance to disease. Those without any built-in opposition don't stand a chance. Don't get me wrong, cucumbers of all kinds are worth the effort, but sometimes it's difficult to remember how you grew that one perfect crop. That's where the garden journal comes into play. Reviewing the pages about when and what varieties you planted will provide better results.

■ *When to Plant*

Cucumbers like warm soil to germinate. In North Florida plant seeds directly into the garden from August to September for a fall garden, and plant from February to April for a spring garden. In Central Florida plant seeds in September for a fall garden and from January through March for a spring garden. South Florida has an extended growing season; plant seeds for a fall garden from September to October, for a winter garden from November to December, and in January for a spring garden. It's generally too hot and humid in South Florida for a summer crop of cucumbers.

■ *Where to Plant*

Plant cucumbers in full sun in well-drained, enriched soil with an ideal pH of 5.8 to 6.5. Keep in mind that cucumbers will grow in soils with a pH outside of their preferred range, but they just won't be as productive.

■ *How to Plant*

The old standby is to direct sow the seeds ½ inch deep into prepared soil in rows 36 to 48 inches apart and the seeds 8 to 10 inches apart. An alternate method, and my favorite, is to grow the vines up strings or on a welded wire fence, like you do with pole beans. Using this method keeps any one from stepping on the vines and keeps the cukes clean and visible. By growing them upright they have better air circulation, are easier to fertilize, weeds aren't a problem, and the plants require less space. When growing up, direct sow or plant seedlings 8 to 10 inches apart.

Care and Maintenance

The most serious problems by far are downy mildew and powdery mildew. Powdery mildew can be lessened by increasing air circulation, reducing overhead watering, and timing daily watering to occur in the early morning so the plants have a chance to dry. It's also important to never walk among the plants while they are wet—diseases can be transferred via wet clothes and skin. During warm, humid nights a light, powder-like dusting called powdery mildew may appear on the upper surfaces of the leaves, causing the leaves to drop off prematurely, ultimately killing the plant. Oils such as Neem or Safer Soap will have moderate results in preventing powdery mildew, but they cannot be used together or when temperatures reach 85 degrees Fahrenheit. If mild to moderate powdery mildew symptoms are present, the horticultural oils and Neem oil can be used to reduce or eliminate the infection. *Bacillus subtilis* (*B.s.*) helps prevent powdery mildew from infecting the plant. While this product functions to kill the powdery mildew organism and is nontoxic to people, pets, and beneficial insects, it has not proven to be as effective as the oils. *B.s.* can be applied up to, and including, the day of harvest. Applying horticultural oils (such as Neem and Sunfine Ultraspray), copper, and sulfur work well to protect plants and eradicate powdery and downy mildew, but they cannot be used together nor should they be used when temperatures reach 85 degrees Fahrenheit. Synthetic products containing chlorothalonil or mancozeb are fungicides registered for cucumbers that both protect and cure downy mildew. Ordinary sulfur and copper applied every seven days works well, too, but only when temperatures are below 85 degrees Fahrenheit. When the plants reach 4 inches tall, add a high-nitrogen fertilizer (blood meal, cottonseed meal, and so forth) or water the plants weekly with fish emulsion. Check the garden daily for harvestable fruits. If mature cucumbers are left on the vine, all production for that particular plant will stop.

Additional Information

For standard slicing cucumbers 'Indio', 'Indy', and 'Dasher II' provide the greatest disease resistance package on the market. For pickling cukes go with the disease-resistant 'Eureka'.

EGGPLANT

My experience is that you either love eggplant or you hate it. There never seems to be any ambivalence. My son-in-law thinks he is even allergic. So, if you can't stand them, turn the page. If, however, you have a passion for eggplant and the numerous dishes that can be made with it, read on. I have won over more than a few eggplant loathers to fanciers just by showing them pictures of the wide range of different types that can be grown in Florida, with colors ranging from deep purple-black to polar white, and from egg-sized to three-pounders. For an average family, six plants are enough. (Really, how much eggplant *can* you eat?)

When to Plant

Eggplant is a heat-loving plant. It loves heat so much that when eggplant is grown in cool temperatures it simply languishes in the cool, damp air until the heat is turned up. Don't plant eggplant too early or it will just sit there and stare back at you. Eggplants are best planted as seedlings from June to September.

Where to Plant

Plant eggplant in full sun in average, well-drained soil. Keep eggplant out of moist, mucky soils.

How to Plant

Eggplants are best planted as seedlings, not directly sown from seed into the garden. However, the uncommon varieties are usually only available as seed. Most garden centers won't carry the oddball variety seed and you will have to search them out. Do it; it's worth the effort. Sow the seeds ¼ inch deep six weeks prior to your anticipated outdoor planting date. Set individual transplants 30 inches apart in 30- to 36-inch-wide rows. The smaller-fruiting types can be spaced closer together.

Care and Maintenance

Eggplants are virtually pest free. Occasionally, aphids, cottony cushion scale, flea beetles, and spider mites will stop by, but only when the plant is stressed by too much or too little water. A simple soap or Neem oil spray will eliminate the bugs, but it's just as easy to prevent them by keeping the plants stress free. In the absence of a soil analysis, a 12-0-12 fertilizer applied 3 to 4 pounds per 100 feet of row is sufficient. Apply the same amount halfway through the growing season and again immediately after the first fruit is picked. Giving eggplants too much fertilizer will delay fruit set. To prevent the heavy fruits from lying on the ground, pound a sturdy ¾-inch × 48-inch-tall wooden stake into the ground beside each plant and gently tie the individual branches to the pole using heavy garden twine or 1-inch-wide strips of old sheets or other fabric. The tall stake will seem like overkill at first, but as the plant grows you'll be glad you started out with the tall stake. Although eggplants can withstand drought, fruit production is severely curtailed if the plants are permitted to go without sufficient water. Keep the soil moist and add a layer of mulch to conserve available moisture. Small yellow fruits that never mature is a sure sign of too little water; simply double up on the watering and the bush will begin to produce full-sized fruit again. Larger yellow fruits mean that the eggplants are overripe and should be discarded. No more than four to six flowers should be allowed to set fruit per plant. If too many flowers appear, clip some off.

▓ *Additional Information*

Harvest the fruits when they are still glossy using pruning shears or a sharp knife. Leave the calyx (the green star at the top) on the fruit to prolong its shelf life. Varieties suitable for Florida include 'Black Beauty' (stocky and black); 'Cloud Nine' (stocky and white); 'Calliope' (stocky and purple-and-white striped); 'Casper' (long and white); 'Florida High Bush' (long and black); 'Green Goddess' (long and green); 'Machiaw' (slender and light purple); 'Rosa Biancha' (round and white with blush of purple); and 'Apple Green' (egg shaped and light green). For the perfect eggplant in a container try "Pot Black'; it can produce ten to fifteen fruits at the same time perfectly sized for kabobs.

Eggplant 'Gretel'

English pea

ENGLISH PEA

English peas are easy to grow in all areas of Florida provided they are grown in the proper season. Make no mistake about it—peas are a cool-season crop and like daytime temperatures that are cool and nighttime temperatures that are even cooler (although short of frost). The variety of peas that can be grown in the home garden is limited only by the amount of space. English snap peas, snow peas, and sugar snap peas can all be grown in Florida. Fresh-off-the-vine peas taste like candy compared to those bought from a grocery store. Trust me, once you have tasted fresh peas from the garden you will look forward to the English pea planting season.

■ *When to Plant*

In North Florida plant peas from January through March. In Central and South Florida plant English peas from October through February.

■ *Where to Plant*

Plant peas where the plants will receive a minimum of 8 hours of full sun. The plants perform best in well-enriched soil that has been deeply tilled.

■ *How to Plant*

English peas, including snap, snow, and edible podded, can be grown on a tall support device similar to climbing beans or as a bush. Many varieties of the bush forms benefit from some support (18 to 24 inches tall) to keep the fruits off the ground. Mesh fencing placed between a double row planted 6 inches apart works very well. After soaking the seeds overnight in warm water, plant them 2 inches apart in rows 30 inches apart. When the new growth emerges from the soil (three to five days after they're planted), the pea seedlings are often the favorite food of birds. They will break off the tender seed that emerges with the new leaves, killing the new sprout. Aluminum pie pans attached to strings and allowed to twirl in the air will scare them off. Plastic snakes and/or plastic lizards work equally well.

Climbing peas produce multiple crops (provided you pick every pod and pick often) and are easier to harvest. Climbing peas can grow to 6 feet tall and need some sort of support. Most often, two poles are placed at either end of a row and a single strand of wire is placed at heights of 5 to 6 feet tall between the posts. Strings are then gently and loosely attached to the pea seedlings below their leaves and then to the wire. Pea vines will naturally climb up the string. Welded wire in a 2 × 4-inch configuration works even better and will last a lifetime. Just stretch the wire tight and secure to wooden poles. Plant the seeds at the base of wire. For shorter varieties of peas 18 to 24 inches tall, pound a 36-inch stake into the ground at either end and stretch a 24-inch-tall piece of one-inch chicken wire or plastic mesh designed for that purpose from pole to pole. At 2- to 3-inch intervals lace a pole through the wire mesh and pound into the ground. Mulch heavily to maintain soil moisture. Both forms benefit from a slight mounding of the soil against the stems for added support.

■ Care and Maintenance

Peas like moisture but not wet feet. Soaking the seeds before planting will require less water initially, but as the flowers bloom and pods develop, the plants will require more water. As you water more, keep a sharp eye out for slugs. Peas are one of their favorite foods, so the addition of slug traps filled with beer works well. Aphids can also be a problem on the tender new growth, but they can be washed off with a stiff stream of water. Adding too much fertilizer will produce nice, new growth but at the expense of fruit. Peas are ready when the pods begin to bulge slightly. Pick the pods just moments before cooking; the sugars will change to starch very quickly.

■ Additional Information

'Little Marvel Improved' is by far the most popular English pea grown in Florida. The vigorous plant grows to 18 inches tall and produces loads of pods. 'Sugar Snap' is a popular tall variety and the entire pod and peas within can be eaten raw or cooked. Other good varieties include 'Wando', 'Oregon Sugarpod II', and 'Green Arrow'.

GARLIC

Given that you can cultivate garlic simply by breaking off a clove and sticking it in the ground, one would think growing garlic in the Sunshine State would be easy. Even though our temperatures are perfect for gardeners, garlic is more accustomed to growing in colder climates and our warm winters may throw a wrench into things.

Garlic comes in two basic types: hardneck and softneck. You can forget growing hardneck types in Florida. They like very cold winters, cool springs, and mild summers. The hardnecks include the categories of porcelain and purple stripe garlic. If you live in Florida and you see these names in a catalog description, just move on to the softneck group.

When to Plant

Plant garlic cloves any time cold weather is on its way. They enjoy the cold weather and after growing all winter, they can be harvested by early summer. It's important that they grow in cool soil as long as possible. When our weather begins to heat up, the garlic matures and the growing portion of the garlic's life is over. If a bulb matures before it's finished growing you will harvest small garlic bulbs. An old rule of thumb prevails when planting garlic: plant on the shortest day of the year and harvest on the longest day of the year. Garlic tolerates different weather conditions. Just remember, every year you grow garlic will be different from the year before. Depending on the weather, rainfall, temperatures, planting date, and so forth, your garlic may be stronger or weaker in taste, hot varieties may become mild, and mild varieties may become hot.

Where to Plant

Plant garlic in good, deep, rich, loamy soil in full sun. Garlic is very self-sufficient and can get what it needs out of the soil. Stay away from dry, tight soils and grow in soils with a pH of 6.5 to 7. Garlic enjoys moist soil but will not tolerate standing water for even the shortest period of time. If it's given too much nitrogen the plant will produce good foliage but only small bulbs.

How to Plant

If you have sandy soil, add organic material to it so it will hold water a little longer and be friable (easily crumbled). Garlic is very susceptible to a wide variety of pathogens, but a little work upfront will help later as the bulb grows. Here's a little tip: Combine seaweed and baking soda (1 tablespoon each) in a gallon of water. Place individual cloves to be planted in the solution; leave overnight. Then, soak the cloves in rubbing alcohol for five minutes. Remove the cloves from the rubbing alcohol and plant directly into the ground; place a 2-inch layer of mulch on top. (The cloves will later grow through the mulch.)

Care and Maintenance

Garlic is very easy to grow after the soil preparation and inoculation are complete. Just keep the weeds down and fertilize every two weeks with a seaweed/molasses combination (1 tablespoon per gallon of water) every two weeks until harvest. Harvest when the bottom one-third of the leaves turns brown and only the top four or five leaves are still green. It's important to harvest the bulbs when the soil is dry, so stop watering one to two weeks before harvest. If it looks like rain, throw a tarp over the bed. Dry the bulbs in a cool, dark place with lots of ventilation. Garlic bulbs are very susceptible to bruising at this stage so be careful how you handle them—don't throw them or handle them roughly. Clean the bulbs down to the last paper skin that wraps around the individual cloves, and cut the dried leaves off. Garlic can be stored up to nine months, depending on the variety, at room temperature. Garlic stored in a refrigerator will sprout prematurely and will not last long.

Garlic

Additional Information

Good varieties for Florida include 'Early Italian Purple', 'Inchelium Red', 'Kettle River Giant', 'Siskiyou Purple', and 'Transylvanian'.

Kale 'Redbor'

KALE

Admittedly, I never considered kale to be an important vegetable. In fact, for years the only kale I grew was the beautiful ornamental flowering kale used as a bedding plant. It wasn't until I started cooking in earnest that I realized how adaptable kale is in a variety of recipes ranging from soups to side dishes. Kale has quickly risen to the top of my "must have" vegetable list, and, if you give it try, I think it will rise on your list, too.

■ *When to Plant*

A cool-season crop, kale should be planted in the cooler months, primarily from September through April. A light frost is not a bad thing; it will only sweeten kale's flavor.

■ *Where to Plant*

Kale is not very fussy about soil, and wherever it's planted it seems to thrive and be perfectly happy. If possible, however, direct sow seeds ¼ inch deep or plant transplants in full sun with rich, water-retentive soil with a pH of 5.5 to 6.5. For transplants, start seeds indoors five to six weeks prior to the expected outdoor planting date.

■ *How to Plant*

Kale can be planted using the wide row method with rows 48 inches wide and the individual plants 14 to 18 inches apart in the rows. Otherwise, kale is planted in rows 24 inches apart and 18 inches apart in the row. There are many different selections of kale and spacing depends solely upon the variety you plant.

■ *Care and Maintenance*

Give kale full sun, plenty of water, and periodic applications of fish emulsion fertilizer and it will provide tasty leaves throughout its growing season. Leaves that are grown on well-tended plants will be sweet and tender; those allowed to dry out will often be bitter and tough. The leaves can be picked based on color—dark and heavy means the kale is tough and bitter, while bright, rich green leaves are sweet and ready for cooking. The leaves are picked from the bottom, encouraging new leaves to grow at the top. The newer, tender leaves can be eaten raw in salads. Like many other cooking greens, kale is susceptible to many of the same pests, such as aphids and slugs, but generally these are not serious problems and most can be removed with a strong stream of water. A 2- to 3-inch layer of organic mulch will moderate soil temperatures, keep weeds under control, and conserve water.

■ Additional Information

Good varieties of kale for Florida include 'Dwarf Blue Curled Scotch', 'Red Russian', 'Redbor', 'Winterbor', and 'Yates Blue Curled'. 'Nero de Toscana' is a unique-looking kale that can also be used as an ornamental in mixed containers.

Kale is very high in beta carotenes; vitamins A, C, and K; potassium, iron, and calcium, and it's an excellent source of fiber. Patients taking anticoagulation drugs should avoid kale because of its high vitamin K content (which promotes blood clotting, thus reducing the effectiveness of the drugs). Kale was popular during World War II in Great Britain because of its high vitamin content, which supplemented a poor diet resulting from wartime food rationing.

Kale 'Lacinato'

KOHLRABI

Mention the vegetable "kohlrabi" in a conversation and chances are good that very few people will know what you're talking about. That's a shame, too; kohlrabi may be one of the most underutilized and fun plants to grow in the garden. Unlike beets or turnips, which hide their "bulb" beneath the soil, kohlrabi has a light-green, 3-inch-diameter, spaceship-looking bulbous growth with dark-green leaf sprouts coming out of its top that appears just above the ground. (In German, the word kohl means "cabbage" and rabi means "turnip.") Being unusual, however, is not its only claim to fame. The bulb is harvested by cutting it off just above the ground. It's peeled like a potato and either eaten raw as crudités or gently steamed to be served with cream sauces. Some say it has a very mild broccoli or cabbage taste while others say it tastes like celery with a nutty flavor. The leaves can be harvested and added raw to salads; they have a slightly spicy taste. Kohlrabi is very easy to grow and will surely elicit a question or two as your friends stroll through your garden.

When to Plant

Grown only in cool seasons, direct sow kohlrabi seeds in September and continue through March on three- to four-week intervals. It matures in 45 to 55 days depending on the variety selected. It can withstand significantly cold weather and even a little frost.

Where to Plant

Kohlrabi enjoys full sun when planted in well-prepared, water-retentive soil with a pH of 5.8 to 6.5.

How to Plant

Direct sow kohlrabi seeds ¼ inch deep in rows that are 18 inches apart. Thin kohlrabi seedlings to 4 inches apart in the row or plant using the wide row method three wide with the same individual plant spacing of 4 inches. If the seedlings are not thinned the resulting aboveground bulb will be small and unusable.

Care and Maintenance

Kohlrabi is one of the easiest plants to grow and has no serious pests or diseases. Occasionally, aphids will stop by but a strong stream of water will wash them away. Sometimes the bulbous aboveground growth will get a black moldy spot, which is indicative of using too much water. Remove the infected plant and reduce the amount of water to stop the problem. It's important to make successive plantings every four weeks during the growing season. If kohlrabi is left to grow too long, it will get pithy like overly mature carrots and will be unusable.

■ *Additional Information*

Good varieties of kohlrabi for Florida include 'Early White Vienna', 'Kolibri' (perhaps the prettiest of kohlrabi with its intense, deep-purple color), 'Grand Duke', and 'Early Purple Vienna'. For the more unusual varieties try 'Kossak' (which grows to 10 inches in diameter) and 'Superschmelz' (which can withstand less water than others without getting pithy). Kohlrabi is high in potassium, vitamin C, and fiber.

Kohlrabi 'Vienna Purple'

Lettuce 'Black Seeded Simpson'

LETTUCE

If you have a vegetable garden of any size, any kind, anywhere, you must have some sort of lettuce. It is a staple of healthy eating and is one of the easiest plants to grow. There are so many different kinds and shapes of lettuce that it's mind-boggling. Tall, short, wide, upright, green, striped—the list goes on and on. It's probably the first vegetable that young gardeners grow because it sprouts so quickly and sustains their curiosity over a long period of time. Planting lettuce, growing lettuce, and eating lettuce are all about instant gratification. It is also about color and texture. Some of my favorite lettuce varieties are those that "perk up" an otherwise boring green salad with their intense reds and shades of green. When I was growing up we only grew iceberg lettuce. That's all. Now, that's not bad, and I remember eating entire heads of iceberg lettuce right out of the refrigerator. Once I moved away from home, however, I realized that there was another world out there, a world of 'Black Seeded Simpson', and 'Deer Tongue', and 'Cardinal' and . . . well, you get the picture.

■ *When to Plant*

Lettuce is a cool-weather plant, and it will be bitter when it's grown in warm weather. In North Florida lettuce is planted from September through October and again from February through March. In Central Florida plant lettuce from September through March. In South Florida plant lettuce from September through February. If frost is imminent, cover lettuce with row cloths or old blankets to retain ground heat. Plant short rows of lettuce every two weeks to ensure you have enough to last throughout the growing season.

■ *Where to Plant*

Plant seeds and seedlings in well-composted, deeply tilled, well-drained but still water-retentive soil that receives at least 8 hours of full sun.

■ *How to Plant*

Lettuce of all kinds can be planted either by sowing seeds directly into prepared soil or by setting out transplants. Plant seeds indoors four to five weeks prior to planting outdoors. Use fresh seed every year and place partially used seed packets in the refrigerator for sowing later in the season. Lay the handle of a rake or hoe in a well-prepared bed and gently press the handle into the freshly tilled soil to create a shallow furrow ¼ inch deep. Carefully sprinkle a small amount of lettuce seed into the furrow every 2 to 3 inches. Barely cover the seed with fine soil. Gently water the seed with a watering can just enough to wet the seeds and make them happy without burying them too deep. Lettuce seeds will sprout in five to seven days. Pelleted seeds, although slightly more expensive, work best because you can see the large seeds and use less that don't need to be thinned later.

Regardless of how careful you are, you'll more than likely sow too many seeds. Once the lettuce plants grow their third or fourth pair of "true" leaves, the plants must be thinned to a distance described on the seed packet (it's different for different kinds of lettuce). Thinning can be done by gently pulling the extra seedlings sideways out of the soil or by clipping the seedlings off at ground level; both methods reduce root damage to the remaining seedling. Trust me, thinning is probably the hardest thing to do in vegetable gardening, but it is absolutely critical that you do so if you want fully and properly formed lettuce plants. Lettuce performs best in soils that have been highly enriched with rotted manure and fertilized well before planting with high-nitrogen fertilizers such as blood meal and cottonseed meal.

■ Care and Maintenance

Lettuce is an average feeder. Water with a little starter fertilizer when planting seedlings and fertilize every two weeks during the growing season with a general-purpose product. Lettuce matures in fifty days so fertilizing after the initial application at planting often isn't necessary. This, of course, depends upon whether adequate nutrients were added to the soil prior to planting the seeds or transplants. If lettuce plants are kept too wet, slugs can be a problem, but slug traps baited with beer usually do the trick. Also, placing boards next to lettuce plants will encourage the slugs to hide beneath the boards after the sun comes up. The slugs can be removed manually from underneath the boards and destroyed.

■ Additional Information

Lettuce can be subdivided into four main groups: crisp head, Cos or romaine, Bibb (sometimes called butter head), and leaf.

Lettuce 'Oak Leaf'

Crisp head is the most difficult lettuce to grow because of its long growing season requirements and its tendency to bolt or flower when the temperatures increase. Slow-bolting varieties are available, and adding a layer of mulch beneath the plants will help reduce fluctuations in soil temperatures. Mulching also helps keep dirt and grit off the leaves. Standard crisp head varieties for Florida include 'Iceberg', 'Ithaca', 'Great Lakes', and an heirloom variety called 'Hanson Improved'. More uncommon and smaller but equally good crisp head lettuce varieties include 'Bronze Mignonette' (slow to bolt); 'Prizehead' (its inner leaves are green and outer leaves are reddish brown); and a French heirloom variety called 'Rouge d' Hiver'.

Cos or Romaine varieties for Florida are some of the most plentiful and colorful varieties. My all-time personal favorite

Lettuce and mustard

lettuce variety, 'Freckles', has regular green leaves speckled with bright red spots. It can really perk up a salad and when I serve it at dinner parties everyone wants to know about it. Another unusual variety is 'Cimarron Red', which has green leaves inside the head and deep red to magenta leaves on the edges. Other more common but equally good varieties include 'Parris Island' and 'Dark Green'.

Bibb lettuce may be the tenderest of all the lettuce varieties and produces well-formed, flat heads of exceptional quality. Bibb lettuce varieties are formed the best and perfectly shaped when the seedlings are spaced properly in the initial planting. Good performers include: 'Bibb', 'Big Boston', 'Buttercrunch', 'May Queen', and 'White Boston'. A French heirloom variety named 'Merveille des Quatre Saisons' is a red-tinted butter head variety. 'Baby Star' produces 5-inch-tall heads of shiny green leaves, with a Romaine flavor.

Leaf lettuce is far and away the largest group and is the easiest to grow. 'Black Seeded Simpson' is the old standby, and it's still very popular. Others include 'Red Sails', 'Oak Leaf', 'Ruby Red', 'Salad Bowl' (red and green varieties), and 'Tango'. 'Deer Tongue' is an American heirloom variety that dates to 1740; it has wonderful taste and texture.

MUSTARD

Mustard

If any plant describes vegetable gardening in the Deep South it's mustard greens. Mention the words, and cheese grits, fried fish, hushpuppies, and "pot licker" comes to mind. (We'll talk more about pot licker later.) If there is an easier vegetable to grow in a Florida garden I don't know what it is. Mustard greens will thrive, and even flourish, in the worst of soils provided adequate water and sun are available. It seems as if every seed will germinate when given a chance, and when someone says that a particular seed is easy to sprout, you will often hear them say, "Those seeds will come up like mustard."

■ *When to Plant*

In North Florida plant mustard seed from September through May. In Central and South Florida plant mustard year round. If it's grown in the long, hot season, mustard with "bolt," or go to flower, quicker than when it's grown in cooler months.

■ *Where to Plant*

Although mustard greens will perform well in any ordinary soil, it grows best in organically enriched soil with a pH of 6.0 to 6.8, in a location in full sun.

◼ How to Plant

Plant short rows of mustard every two weeks in order to harvest a succession of tender greens. Direct sow the seed ¼ inch deep, 8 inches apart, in rows that are 24 inches apart.

◼ Care and Maintenance

For a constant supply of tender greens it is important to encourage mustard to grow quickly. Make sure it has plenty of water and plentiful amounts of high-nitrogen fertilizer, manures, or compost to promote the fast growth of tender, green leaves. Water plants during dry periods; otherwise, the greens will be bitter. Keep mustard plants well weeded; weeds compete for water and fertilizer and provide hiding spots for pests. Occasionally, cabbage worms can be a problem, in which case a light dusting of Dipel® (*B.t.*) will solve the problem.

◼ Additional Information

Although literature says that mustard greens can be eaten raw in salads for a little "bite," my experience has been cooking mustard greens is the only way to eat them. Pick individual leaves from the bottom (like collards) or harvest the entire plant. During the summer months, a teaspoon of sugar in the cooking water will take away the bitterness. Nearly everyone I know places a smoked ham hock or neck bone in with the leaves for better flavor.

Mustard 'Garnet Giant'

Talk to the ol' timers and they will tell you that 'Florida Broadleaf' and 'Southern Giant Curled' are the best mustard greens to grow; both mature in about 45 days. 'Misuna' is decorative mustard with finely divided leaves; it has a spicy flavor and can be used raw or cooked. 'Tah Tsai' is an Asian mustard with dense whorls of compact leaves; it matures in fifty-five days. 'Garnet Giant' is tall mustard with very dark, garnet-colored leaves that can be eaten cooked or raw in salads and look beautiful in mixed containers of annuals and perennials.

Okra

OKRA

If you live in Florida you need to grow okra for several reasons. First, it's one of the few vegetables that will grow in Florida's summer heat and humidity. Give okra plenty of water and ordinary soil and it will repay you with hundreds of tiny okra pods. Second, okra is one of those vegetables that deserves a chance. Even if you don't like okra, it grows so well and is so pretty as a plant (it's a member of the hibiscus family) that you could grow it as an ornamental. Finally, it's important to try at least one new vegetable every year, and this may just be the year for okra in your garden. Pick the little 2- to 3-inch pods, slice them up with some green pepper and fresh tomato, and you have a meal. Plus, fried okra is a southern tradition, and what would gumbo be without okra?

■ *When to Plant*

In North and Central Florida plant okra seed directly into the ground from March through July or August. In South Florida plant okra from August through September.

■ *Where to Plant*

Plant in the full, hot, blazing sun—just make certain there is plenty of water nearby. Okra will exceed even your wildest expectations when grown in well-drained, composted (and thereby water-retentive), and deeply tilled soil. Avoid wet, poorly drained soils.

■ *How to Plant*

Direct sow okra seed 1 inch deep after the danger of frost has passed and the soil has warmed up a bit. Okra planted in cool soil will sit there; the seed will not germinate until everything starts to warm up a bit. If you want to get a jump on the season, plant individual seeds in peat cups indoors, give them plenty of bright light, and transplant outdoors when the soil temperatures are warm to the touch. Give okra plenty of room—plant seed 24 inches apart in rows 36 inches apart.

■ Care and Maintenance

It took me a little while to get used to okra, but once I did, I became a real fan. I recommend both growing the plant and using the little pods in cooking, with little being the operative word. Show no mercy: you must be unrelenting when it comes to picking okra. Once the pods get beyond 3 inches long they are virtually inedible, so it's important that you pick okra every day, or no less often than every two days. If you are only growing a few plants, it may be necessary to store the pods in the vegetable drawer in a zippered plastic bag until you have enough to cook. Refrigerated okra will last at least five to six days. Once the unpicked pods are allowed to get more than 3 inches long, the plant will think it's done its job and will stop forming seedpods. In well-drained soil, you can't water okra too much. Harvest okra with handheld clippers or scissors; do not twist the pods off! Also, most varieties have pods that have very fine little "spines" that can irritate your skin, so wear gloves.

■ Additional Information

The old standby 'Clemson Spineless' is just that—spineless. If ever you grow any other variety you will appreciate the spineless part. Other varieties include 'Alabama Red', 'Baby Bubba' (which is perfect for small gardens and containers), 'Cow Horn', 'Evertender', 'Little Lucy' (which is another dwarf, but this one has burgundy foliage, stems, and pods), 'Red Burgundy', and 'White Velvet'. Don't you love that name?

Pick okra by snipping off pods before they reach 3 inches in length.

ONION

Onions, shallots, bunching onions, and chives are easy to grow in Florida. Bulb onions come in a variety of colors, including white, yellow, and red; red is the sweetest of the group. Shallots have a more refined, less harsh flavor compared to onions, and bunching onions have green tops and small, slender white onions at the bottom. Chives are very easy to grow and can be grown either in pots on the windowsill or in the ground. Onions and their many relatives can be harvested and eaten at any stage in their development.

■ When to Plant

Onions prefer cool weather. In North, Central, and South Florida plant all types of onions from September through March.

■ Where to Plant

Onions enjoy full sun in a well-prepared, deeply tilled sandy loam or muck soil. Any amount of organic matter will enrich the flavor and increase the size.

■ How to Plant

Bulb onions that have been grown from seed the previous year are purchased in bulk by the pound and are called "onion sets." The bulbs should be the size of a large marble. Individual onions are placed halfway into the prepared soil, pointed side up, 2 inches apart in a row. After about eight weeks, thin the row by pulling every other onion out; they can be eaten as fresh scallions or boiled. The extra space between the remaining onions will give them plenty of room to grow. Onions can be double planted in a row; that is, set in two smaller rows 3 to 4 inches apart next to each other and 18 to 24 inches between these two rows. "Transplants" are just that, onions that you have grown from seed earlier in the summer and then transplanted out into the garden. Make certain that when you buy seeds from mail-order sources you order "short day" onions, not the "long day" onions that would be grown in northern states. Another method is to direct sow seeds into the prepared seedbed. This method is usually reserved for bunching onions, which are also known as scallions or green onion. Plant them ½ inch deep, and thin when they get about 4 inches tall. Eat any thinned onions.

Onions can also be planted using the newspaper-and-straw method. Lay a single layer of newspaper over a prepared seedbed, cover lightly with straw, and water the seedbed. While the newspaper is still wet, gently push the onions through the newspaper halfway into the soil, and grow as you would otherwise. The thin layer of newspaper and straw will virtually eliminate weeds.

Care and Maintenance

The biggest problem with onions is keeping the weeds away. Not only are they unsightly and a nuisance, weeds compete for water and fertilizer. Cultivating is difficult around the small, thin onion plants, so extreme care is needed when weeding. I've learned the hard way about proper fertilization of onions. For years, my onions were always sub-par. Then, someone told me that onions were heavy nitrogen feeders. Ever since, I have added a 12-0-12 fertilizer about every three weeks or a water-soluble 20-0-20 every week, and my onions have never looked better.

Onion

Additional Information

For standard bulbing onions try 'Crystal Wax Bermuda' (flat and white); 'Excel' (flat and yellow); 'Red Creole' (red-skinned with a strong flavor); 'Granex White' and 'Granex Yellow' (very large bulbs with mild flavor). 'White Lisbon' bunching onion is a popular salad onion with long white stems and no bulb. For a real twist try 'Crimson Forest' bunching onion; it's a standard salad onion but it has a beautiful burgundy color. 'Barletta' onions are used primarily for pickling and with shish-ka-bobs. Shallots are sometimes difficult to find, but if you look hard enough you can find 'Matador' shallots from France; they are a very fine addition to any garden. Chippolini White is a smaller (to 2-inch diameter), very flat onion with a subtle onion flavor— many consider it to be the best onion available.

PEPPER

Peppers are great plants for the summer vegetable garden because they are very easy to grow, and they can be grown in the ground or in containers. And—big plus—they enjoy the heat and humidity of Florida summers. There are many different types of peppers, and you can cook with them so many different ways. Bell peppers by far are the most commonly grown; however, if you are looking for hot and spicy peppers, the list is virtually limitless. The hardest part about growing peppers may be deciding which to grow!

Green bell pepper

■ *When to Plant*

Peppers enjoy warm temperatures. Plant seed into peat pots three weeks before the last anticipated frost. In North and Central Florida plant pepper transplants outdoors from February through March and again from July through September. In South Florida plant peppers outdoors from August through September.

■ *Where to Plant*

Plant peppers in locations where they receive at least 8 hours of full sun and where there is an ample water source close by. Although peppers are not particular about soils, they perform best in compost-amended, well-drained soil. The soil pH should be about 6.5.

■ *How to Plant*

Peppers are very easy to grow by seed, and seeds are much less expensive than transplants. Sow seeds indoors three to four weeks before the last anticipated frost of the season. Recycled seed trays or biodegradable pots work best. Fill the containers with a good, sterilized soil mix and press the seeds ⅛ inch into it. Cover the seeds with fine, sifted soil mix. Label every pot or tray with a plastic marker and a china marker. Because the fine seed can be washed away by a strong stream of water from a watering hose, it's best to water the seeds from the bottom. (This is the reason why it is very difficult to grow peppers from seed sown directly in the garden.) Place the entire tray or peat pot into another, larger tray filled with shallow water and allow the soil mix to absorb as much water as it can; usually fifteen minutes is enough time. Afterwards, place the container in full sun or indoors in bright light. Water using this method every day until the seeds pop out of the ground, usually in seven to ten days. Place newly germinated seeds in a little more bright light every day over a period of two weeks until they are growing in full sun every day. Once you see roots growing out of the pot or you can see roots twirling around in the bottom of a seed tray, they are ready to be planted into the garden, generally when they are about 6 to 8 inches tall.

Plant the individual plants using the recommended spacing on the seed packages. For sweet bell peppers, for instance, plant individual plants 18 inches apart in rows 24 inches apart. For many of the larger varieties, however, more space will be required. Some peppers can reach a maximum height of 4 feet and can get 4 feet wide. Peppers also like a little sulfur when they are planted, so place a few (five or six) matches in the bottom of the planting hole, and place the transplant directly on top. Complete the planting as you would any other transplant. I am not kidding; this really works.

■ Care and Maintenance

Peppers are major feeders at all stages of their growth, and if I have learned anything over the years it's that peppers like a little bit of fertilizer frequently. An 8-0-8 fertilizer applied every three weeks is ideal. Peppers like moist, but not wet, soil, and dry soil can limit fruit production. A good layer of mulch will help moderate soil temperatures and retain moisture. Cultivate lightly to keep weeds out of the pepper patch. As the peppers begin to set fruit, reduce the nitrogen fertilizer and increase the level of potassium. Too much nitrogen will produce loads of green leaves at the expense of little or no fruit production. Peppers can produce many fruit on a single plant at the same time. If allowed to stay on the plant, green peppers will turn red and their taste will be sweeter. The sheer weight of the fruit can cause a pepper plant to fall over. Before they have a chance to do that (and possibly break off at the ground), place a 4-foot wooden stake or similar tall stick into the ground and gently and carefully attach the main stem to the stick. Outdoor paper Velcro strips work best and can be adjusted, if necessary. I caution you about using plastic coated wires—they can scrape the stem, allowing disease organisms an opportunity to get a foothold. Strips of recycled sheets or pillowcases work well, too.

Occasionally, aphids can be a problem, especially on emerging growth. A firm stream of water is usually sufficient to wash them away. Chili thrips are common and can prevent a plant from growing and producing fruit. Any organic or synthetic insecticide will control them, but be sure to change product every other application.

■ *Additional Information*

If you plan to store seed from your peppers for the following year, make sure you separate the hot and mild varieties in the garden. Peppers are self-pollinated but sometimes bees will stop by after they have visited another plant. The mix in flavors won't affect this year's fruit but may in the cross-pollinated seeds.

Chili pepper

There are too many different pepper varieties to mention all of them. However, some of the best in each category include:

Standard sweet varieties: 'Yolo Wonder', 'Cubanelle', 'Sweet Banana', 'Early Calwonder', 'Keystone Resistant Giant', 'Purple Beauty', 'Pimento'
Hybrid sweet varieties: 'Big Bertha', 'Gypsy', 'Fooled you'
Standard hot varieties: 'Caribbean Red', 'Chili Jalapeno', 'Habenero', 'Hungarian Yellow Wax', 'Long Thin Cayenne', 'Serrano Tampiquero', 'Scotch Bonnet'
Hybrid hot variety: 'Super Chili'

Pepper 'Yellow Banana'

> *Why do the flowers on my pepper plants fall off?*

Peppers are very sensitive to temperatures and fruit set is best achieved when daytime temperatures are between 70 to 80 degrees Fahrenheit plus/minus and when nighttime temperatures are in the 60 to 75 degree Fahrenheit range. Poor pollination can also be a cause. With fewer and fewer pollinators around to help out, bud drop of peppers is becoming a real problem. To help with pepper pollination, interplant pepper plants with flowers that attract bees, such as African Blue Basil and Agastache. The more pollinators there are the less bud drop will occur. Although there is no significant data to back it up, many gardeners think that poor air circulation might also be a cause of bud drop. By placing peppers on the outside rows of a garden rather than deep inside among taller plants, the plant will get better air circulation and less bud drop. It's important to maintain consistent irrigation levels and keep the pepper plants moist but not overly wet. Be careful not to apply too much nitrogen fertilizer on peppers; the extra nitrogen will produce lots of new growth but at the expense of flower buds. Finally, place one teaspoon of Epsom salts in a quart of water and spray the open flowers to encourage fruit set.

Potatoes

POTATO

Potatoes are fun, easy to grow, and they are good for you. Dig a trench, throw an "eye" (the sprouting part of the potato) in the ground, and watch them grow. Every time I grow a crop, whether they are the big Idaho potato baking type or the cute little Irish red type, the entire process fascinates me. Years ago, while I was living in Tallahassee, I gave a tour of a vegetable garden to a few Girl Scout Brownies. When I asked them about what they knew about growing plants it was clear that they had never set foot in a food garden before. When asked, not one of the ten girls had a clue where potatoes came from other than the ever-popular "grocery store" response. We encouraged them to drop to their knees and dig in the soil, apparently for the first time. Lo and behold, what did they find? Tiny potatoes. To them the little red potatoes were little treasures. You should have seen their eyes light up! Since then, whenever I have asked someone to dig potatoes for the first time, I get the same response. Soon thereafter they want to know about how to grow lettuce, and tomatoes, and beans, and . . . you get the picture. And so it begins.

◼ When to Plant

In North and Central Florida plant potatoes from January through March. In South Florida plant them from September through January.

◼ Where to Plant

Plant potatoes in full sun with compost- or manure-enriched, well-drained soil. Potatoes can grow well in muck but not in soil that is constantly wet.

■ *How to Plant*

Growing potatoes for the first time is a fascinating process. First and most important, use potatoes that have not been treated with hormones to prevent them from sprouting (such as those found in a grocery store). "Seed potatoes" are available from local feed stores or through online web sources. Potatoes found in organic grocery stores haven't been treated with hormones either and are very inexpensive. Locate a potato "eye" (a small, dark, depression on the potato's skin). With a sharp knife, remove a ¼ inch "scab" (including an eye) from the potato. The scab should be about 1 inch in diameter, including the eye and some of the white of the potato. Dust the scabs with sulfur dust or allow the scab to dry for several days. Dig a 6-inch trench 4 to 6 inches wide and 6 inches deep; place a scab in the trench every 8 to 10 inches with the eye facing up, and cover with 4 inches of soil. Rows should be 36 inches apart. In ten to fourteen days the scabs will sprout, and new growth will emerge from the soil.

■ *Care and Maintenance*

Once the sprout reaches 8 to 10 inches in height, pull the soil up around it leaving just the top leaves above the mound. (Add a few handfuls of an 8-0-8 fertilizer in the soil to be mounded as you work.) As a potato continues to grow, keep pulling the soil up to the sprout until there is a mound about 12 to 14 inches high. It is in the mound where the stem, now surrounded by soil, will sprout to produce potatoes. Tubers in the mounded soil can be harvested when the foliage begins to turn yellow. For smaller potatoes, harvest anytime during the growing season. Potatoes have no real problems except an occasional potato beetle, and they can be controlled with spinosad or Sevin dust.

■ *Additional Information*

For Florida the best varieties include 'Kennebec', 'Yukon Gold', 'Gold Rush', and 'Red Pontiac'. Other varieties that are fun to grow include 'French Fingerling', 'Adirondack Red', 'Adirondack Blue', and 'Russian Banana'.

GROWING TIP

Early varieties of potatoes are ready to harvest when their flowers bloom.

PUMPKIN

At one time or another I think every gardener who grows vegetables dreams about growing pumpkins. When new gardeners ask me about growing them, I try to remain positive, but the reality is they take lots of room to grow. If you have plenty of space, then have at it! For those with smaller spaces, the smaller pumpkin varieties are just fine. Just be aware that pumpkins need lots of water, too. If supplying water is a problem, then you'd better look for something else to grow. If your supply of water is plentiful, then having a pumpkin maturing into a nice fruit ready for Halloween carving is just around the corner.

In my case, I usually remember that I want to grow pumpkin about two weeks before Halloween, and I get mad at myself for not starting early enough. I promise myself that next year will be different. One year, I actually went as far as purchasing a package of pumpkin seeds only to realize when I got home that I was already two months late. Next year will be the year—you can count on it.

■ *When to Plant*

To have pumpkins ready to harvest by Halloween, you have to plant the seeds July 1. Planting any vegetable, let alone pumpkins, at that time is fraught with risk—bugs and diseases are at their high point. If you are growing pumpkins for pie making, it's better that you plant immediately after the danger of frost has passed in your area. Try to beat the pest invasion. It can be done, but the timing is critical. You can get a head start by planting pumpkin seeds in peat cups three to four weeks before the last frost and then planting them outdoors as quickly as you can after that.

■ *Where to Plant*

Pumpkins need lots of room (100 square feet per plant), full sun (at least 8 hours), well-drained and well-composted soil, and lots and lots of water. Pumpkin plants do not tolerate wet, poorly drained soil or standing water even for the shortest period of time; it will put the plants into a tailspin.

■ *How to Plant*

Given the space needed to grow pumpkins and the number of weeds that would enjoy living in the same space, pumpkins are best grown on black plastic to eliminate weed competition.

Place a 10 × 10-foot piece of black plastic over the garden space and pin it into place. Make a 6-inch "X" in the center of the plastic and plant three seeds into the exposed soil. The seeds should germinate in five to seven days. After the seedlings reach 4 to 5 inches tall, remove all but the strongest seedling.

■ Care and Maintenance

One plant will produce one pumpkin in a 10 x 10-foot garden space. Pumpkin vines will produce a pumpkin 110 days after the seeds have been sown into the soil. That's why seeds should be planted about July 1 to have a pumpkin ready for Halloween. Insects and diseases are a real problem so be prepared to spray a variety of chemicals weekly (pages 234 to 253) to keep the plant alive and well.

Water and sunlight are the key ingredients. An application of 10-10-10 fertilizer (½ cup) every four weeks is needed to keep the fruits and vines growing well. One cup of 10-10-10 fertilizer added to the initial planting area has very positive results.

■ Additional Information

Good varieties of pumpkins for Florida include 'Connecticut Field', 'Spirit', 'Half Moon', 'Big Moon', 'Howden', and 'Jackpot'. For pumpkin pies, grow 'Small Sugar'. For small pumpkins try 'Apprentice', 'Bumpkin', and 'Munchkin'.

Pumpkin

Radish 'Easter Egg'

RADISH

Sometimes salads can be so drab and unappealing. Many people simply throw a few lettuce leaves in a bowl, sprinkle them with dressing, and call it a salad. But salads can be much more than that given the different varieties of fresh vegetables you can grow and add to them. For example, radishes are a main component of any salad in our house. But if you only know the little, red, round radish from the local markets, well then, you're in for a real surprise.

When you open any seed catalog or visit an online site selling vegetable seeds, you will be amazed at the number of different radishes that are available now. Recently, I counted seventeen different varieties in just one catalog. Radishes are now available with different heat intensities, in different colors, and in different sizes. Second only to growing mustard, radishes have to be one of the easiest vegetables to cultivate. Because they are so easy to grow, and the seeds are relatively inexpensive considering the number you receive in a seed package, it's a great vegetable to help children get started in gardening. Many radishes can be harvested only forty-five days after sowing the seed. When they're planted at weekly or biweekly intervals, radishes can keep a child's attention over many months.

■ *When to Plant*

In North Florida radishes can be planted from April through November. Radishes don't like intense heat (which translates into hotter bulb flavors), so in Central and South Florida plan to sow them from October through April.

■ *Where to Plant*

Radishes are very forgiving of a variety of soils. They can grow in any natural soil in Florida (including South Florida's rockland soils) and can be planted in a wide variety of containers filled with a good quality potting soil. Because they are so small, radishes are a perfect candidate for planting in mixed containers with flowering annuals and perennials; just harvest before the flowering plants "fill in." Radishes still need full sun like other vegetables and they need ample water to prevent a harsh flavor (which sometimes can be caused by too little water).

■ *How to Plant*

Radish seeds are easy to handle and should be planted 2 to 3 inches apart in a furrow or broadcast evenly in a wide planting bed and covered with ¼ inch of fine soil. Thin the wide row of seedlings to 2 to 3 inches apart when the seedlings produce their second pair of true leaves. Radishes can be used as "marker" vegetables. For instance: carrots are notoriously slow to germinate and sometimes get "lost" in the garden. Plant a radish seed every 10 to 12 inches in the carrot row to mark the location of the carrots. Once the radishes have matured forty-five days later, they can be harvested; in the meantime, the carrots will have grown tall enough to be seen.

■ *Care and Maintenance*

Just make sure radishes get adequate water so the soil remains moist but not soaking wet. Radishes that are allowed to go dry will have a much more intense, harsh, and bitter flavor; and keep an eye on the number days since you planted the seed. Although it may be fun to watch a radish plant grow to 18 inches tall with a fist-sized bulb, ones that large aren't very tasty. Harvest radishes within ten to fourteen days of the harvest schedule printed on the seed packet.

■ *Additional Information*

For traditionally sized and flavored radishes, try 'Easter Egg' and 'Cherry Bell'. For more exotic shapes and colors, try 'White Icicle', 'Fire and Ice', 'Watermelon', and 'Zlata'. For a Daikon variety try 'Minowase'.

SPINACH

Versatility is the key word when talking about spinach. It can be eaten raw, steamed, added to pasta dishes, and used in dips. Once you get few of the details down it's easy to grow, and a few rows a can feed a family of four without much work. In addition to using it in the vegetable garden, its wrinkled, emerald-black leaves work well as a border plant in the landscape or as a filler plant in a mixed container of bedding plants and perennials.

▧ When to Plant

Spinach is a cool-weather plant and bolts, or goes to flower, when the weather turns warm. Most spinach is planted in the fall and it will continue to grow until warm weather returns. In North and Central Florida plant spinach from October through November and in South Florida plant spinach from October through January. If you plant successive crops of spinach every three weeks you'll be able to harvest a continuous crop.

▧ Where to Plant

If you ever need to improve your garden soil with compost or manures, spinach would be the crop to do it. Rich, deep loamy soil that drains well will produce crisp green leaves for

Spinach

harvesting. Full sun is a must and so is moist, but not wet, soil. Spinach prefers locations with good air circulation. If that's not possible in your garden, try growing spinach in aboveground containers or in raised beds.

How to Plant

Spinach can be direct sown into the garden or started from seed indoors four weeks before planting in the garden. Soak in warm water overnight before planting. For transplants, plant the seed ½ inch deep in biodegradable containers and keep the soil moist for good germination. Transplants can be planted out when the seedlings are 3 to 4 inches tall. When planting seed outdoors directly into the garden, plant seeds 3 to 4 inches apart. Later, thin to 6 inches apart in rows that are 14 inches wide. Spinach lends itself to wide row plantings.

Care and Maintenance

Spinach likes to be fed a little bit at frequent intervals. Fertilize with a general 12-0-12 fertilizer every two to three weeks, and keep the soil moist. An occasional liquid feed of 20-20-20 wouldn't hurt, either. Remove weeds often to reduce the competition for food and water. Harvest the single, outside leaves of spinach or cut the entire plant for cooking. Mulching with hay around the plants will reduce weeds, conserve water, and reduce the amount of dirt and grit that splashes up on the plants during rainstorms. As the weather begins to warm up watch for flower stalks and harvest immediately, otherwise the foliage becomes very bitter quite quickly. After it has been washed, fresh spinach can be refrigerated in an airtight container for up to one week.

Additional Information

Spinach is rich in calcium, iron, and vitamin A, and there are several different types. Of the crinkled leaf varieties 'Bloomsdale Longstanding' performs well in Florida. Good medium savoyed varieties include 'Melody' and 'Vienna'. 'Tyee' is a good, slightly savoyed spinach with very upright leaves that help it stay cleaner than most others. Good plain-leaf varieties for Florida include 'Giant Nobel', 'Space', and 'Olympia'.

SQUASH

Squash 'Peter Pan'

Of all the vegetables, I must admit squash is my favorite. There are so many different kinds that one never grows tired of it. It can be prepared in a nearly infinite number of ways, which makes it a preferred vegetable of chefs around the world. Stir-fried, baked, sautéed, grilled—the list of preparation methods is endless. It's also very, very easy to grow. Just stick a few seeds in the ground and sixty days later you'll have edible fruit. That's why it is so popular in children's gardens, too; it grows fast and the fruit are easy to find during harvesting. I encourage you to try some new squash varieties in your garden this year. It's a great way to learn more about growing plants, and a new vegetable on the dinner table might be a nice change!

■ *When to Plant*

The traditional terms of summer and winter squash really don't mean a thing in Florida. Let's talk about summer squash first. In North Florida summer squash should be planted from March through April and again from August through September. In Central Florida summer squash is planted from February through March and again from August through September. In South Florida summer squash should be planted from January through March and again from September through October. Now let's talk about winter squash (which is usually the vining type). In North Florida plant winter squash in March and again in August. In Central Florida plant winter squash from February through March and in South Florida plant winter squash from January through February and again in September. Whew! That's a lot of squash.

■ *Where to Plant*

Plant squash in full sun in a compost-enriched, well-drained soil that has been deeply tilled and that has a pH of 5.8 to 6.8.

■ *How to Plant*

Although our northern friends plant squash in hills, in Florida they are planted in rows just like other vegetable crops. The use of hills in northern gardens allows the seed to dry out and stay above any wet soil, a problem we don't generally have here. Plant two or three seeds every 36 inches in rows that are 36 to 48 inches apart. Five to six fruit-producing plants are enough for an average family.

■ *Care and Maintenance*

Although they are very easy to grow and care for, squash plants do have a few problems that may arise. The number one problem is stem borers. Very large, cream-colored worms burrow into the thick but hollow squash stems and ultimately kill the vine beyond the spot where the pest has eaten. An application of spinosad, Sevin, or a pyrethroid every two weeks will deter stem borers. Once inside the stem they can be detected by their light-green "frass" (a somewhat nicer word for poop) found on the outside of the stems. If stem borers are caught early enough, the

Squash Scallopini 'Flying Saucer'

Zucchini squash 'Cheetah'

home gardener can carefully cut an infected stem lengthwise with a sharp knife and kill the worm. Piling 4 to 6 inches of dirt in mounds on the cut vine will cause the vine to root at those locations and will help overcome any borer damage. Once a worm is inside a vine or the fruit itself, insecticides will not work.

The other serious problems for squash are powdery mildew and downy mildew. As a result of our warm, humid nights, the disease powdery mildew appears, as the name implies, as a powder-like dusting on the upper surfaces of the leaves, causing the leaves to drop off prematurely and ultimately kills the plant. One method of control is prevention. Plant mildew-resistant varieties if they are available (unfortunately only a few are available at this time), and avoid those varieties that are regularly susceptible. Downy mildew on squash appears as purplish, dark gray angular spots on the underside of leaves and eventually will kill the plant if not controlled. Planting in full sun, watering in the mornings, and selecting sites with good air circulation will help. Applying horticultural oils (such as Neem and Sunfine Ultraspray), copper, and sulfur works well to protect plants and eradicate powdery and downy mildew, but they cannot be used together nor should they be used when temperatures reach

---

GROWING TIP

Winter squash is ready to harvest when the skin is hard enough so that a scratch from a thumbnail will not leave a mark.

---

85 degrees Fahrenheit. Any product that has *B.s.* as the active ingredient can be used on squash. It must be applied every seven days once the disease has been identified and can be applied up to and including the day of harvest. Synthetic products containing chlorothalonil or mancozeb are fungicides registered for squash that both protect and cure downy mildew on squash.

◼ Additional Information

Do not try to pull the fruits off a squash vine; instead, cut the fruit so there are 1 to 2 inches of stem remaining. Squash store longer if their stems are left intact. Remember, both summer and winter squash can grow in fall and spring, but for the sake of simplicity I will use "summer squash" (those with a tender skin) and "winter squash" (those with a tough, hard skin) for descriptive groupings only. Good disease-resistant varieties of summer squash for Florida include 'Cheetah', and 'Lioness'. Good winter varieties include 'Spaghetti', 'Table King', 'Table Queen', 'Table Ace' (acorn), 'Waltham', and 'Early Butternut'. Good Florida disease-resistant zucchini varieties include 'Reward' and 'Eight Ball'.

Wrinkled and premature fruit drop is common when growing squash and indicates poor flower pollination. Planting African blue basil, agastache, marigolds, or any flower that attracts pollinators to the garden should solve the problem. Or, they can be pollinated by hand.

> *Can I save the seeds of squash for planting next year?*
Yes, provided they are not hybrids. Remove the hard seeds from mature squash and allow them to dry in the sun, turning them daily so they dry evenly. Remove any pulp, and store the seeds in a resealable plastic bag in the bottom of the refrigerator. Inspect the seeds periodically, and remove any seeds that have mold on them. Seeds stored in this way can be used for several years.

Strawberries

STRAWBERRY

If ever there were a sweeter berry than a strawberry, I don't know what it would be. One of my favorite memories growing up was the delicious aroma of strawberries in the air riding along the sandy roads through Plant City (near Tampa) in the springtime. The air was heavy with the deep, rich scent, and afterwards I was determined to learn how to grow them myself. I have since learned how to do it, and I still enjoy the springtime ritual of riding through Plant City in the spring.

Just a word of caution, however. If you enjoy fresh strawberries, think how much the bugs, slugs, birds, spider mites, mice, raccoons, and opossums like them, too. As with sweet corn, I encourage you to grow strawberries once or twice, but chances are you will find that going to the store or to a strawberry festival may be much easier and less costly!

■ *Where to Plant*

Plant in full sun in rich, very well-composted, well-drained garden soil with an acidity of 5.5 to 6.5.

■ *How to Plant*

Bare root, single-crown strawberry plants planted in the fall will produce up to three cycles of berry production, with the most abundant in the spring months. The cycles can be interrupted by frost and water availability. Strawberry plants are grown in raised linear beds about 8 inches high. Drip irrigation or soaker hoses are placed 2 to 3 inches below the top of the soil. If you cover each row with an opaque, polyethylene plastic it will control weeds, keep the fruit clean, and conserve water. Small slits are made in the plastic in an alternating pattern 12 inches apart along the row and 12 to 18 inches wide, and the plants are planted into the soil beneath. It is very difficult to grow strawberries any other way given their long growing season and the abundance of weeds in Florida gardens. The only alternative would be to use newspaper and coastal hay (with or without mounding the soil and with or without soaker hoses).

Care and Maintenance

A fertilizer formula containing nitrogen (N), phosphorus (P), and potassium (K) is essential for successful strawberry growth and fruiting. Two pounds of a 10-5-10 or similar garden fertilizer with micronutrients (such as zinc, copper, iron, manganese, and boron) per 10 feet of row should be incorporated into the bed before planting. At least half of the nitrogen should be slow release. Protect fruit and flowers from temperatures below 32 degrees Fahrenheit by covering them with old blankets or commercially available polypropylene row covers.

Strawberries are the favorite among many pests. Birds, field mice, raccoons, and so forth can be repelled by placing fine mesh bird netting over the plants. The netting won't bother the strawberries but it infuriates the animals. For slugs, a very common pest, beer traps work best. For spider mites and insects, apply Neem oil as necessary. For spider mites, at least three applications will be necessary five days apart.

Additional Information

Recommended varieties for Florida include 'Camarosa', 'Sweet Charlie', and 'Festival'. All three varieties produce attractive, flavorful berries suitable for eating fresh or for freezing. 'Camarosa' has been the most productive variety in North Florida, while 'Festival' has been the most productive variety in Central Florida. These varieties are capable of producing one to two pints of fruit per plant over the season.

SUMMER PEA

It's confusing, I know, but in Florida you can plant two types of peas. The first is the English pea; that's the kind that is green, sweet, and grown in the cooler seasons of the year. The second is the summer pea, which are similar to beans and can be eaten fresh or dried to be used later. Black-eyed peas and purple hulls are examples of summer peas. Summer peas are usually long and narrow, with tiny beans or "peas," and they enjoy the hot, humid summer months. Summer peas and a few other vegetables, such as okra, sweet potatoes, peppers, and peanuts, are about the only things that can take the full sun and summer heat of Florida. People from our northern neighboring states may think it seems odd not to plant anything in the summer, but that's Florida—it's just too hot and too humid for most vegetables.

When to Plant

Plant the seeds when it's hot—the hotter, the better. Once soil temperatures reach 70 degrees Fahrenheit, it's pea planting time. In North and Central Florida plant summer peas from April through August. In South Florida plant summer peas year round.

Where to Plant

Plant summer pea seeds in full, hot, steaming sun in a location that receives at least 8 hours, more if you can get it. Summer peas will grow in just about any kind of soil from rich, organically improved soils all the way to the other end of the spectrum—muck. They are not fussy plants and will grow just about any where, provided they have sun and water.

How to Plant

Summer peas are easier to grow than radishes. Plant the seeds 1 to 2 inches deep, 3 to 4 inches apart, in rows that are 30 inches apart. The seeds will germinate in five to seven days. The peas will be ready to harvest in eighty to ninety days. Summer peas must be planted directly into garden soil—do not transplant.

■ Care and Maintenance

Fertilize the plants once at planting with a general-purpose 8-0-8 fertilizer, or fertilize according to the results of your soil analysis. When new growth emerges from the soil the bean seedlings are often the favorite food of birds, especially brown thrashers. They will break off the tender seed that emerges with the new leaves, which will kill the new sprout. My daughter's 30-inch-long, lifelike plastic monitor lizard will scare them off most years, but aluminum pie pans attached to strings and allowed to twirl in the air will work, too. Many of the pea pods can be eaten like snap beans if they're picked early enough. Otherwise, the pods should be allowed to grow until the pods have turn buff colored and the peas inside the pods are fully formed. Shell them like English peas.

■ Additional Information

Summer peas are easy to grow and even easier to cook. Just place dried peas in a pot and cover with water; let it stand overnight. The next day, pour the water off, add new water to cover, add a ham hock or neck bones, and season to taste. Make some corn bread, too, to sop up the leftover liquid. Wow!

Varieties of summer peas that perform well in Florida include 'Brown Crowder', 'California Blackeye', 'Knucklehull Purplehull', 'Hercules', 'White Acre', 'Calico Crowder', 'Iron and Clay', 'Washday', and 'Zipper Cream'.

Black-eyed peas

SWEET POTATO

If you are looking for a problem-free summer vegetable that requires very little car,e then sweet potato is for you. These tender, sweet, orange tubers and their vining, heart-shaped leaves thrive in Florida's summer heat. All you have to do is prepare the soil properly before planting and walk away. Sweet potatoes are grown from tip cuttings of growing tubers, and not that long ago a gardener would simply take cuttings of the vine tips, called "slips," and plant them directly into long, mounded hills. Then the growers came out with rooted slips in bundles of twenty five, which made life much easier; with the old way you had to watch the new cuttings to make sure they didn't dry out. Now, however, slips are considered old fashioned. Growers now put cuttings in plastic, nine-count cell packs. When you buy them they are fully rooted and ready for planting out into the mounds. Isn't technology grand?

▓ *When to Plant*

Plant sweet potatoes from March through June throughout Florida.

Sweet potato

■ *Where to Plant*

Plant in full sun, in mounds of compost-enriched soil. Be sure there is an ample water supply nearby.

■ *How to Plant*

Create 10-inch tall, 12-inch-wide linear mounds with surrounding garden soil. A little 10-10-10 fertilizer (2 to 3 pounds) sprinkled on the soil used to make the mounds should be enough for the entire growing season. Place the rooted slips into the top of the mound 12 to 14 inches apart in rows that are 48 to 60 inches apart.

■ *Care and Maintenance*

Once the slips are planted, make certain that the plant receives enough water to produce large tubers. In the final two weeks reduce the amount of irrigation the plants receive. The tubers can be harvested at any time during the summer, but they are finished growing when the vines begin to turn yellow. Cut the vines away from the mounds and gently lift them, shaking carefully to remove the soil. The tubers that have grown in the mounds can be eaten after two or three days of "curing" in the sun. The only real problems with sweet potatoes are deer; deer will walk a hundred miles to eat sweet potato vines. Let them eat all they want; deer eating the vines every so often won't have an adverse effect on the size or quality of the tubers. Store the tubers in a cool, dry location.

■ *Additional Information*

For Florida the best sweet potato varieties include 'Beauregard', 'Hernandez', and 'Picodito' (boniato). Sweet potatoes perform best where the soil has been turned over two to three months prior to planting. This reduces the number of nematodes and helps any plant debris that was turned under to decompose. Soils with high levels of nematodes (more than two percent) are not well suited for sweet potato production, and planting in that location will result in cracked tubers. Avoid garden areas that have been allowed to go fallow or where sweet potatoes have been grown in the last three years. Sweet potatoes will continue to grow as long as there are green tops. For that reason, sweet potatoes can be harvested anytime their size fits your particular need.

SWISS CHARD

There is something satisfying about growing greens in the home garden. I guess it's like having money in the bank; as you walk through your garden you know at the very least you won't starve no matter how tough things get. Swiss chard is a staple in any fall-spring garden, and on the dinner plate it complements just about everything. Many people eat it raw in salads like spinach and just about everyone eats it cooked with a piece of smoked meat for additional flavor.

■ When to Plant

Swiss chard can be planted as early as mid-October and can be successfully grown through early May. Seeds can be started in biodegradable pots in late September and planted out into the garden in mid-October. Plant three to four successive plantings in 15-foot-long rows of chard, three weeks apart, to provide an adequate supply for an average family.

■ Where to Plant

Plant in full sun in compost-enriched, deeply tilled soil with a pH of 6.0 to 6.8. Swiss chard prefers to have moist, but not wet, soil, so be certain an adequate supply of water is nearby.

■ How to Plant

Plant Swiss chard seeds directly into the garden every 4 to 5 inches apart in rows that are 24 inches apart. Soak seed overnight in warm water and plant the seed ½ inch deep. One seed will produce several seedlings when it begins to sprout so it is necessary that the small seedlings be thinned to 12 inches apart. Seedlings grown in biodegradable pots should be planted 12 inches apart when the seedlings reach a height of 6 inches.

■ Care and Maintenance

Swiss chard is grown like spinach or mustard. If the seedlings don't sprout uniformly, interplant with more seed to make a complete row. A standard 12-0-12 fertilizer applied every three weeks will provide adequate nutrition. Apply a layer of hay or leaves to maintain soil moisture, keep the foliage free of dirt and grit, and minimize weeds. Not only do weeds compete for nutrients and water, many of the critters that can eat the leaves on Swiss chard begin their life cycle in weeds. Swiss chard should be harvested like collards—the leaves at the bottom of the plant are picked first. Picking from the bottom encourages new growth on top.

Speaking of bugs, Swiss chard doesn't have many pests. If the soil is kept too wet, slugs can be a problem, but they are easily eliminated with beer traps. Wide boards placed near the base of the plants will attract slugs, too. Simply flip the board over in the morning and eliminate the slugs that have accumulated beneath the board during the evening.

■ Additional Information

In addition to its other good qualities, Swiss chard is a handsome vegetable that can also be used as an attractive border plant in the landscape. Most notably, 'Bright Lights' has large, broad stems with orange, red, yellow, and light-green stems. Other good chards include 'Erbette', 'Monstruoso', 'Fordhook Giant', 'Italian White Ribbed', and 'Ruby Red'.

Swiss chard 'Bright Lights'

TOMATO

If you mention the words "vegetable garden," often the first thing many people think about are tomatoes. Juicy, firm, vine-ripened tomatoes. Of all the vegetables, tomatoes are king in the garden. People grow more tomatoes than any other kind of vegetable. (Technically tomatoes are fruits, but let's not get into that.) They can be grown indoors and outdoors, in the ground and in containers—even in hanging baskets! Tomatoes can grow several feet tall or fewer than 12 inches tall and still produce loads of fruit. There are hundreds of different varieties to choose from, and because tomatoes are so easy to place in your garden, the real difficulty is trying to decide which variety to grow.

Let's talk for just a minute about how tomato plants grow. They can be divided into two main groups: indeterminate and determinate. Knowing these terms will save you time in the garden later. If you have ever grown tomatoes, you know that most grow and grow and then grow some more. More often than not they grow taller than the stake you tie them to or the cage you placed them in. The majority of tomato seeds sold today are the vining type of tomatoes, which are the indeterminate type. That means, given adequate water and fertilizer, they will grow to an indeterminate height. Then there are the determinate-type tomatoes, and, if you haven't guessed by now, they grow to a (genetically) determined height (usually 4 to 5 feet tall) and stop. Determinate tomato varieties are great because you know at what height the tomato will stop growing and thus the length of stake or the size cage you will need.

One more thing; have you ever noticed the letters "VFN" after the variety name on the plant label? The "V" stands for Verticillium wilt (which is a deadly tomato disease); the "F" is an abbreviation of Fusarium wilt; and "N" stands for nematodes. When these letters, and occasionally a few others, appear on a label it means that hybridizers have created a built-in resistance to these problems and the plants have a better chance of survival in the garden.

■ When to Plant

It seems the "when to" part of growing tomatoes is a little tricky in Florida. In most areas of the country, tomatoes are planted in the spring and allowed to grow all summer. If you haven't already guessed it, that's not true in Florida. In North Florida plant tomatoes from February (after the last frost) through March (so they will produce loads of fruit before the heat sets in). Plant again in August (so the plants will produce fruit before first frost). In Central Florida plant tomatoes from January through March and again in September until frost. In South Florida plant tomatoes from August through March.

Florida has a perfect climate for growing beautiful tomatoes.

■ *Where to Plant*

Plant tomatoes in a location where they will receive at least 8 hours of full sun. More is better; less will cause the plant to "stretch," and it will produce low-quality and fewer fruit. Tomatoes can tolerate a variety of soils; just make certain the soil is compost rich and well drained. Tomatoes prefer constantly moist soil—inconsistent moisture will produce poorly formed fruit. Tomatoes will not tolerate soggy or wet roots. If you are planting in containers on a patio or terrace, be sure to plant them where the roots have plenty of room to grow. A deep, 24-inch-diameter container or larger works best.

■ *How to Plant*

Tomatoes are very easy to grow from seed and can be sown indoors six to eight weeks before the danger of frost is past. In mid-Florida the magical dates are January 1 and July 1 to plant seeds. Sow individual seeds in a high-quality, sterile potting mix and grow in full sun until planted outdoors. More often than not when customers buy ready-to-plant transplants in the store they overlook the tall and spindly plants and buy the short, stocky plants instead. Actually, the taller plants are better. Tomato plants should be planted deep into garden soil; they are the only vegetables that can be treated that way. A deep, narrow hole is best and only 4 inches of a tomato plant should poke its head out of the hole. Backfill the planting hole with native soil and good compost to a height 2 inches less than the original soil line to create a water reservoir. Because it is planted so deep, in addition to the roots at the bottom of the plant, roots will also form along the entire length of the stem. This allows more water and nutrient absorption.

■ *Care and Maintenance*

The less you fuss with tomatoes, the better. Tomatoes are highly susceptible to a variety of diseases, and any activity that reduces contact with dirty, germ-ridden human hands is a good idea. Do not pick tomatoes or groom plants when the leaves are wet; that's when they are particularly vulnerable to transmission of diseases. Blossom drop is the result of cool temperatures (below 55 degrees Fahrenheit), hot temperatures (above 90 degrees Fahrenheit), not enough water, and too much nitrogen fertilizer.

Tomatoes are commonly attached to wooden stakes with stout twine or thin straps of remnant cloth tied into a figure-eight shape. Velcro strips designed for outdoor use work very well, too. I prefer cages made from concrete sidewalk reinforcing wire (often available for free at construction sites), formed into a tall column, and placed around a newly planted tomato plant. As the stems grow they are pushed into the column and the stems/leaves are supported by the wire mesh. This method requires minimal gardener-to-foliage contact. (A gardener friend of mine once made a cage of one-inch chicken wire to grow his tomatoes. The tomatoes grew very well, but he couldn't get the fruit through the chicken wire!)

Grape tomatoes

GROWING TIP

Use a thin piece of cloth to wind a figure-eight shape between the stem of a tomato plant and its stake. The cloth will support the plant but will also allow it to move with the wind as needed.

A common method of growing tomatoes in the South is the wire-and-string method, which is similar to the system one would use to grow pole beans. Place a stout, 6-foot-tall pole at either end of a planned tomato row and place a heavy wire across the top of the poles, stretching the wire from pole to pole. After planting the tomato plant, gently tie heavy string to the lower stem of a tomato plant, and attach the other end to the wire. As the tomato grows, simply tie or clip the tomato stems to the upright string. Another method of staking tomatoes is called the "Florida weave." It starts out with two very stout poles located at either end of the row as described, but in addition, smaller-diameter poles are pounded into the ground along the row every 2 feet. Heavy garden twine is then woven back and forth from one end of each row at 6-inch intervals to create a basketlike effect. The tomatoes are planted along the row and as they grow, the stems are "woven" in and out of the supporting twine.

■ Additional Information

Deciding which tomato to grow is based on a variety of criteria, such as how much space you have, the size of tomato plant you ultimately want to have, whether you want to grow modern versus heirloom varieties, and so forth. Several varieties that perform well in Florida are:

Indeterminate (large fruit): 'Better Boy' (VFN), 'Bonnie Best' (North and Central Florida only), 'Bragger', 'San Marzano' (plum shaped), and 'Striped Cavern' (hollow for stuffing)

Indeterminate (small fruit): 'Red Cherry', 'Sweet 100', 'Sweet Chelsea', 'Husky Cherry', and 'Everglades'

Determinate (large fruit): 'Walter' (F), 'Sun Coast' (VF), 'Floramerica' (F), 'Flora-dade' (VF), 'Duke' (VF), 'Sunny' (VF), 'Celebrity', and 'Tasti-Lee'

Determinate (small fruit): 'Floragold', 'Florida Petite', 'Patio', and 'Micro Tom'

TURNIP

Can you have a garden in the South and not grow turnips? I have to confess I am a real fan of turnips, but I also have to come clean. For half my life, I used to throw the tops away and eat only the roots. It wasn't until I was in my mid-30s that I tried eating the tops, when an old-timer walking by my house while I was sitting on my porch pointed out that I was throwing out the wrong part. Since then, turnip greens, with a few diced roots and a ham hock, is one of my favorite meals. Add some cracklin' cornbread to sop up the pot licker on the bottom of the pan and you're livin' the high life! For the Irish in us, turnips are perfect in lamb stew and cooked with corned beef. Mashed turnips make a great side dish, too.

■ When to Plant

In North Florida plant turnips from January through April and again from August through October. In Central Florida plant them year round. In South Florida plant turnips from October through February.

■ Where to Plant

Turnips are the least fussy of all southern garden plants. Give the plants full sun (8 hours minimum) and plenty of water in well-composted or manure-enriched, well-drained, and deeply tilled soil, and you're home free. To prevent the occasional root maggot, sprinkle the soil with a little wood ash from a fireplace (one cup to every ten feet of row) over the soil before planting the seed. Leaf-eating worms are also sometimes a problem. A light dusting of Dipel will make them disappear. When too much water is added to turnips, slugs can be a pest, but beer bait traps can make quick work of them.

■ How to Plant

Direct sow turnip seed ½ inch deep, 2 to 3 inches apart, in rows 18 inches apart. After they are about 3 inches tall, thin them to 3 inches apart. Because turnips are a root crop, they don't perform well when they are transplanted. If you want to grow primarily tops and not roots, turnips can be planted closer together.

■ *Care and Maintenance*

Keep the plants weed free and cultivate regularly but lightly. A layer of coastal hay between the rows will also reduce weeds and prevent soil and grit from splashing up on the greens. Every three weeks or so feed the turnips with a water-soluble fertilizer, containing some minor elements, including boron. Harvest turnips when they are about 3 inches in diameter; any larger and they are likely to be pithy and tough to eat.

Turnip 'Tokyo Cross' hybrid

■ *Additional Information*

'Purple Top White Globe Turnips' are by far the most popular turnip for both greens and roots. An unusual turnip 'Scarlet Ohno Revival' produces a beautiful bright red skin with white flesh. If you are interested primarily in growing turnips for their tops only, then try 'Seven Top', 'Southern Green', 'Shogoin', and 'Topper'. Varieties you want to grow for the roots include 'Golden Ball', 'Just Right', 'Lunga Bianca A Colletto Viola', 'Tokyo Cross', and 'White Lady'.

➤ *What are the two kinds of turnips?*

The rutabaga is considered by some to be the yellow turnip or the Swede, and the white turnip is the "true" turnip. The true turnip includes the 'Purple Top' and 'White Lady' cultivars. Both belong to the Brassica family, which also includes cabbage, broccoli, Brussels sprouts, mustard, and cauliflower. All members of the Brassica family contain very high levels of vitamin C, and, according to the researchers at UC Berkley, they provide potent antiviral, antibacterial, and anticancer properties.

WATERMELON

Florida provides the perfect growing conditions for producing watermelon: well-drained soil, a long growing season, plentiful sunlight, and abundant rainfall. The multitudes of semi-trailer trucks running down the roads loaded to the brim with bright-green watermelons is a testament to that. Watermelon fields in Florida are like peanut fields in Georgia or cotton fields in Alabama—it's a sign of who we are. We are proud to be able to grow them in such quantities. In fact, Florida is the nation's leading producer of watermelons, and from December through April, Florida is the only producer of watermelons in the entire country.

■ *When to Plant*

Watermelons grow best when daytime temperatures are between 70 to 85 degrees Fahrenheit; they can tolerate temperatures up to 90 degrees Fahrenheit. In North Florida that means planting seeds from March through April and again from July to August. In Central Florida plant seeds from January through March and again in August. In South Florida watermelons can be planted from January through March and again from August through September.

■ *Where to Plant*

Watermelons can grow in a wide variety of soils but they have a tough time growing in muck. The soil pH should be in the 6.0 to 6.5 range, but they can tolerate a pH as low as 5.0. Plant watermelon seeds in full sun with an ample water supply nearby. They are thirsty plants.

Watermelon

■ *How to Plant*

Seeds planted 1½ inches deep, 36 inches apart, in rows that are
7 to 8 feet apart will provide the best possible yields. Watermelons
reach maturity within 80 to 100 days after planting seed,
depending on the variety. Given the amount of water necessary
to grow ample-sized fruit and the fact that competing weeds
also like the same water, many gardeners will stretch black
plastic over the garden and plant the seeds through the plastic.
The plastic eliminates the weed problem, conserves moisture,
and keeps the fruit clean. A thin layer of newspaper covered
with coastal hay will work instead of the plastic, and it can be
tilled under when the season is over.

■ *Care and Maintenance*

Aphids are the primary insect pests affecting watermelons
grown in Florida. Normally these are not a huge problem on
most vegetables, but aphids are vectors for a variety of viruses
that can directly affect watermelon production. Cucumber
beetles also carry viruses. For that reason it's important that
aphids and cucumber beetles are controlled. Applications of
soap or any product containing pyrethroids in the late afternoon
or at dusk, when pollinators are least active, is most effective.
Any worms that feed on the fruit are called rind worms. Beet
armyworms and cabbage loopers are the worst rind worms,
and they can be controlled with Dipel (*B.t.*), spinosad, or Sevin.

■ *Additional Information*

There is no sure way to determine when a watermelon is ripe.
Generally, when the fruit is ripe, the bottom of the melon will
turn a bright golden yellow. Additionally, look for the tendril
closest to the fruit—when the tendril turns from green to
brown, more often than not the melon is ripe.

For large watermelons in Florida try 'Jubilee' (also known as
'Florida Giant'), 'Crimson Sweet', 'General Lee', and 'Charleston
Grey 133'. For smaller varieties or "icebox melons" try 'Sugar
Baby' and 'Mickeylee'.

AVOCADO

Personally, I don't think it's a coincidence that many avocado varieties ripen at the same time that college football season starts. Guacamole is a staple at our house during the fall gridiron season, and you can't get any fresher than going out to the backyard a week before the big game to pick a few avocados. Sushi couldn't exist without the California roll and its avocado contents, and a summer salad with ripe, buttery avocado is just the thing to cool down a hot afternoon. In addition to fruit production, avocado trees make good landscape specimens, ranging in height from 30 to 60 feet tall depending on the variety.

■ Where to Plant

Traditionally, avocados were only planted in the warmest areas of the state, primarily the southeastern and southwestern corners. With the advent of hybridization and the introduction of cold-hardy selections, avocados can now be grown in cooler areas of the state as well. Regardless of where you live, follow the guidelines found in the chart that follows and talk to

gardeners in your area to determine whether or not planting avocados is a viable option. Plant avocados in full sun and be sure to give them plenty of room. For the first four to five years make certain to water during prolonged dry spells.

■ How to Plant

In areas where the soil depth is shallow, planting an avocado tree will take some work. Hand picks,

Avocado

augers, or backhoes will do the job. Any underlying hard rock will have to be removed to twice the depth of a containerized root ball and three times its width. Plant the root ball 1 to 2 inches above the soil line to compensate for settling. In areas where flooding can be a problem, plant an avocado tree on mounds of native soil (2 to 3 feet deep by 10 to 12 feet wide) and install as described. In sandy soils plant as you would any containerized root ball but do not add any amendments (such as peat moss, top soil, and so forth) to the backfill.

■ Care and Maintenance

Nutrition for avocados can be a little confusing because there are different amounts and types of fertilizers added to the underlying soil at different stages of an avocado tree's life. During its first three years, fertilize an avocado tree with 1 cup of a 10-10-10-4 (NPKMg) fertilizer every two months. A generic palm fertilizer will also work. After its first three years, four fertilizer applications per year are recommended (in increasing amounts proportional to the size of the tree)—but never exceed 20 pounds per year. One more thing: four times in the spring and summer during a tree's first four years, use a hose-end sprayer to apply a foliar spray containing copper, zinc, manganese, and boron. After its fourth year, a spray of zinc, manganese, molybdenum, and boron during spring and summer will do the trick. Finally, watch for iron deficiencies that will appear as a general yellowing of the leaves. A granular application of chelated iron will soon correct any problems (but foliar sprays of iron won't help).

■ Additional Information.

Oddly enough, avocado fruits do not ripen on the tree. Generally, the fruit is picked when it's at its maximum size (as noted on the following chart), but this can change from year to year depending on weather conditions. I use this simple test at home: when you think the fruit is ready, pick the largest fruit and leave it on a table without refrigeration. If the fruit softens within four to eight days the remaining fruits on the tree are ready, too. On the other hand, if the fruit gets wrinkly or becomes rotten, it's not ready and you can test again in a week or two. That's the great thing about avocados—they don't all have to be picked at the same time. But remember, once they are harvested, expect them to ripen within four to eight days.

One more thing: when you select an avocado variety for your garden, why not select several that have different ripening seasons, if you have room? When you refer to the chart you can see that avocados have a wide range of dates to maturity. Ideally, it would be great to have early, mid-, and late maturing varieties in your garden.

I haven't said anything about critters because avocados have only a few diseases and bugs that can affect the appearance of the fruit, but they seldom reduce the number of fruit produced. Loopers, aphids, thrips, and scale are sometimes a problem, but if the trees are well fed and watered they hardly ever have serious insect problems. On the other hand, you may have heard of a disease called laurel wilt, which is a disease of trees in the laurel family, including avocado. It is caused by a fungus that stops the flow of water, causing the leaves to wilt. The fungus is carried into host trees by a non-native insect, the redbay ambrosia beetle. Laurel wilt causes the leaves of avocado trees to droop and take on a reddish or purplish discoloration.

If you only need to use half an avocado, use the half without the pit first. The side with the pit will keep longer.

Wilted foliage usually is seen in the top of the tree at first but the remaining leaves drop soon thereafter. Sometimes this process can only take 7 to 10 days. Unfortunately, once the avocado tree gets the laurel wilt the tree is dead and there isn't anything you can do to stop it. Nor is there anything you can do to prevent it. However, it's important to remove the dead tree and take it to a landfill close to your housie to prevent spreading the disease to other trees. Report your dead tree to the State of Florida's Division of Forestry so they can keep track of the disease.

Variety	Season of Maturity	Fruit Weight (ounces)	Cold Tolerance	Production
'Bernicker'	mid-Jul to late Aug	18-32	Low	Moderate
'Brogdon'	mid-July to mid-Sept	8-12	High	Moderate
'Choquette'	Dec to mid-Jan	18-40	High	High
'Day'	mid-Jul to mid-Sep	8-16	High	High
'Hall'	mid-Nov to early Feb	20-30	Moderate	Moderate
'Lula'	mid-Nov to early Mar	14-24	Moderate	High
'Marcus Pumpkin'	early Oct to mid-Nov	30-48	Moderate	Moderate
'Mexicola'	mid-May to mid-Jun	6-8	High	High
'Monroe'	Dec to mid-Feb	24-40	Moderate	High
'Pollack'	mid-Jul to mid-Sep	18-40	Low	High
'Russell'	July to mid-Aug	16-24	Very tender	Moderate
'Simmonds'	mid-June to mid-Sep	16-34	Low	Moderate
'Winter'	mid-Oct	8-12	High	High

BANANA & PLANTAIN

It may be cruel, but when I hear the national weather service report that snowstorms have swept through the Midwest, I often call my sister to tell her that I picked a fresh banana for my corn flakes and had fresh-squeezed orange juice for breakfast. Then I ask, "So, how *is* the weather in Cleveland?" Banana plants can range from 4 to 18 feet tall and are very easy to grow where heavy freezes are not a problem. In the more northern areas of the state, many smaller but equally fine banana varieties can be grown in pots and brought indoors when cold weather passes through. Consider this, though, when you think about Florida's winter weather: wherever you are in Florida, it's still warmer than it is in Cleveland.

▪ *Where to Plant*

Plant bananas and plantains where the temperatures are hot, generally in the 75 to 85 degrees Fahrenheit range; fruiting is best at temperatures of 80 to 85 degrees Fahrenheit. Full sun to part shade is required for growth, and full sun is best for fruit production. Bananas can withstand wide ranges in soil acidity, from 5.5 to 7.0, but they require well-drained, deep soils enriched with plenty of compost. Do not locate banana plants where flooding occurs; occasional flowing water won't hurt the plant long-term, but standing water is life threatening.

▪ *How to Plant*

In South Florida plant bananas from March to May. Elsewhere, wait until the spring drought is over and plant when the daily rain showers begin again. In the rockland soils of southeast Florida, where the soil profile is shallow, planting a banana will take some work. Hand picks, augers, or backhoes will do the job. Any hard rock will have to be removed to twice the depth of the containerized root ball and three times its width. Plant the root ball 1 to 2 inches above the soil line to compensate for settling. In sandy soils dig a hole in well-prepared soil and place the top of the root ball 2 inches above the native soil to compensate for settling. In both soil types, mulch well to maintain adequate soil moisture and reduce weeds.

GROWING TIP

Don't throw away the banana peels. Cut them into three inch pieces and bury them near eggplants, peppers, and tomatoes. The tomatoes will enjoy the potassium.

■ Care and Maintenance

Bananas are virtually trouble free provided they receive adequate sunlight; are planted in well-drained, highly enriched soil; and receive plenty of water. There are a few diseases that affect bananas, but these are more common on large commercial farms than on single backyard plants. A regular fertilizer regimen should begin when a banana tree grows two new leaves after planting. Later, as the plant grows, it should be fertilized monthly with a 6-2-12-2 (NPKMg) at a rate of 1 to 2 pounds for every three to four stemmed plants. Once a banana plant grows five stems it should be divided and the process started again. An annual nutritional spray containing manganese and zinc will help. For proper fruit production, bananas need at least 1½ inches of water per week.

■ Additional Information

Good fruit-producing bananas include 'Manzano' or 'Apple' (14 feet, zones 9 to 10); 'Dwarf Cavendish' (6 to 7 feet, zones 8 to 9); 'Dwarf Orinoco' (6 to 8 feet, zones 7b to 10); 'Dwarf Red' (6 to 7 feet, zones 8 to 9); 'Goldfinger' (14 feet, zones 8 to 9); 'Blue Java' (12 feet, zones 8 to 10); 'Lady Finger' (14 to 16 feet, zone 9); 'Mysore' (10 to 14 feet, zones 8 to 10); 'Rajapuri' (8 to 10 feet, zones 8 to 9); and 'Williams Hybrid' (8 to 10 feet, zones 8 to 10).

Banana

BLACKBERRY

Blackberries have always performed well in the northern and central areas of the Sunshine State, and several new varieties have made growing them even easier. There are two main types of plants: erect and trailing. Trailing types, also known as dewberry or boysenberry, have long stems and need a support of some sort on which to grow. The erect types have stiff stems and grow 4 to 6 feet in height. They are the easiest to grow given their low-maintenance requirements. Regardless of the type you plan to grow, give them ample room and enjoy some blackberry jam!

Blackberries

■ *Where to Plant*

Blackberries like mildly acidic, well-drained soil. Add a good layer of organic mulch to help moderate soil temperatures, conserve water, and keep the weeds down. Although the plants themselves can withstand very cold temperatures (to the mid-teens), the flowers are very susceptible to cold temperatures and will not fruit if they get even a touch of frost.

■ *How to Plant*

Blackberries are often sold bare root, that is, without soil or a container. If this is the case, plant in the cooler months of the year (December to February), and plant immediately after you purchase them. Clip the roots to 6 inches long and set in a hole 7 to 8 inches deep. The crown of the plant (just above where the roots begin) should be set slightly higher than the level of the native soil. Alternate adding soil from the planting hole and watering until the hole is filled to remove any air pockets that might injure the roots. For containerized plants (which can be planted any time), dig a hole a little larger than the plant, set the root ball slightly above the native soil level, and fill the hole with unimproved native soil.

Care and Maintenance

All blackberries produce fruit in summer. Trailing types ripen earlier, the berries are smaller, and the clusters of fruit are more open than the erect types. After the first year, prune the primary canes to 36 inches to initiate new cane development from below. Blackberries produce fruit on one-year-old canes, so the more you prune the more berries you will have. However, don't prune more than one-third of the canes down to the ground in a single season.

Additional Information

A thornless variety named 'Apache' has made the lives of gardeners everywhere a little less painful. Its fruits are glossy black and blocky, and the canes are more erect than most so a trellis won't be needed. 'Arapaho' and 'Navaho' are very similar to 'Apache', and the fruit quality is quite good, maybe even better. 'Chester' is another good thornless variety; it's very cold hardy and a semi-erect type. 'Chickasaw' produces the sweetest and greatest number of blackberries of any variety available but, unfortunately, this variety has a good number of thorns. The canes are erect.

➤ *What's the difference between blackberries and raspberries?*
One sure way to tell is to look at the fruit after it is picked. Raspberries will leave a "plug" on the plant and the berries will have a hole at the top. Blackberries will not leave the plug and therefore the fruit is complete (with no hole).

➤ *My blackberry plant produces many leaves; can I do anything with them?*
Blackberry leaves contain powerful antioxidants, and tea made from dried leaves can be used to treat inflammation of the mouth and throat and is reported to be helpful in reducing blood sugar levels. Try one heaping tablespoon to one cup of water, steep for ten minutes, and sweeten to taste.

Blueberries

BLUEBERRY

Blueberries are a surefire sign that summer has finally arrived and that the accompanying heat will be with us until fall. Blueberries are harvested from late spring to early summer. Our warm winters throughout Florida make it important to purchase varieties of blueberries that have been specifically grown for Florida gardens. Either rabbiteye or southern highbush blueberries can be grown in Florida, depending on your location. Give them a try; a blueberry smoothie on a hot summer day always hits the spot.

■ *Where to Plant*

Plant blueberries in highly acidic soil or mulch, pH from 4.0-5.5, that is high in organic matter and well drained to a depth of at least 24 inches. Although blueberries need 45 inches of rain each year, they will die if their roots are flooded or stand in water for even the shortest period of time. Blueberries must have full sun and cannot be planted near hardwood trees (because the blueberries will produce less fruit), and they should be located at least 20 feet from a house or other structure. Wherever you plant them give them plenty of room. Rabbiteyes can reach 12 inches tall and 8 feet wide. Southern highbush are a tad smaller. A space 10 × 10 feet for rabbiteye or a 6 × 6-foot area for southern highbush will work just fine.

■ *How to Plant*

The best time to plant blueberries is during winter, and there are two ways to do it. In the first method adding plenty of sphagnum peat moss to the planting hole will help the shrub get a good start; a good 2-gallon bucketful added to the native soil and backfilled into the hole will do the trick. Be sure to plant the top of the root ball 1 to 2 inches above the native soil level to compensate for settling.

Pine bark may be the best friend of blueberries. Composted types work best but any form will do. Place a 2-foot-wide band around every plant after it's planted and continue even after the plant has been established. As the bark breaks down, it releases acid and improves the soil even more.

The second, and my personal favorite method, is to build a box of 2 × 10 inch pressure-treated lumber of what whatever length you like. (A 12-foot box will have sufficient room to grow four plants.) Pull the plant out of its container and place it *on top* of the ground inside the box. Do not dig a hole. Fill the box to the top and around the plants with composted pine bark, available at any bulk mulch business in your neighborhood. I can't emphasize this enough; blueberries need exceedingly acidic soil—far more acidic than you will ever be able to create in the ground. The box filled with pine bark is fool proof.

■ Care and Maintenance

Once established, blueberries enjoy a little fertilizer often. Use 2 pounds per plant of 12-4-8-2 (NPKMg), four times per year beginning in April. Apply the fertilizer in a 2-foot circle around the plant, and maintain a good layer of mulch. After the first year, increase the amount by 1 ounce each year for four years and spread the fertilizer in a 4-foot circle in the final year. After that maintain the 4 ounces per application in a 4-foot circle around the shrub.

■ Additional Information

If you live in Central or South Florida you should grow southern highbush blueberries (their early flowering makes them susceptible to early frost in northern areas of the state). Good southern highbush blueberry varieties include 'Emerald', 'Gulf Coast', 'Millennia', 'Sharpblue', 'Jewel', 'Star', and 'Windsor'. Good rabbiteye early varieties are 'Beckyblue', 'Bonita', and 'Climax'. Mid- to late-maturing varieties are more productive than the early types, and good varieties include 'Brightwell', 'Powderblue', 'Tifblue', and 'Woodruff'.

➤ *My blueberry bush produced so many berries I couldn't eat them all. Can I freeze some for eating later?*
Yes, you can freeze blueberries. After picking the berries, place the unwashed berries on a cookie sheet and freeze until they're frozen solid. Once they're completely frozen, place the berries in an airtight container or plastic bag and store in the freezer until you need them. Thoroughly wash the berries before using them.

CARAMBOLA

Even if Carambola, also known as star fruit, didn't produce its delicious, golden-yellow, ribbed fruit, I would plant it as a small landscape tree. It never gets very large (less than 20 feet tall), and it has a round habit that makes it a good candidate for a small yard or as a street tree to be planted between the sidewalk and the pavement. The tree gets its name because its fruit, when cut, is in the shape of a star. The fruit is slightly waxy, and it has been said the juice tastes like a combination of papaya, pineapple, and orange flavors.

■ *Where to Plant*

Plant a Carambola tree in full sun and in well-drained soil. Although the Carambola can withstand some cool weather, it prefers the hot and humid climate of Central and South Florida. While too much water will hinder fruit production, a Carambola will not tolerate drought. Make certain you have ample water nearby—give it at least 1 inch of water per week. If the leaves begin to wilt or fold up during the day, the tree is not getting enough water. Depending on the variety, many star fruit trees will produce several crops of fruit a year.

■ *How to Plant*

Carambola trees are nursery grown in plastic containers throughout Central and South Florida and therefore can be planted any time. Remember—plant in full sun with a source of water nearby. Dig a hole twice as deep and as wide as the container and place the root ball in the hole so that the top of the root ball is 1 to 2 inches above the native soil level. Water well and add a 2- to 3-inch layer of mulch to conserve water, moderate soil temperatures, and keep the weeds down. If you live where flooding may be a problem, create a mound of native soil 2 to 3 feet high and 8 to 10 feet and plant as described. If you live where there is rockland soil, you'll have to use a hand pick, auger, or even a backhoe to dig the planting hole, depending on the size of tree.

■ Care and Maintenance

Carambolas are virtually trouble free. Occasionally aphids may invade the new growth, but a firm stream of water will wash them off. Fruit flies can be a problem, but if you keep the fruit picked they won't stay around where there is nothing to eat. Fertilize young trees with ½ pound per application of a complete 10-10-10-2 (NPKMg) fertilizer six times per year. Trees grown in soils with a high pH should be sprayed with a micronutrient spray containing manganese and zinc.

Carambola

■ Additional Information

Good Carambola varieties for Florida include 'Arkin', 'Fuang Tung', 'Kari', 'Sri Kembangan', and 'Thai Knight'.

Star fruits contain high amounts of oxalic acid, so if you have kidney disease it's probably best to leave the Carambola fruit alone.

➤ *How do I know when my star fruit is ready?*
The best answer is to pick one and see if it is sweet enough to eat. Otherwise, shake the tree, and any that fall should be ripe. If you try to pick a fruit and it "tugs" back or does not come off easily, then it probably is not ripe.

➤ *How do you eat a star fruit?*
Star fruits do not have to be peeled to be eaten. They can be sliced across the "ribs," which will give you the "star" from which the star fruit gets its name. Or, the fruit can be eaten raw, like an apple, right off the tree. Bon appétit!

CITRUS

When you think of Florida you think of citrus—oranges, lemons, and grapefruits. For more than 150 years, Florida has been king of the citrus world. It wasn't until the 1980s, when killing freezes swept through the state, that this mainstay of the Florida economy was threatened. Citrus trees were decimated in those freezes as temperatures plunged to 15 degrees Fahrenheit for more than three days. Many commercial trees were not replanted. Another problem might now have the Florida citrus industry on the ropes.

Citrus greening is one of the most serious citrus plant diseases in the world. It is also known as Huanglongbing (HLB) or yellow dragon disease. Once a tree is infected, there is currently no cure. While the disease poses no threat to humans or animals, it has devastated hundreds of thousands of acres of citrus crops in the United States and abroad. Named for causing green, misshapen fruit, citrus greening disease has now killed

Orange

millions of citrus trees in Florida and is threatening to spread to other citrus-producing states. Citrus greening is spread by a disease-infected insect, the Asian citrus psyllid, and has put the future of America's citrus at risk. When the bug feeds on an infected tree, it becomes a carrier, spreading the disease from one tree to another. Citrus greening can also spread from place to place when infected citrus, trees, clippings, or equipment are moved from one place to another.

Infected trees produce fruits that are green, misshapen, and bitter, unsuitable as fresh fruit or for juice. Most infected trees die within a few years. The Asian citrus psyllid, which spreads citrus greening, is no bigger than the head of a pin. The infected insect spreads the disease as it feeds on the leaves and stems of citrus trees. Symptoms of the disease include yellow mottling of the leaves, lopsided fruit, and excessive fruit drop. Psyllids and eggs are typically found on new shoots. Once the Asian citrus psyllid picks up the disease, it carries it for the rest of its life. Citrus greening is also spread by moving infected plants and leaves.

The state and federal governments and the citrus industry have taken steps to stop the spread of citrus diseases, including quarantines of affected areas, inspection of host plants, removal of infected plants, confiscation of illegally shipped plants, USDA certification of citrus, and public education campaigns. If you are growing or plan to grow citrus at home, there are some things you can do to prevent the spread of citrus greening:

- Inspect citrus plants regularly for disease and insects.
- If you detect an infected plant report it immediately to the local USDA in your area.
- **Keep your home-grown citrus at home.** Help reduce the spread of citrus diseases by not moving your home-grown citrus fruit or plants across state lines. Enjoy your fruit with friends and neighbors, but be sure to obtain a federal certificate if you transport your home-grown citrus, citrus plants or plant materials outside of Florida.
- Gift citrus fruit sold in Florida must be packed in a certified packinghouse and accompanied by a USDA certificate. Commercial fruit packers should be able to prove they are in compliance with the federal quarantine. Before you buy, ask the vendor if their product is in compliance.

FIG

It was my fifth grade teacher who introduced me to figs in a world culture class. We were studying Greece, and she shared with us food from that area of the world. When I bit into a dried fig I thought it was the sweetest and tastiest thing I had ever eaten—until I ate a fresh fig right off the bush some thirty years later. Naturally sweet and highly versatile, figs can be eaten fresh, in desserts, or as preserves and jams. The list is virtually limitless.

Fig plants from fifty years ago had one big problem: the fruit had a hole in the bottom (opposite the stem) that allowed pollinating insects access to the

Figs

plants' sexual parts inside. The problem, if you haven't already guessed by now, is that you sometimes unknowingly ate a bug as well as the fruit. Well, technology is a grand thing, and in the last several years plant hybridizers made it possible for a fig to pollinate itself and got rid of the hole. Figs are now sweet, nutritious fruit without any added protein!

■ Where to Plant

Plant figs in full to part sun in a location where they have plenty of room to grow—figs can grow to 12 feet tall and 12 feet wide. Well-drained soil with a good layer of mulch is all you need to grow nice, healthy fig bushes. Keep them away from standing water or overly wet soils.

■ How to Plant

You can still buy figs bare root; that is, the shrub is sold without soil on its roots. Plant bare-root plants in fall. Dig a hole twice as wide and as deep as the root mass and position the top of the root ball 2 inches above the native soil line to compensate for settling. Be extra careful to water thoroughly as soil is added to the hole. Once planting is completed, leave a soil ring around the top of the hole to be used as a water reservoir. Water every day for the first two weeks, reducing the frequency as time goes on. Plants purchased in containers can be planted any time. For some unknown reason, figs enjoy a dose of calcium every now and then. After a shrub has become established, give a fig plant 1 cup of calcium nitrate under its canopy once a year, increasing the amount as the plant gets larger.

■ Care and Maintenance

Figs have healthy fibrous root systems, so deep cultivation is not recommended. Place a 2- to 3-inch layer of mulch under a shrub's canopy, and keep the weeds in check. Fertilize once a month with an 8-8-8 fertilizer during the growing season. Pruning is generally not required. There are no insect pests to speak of, but be aware that ripe figs are highly prized by birds.

■ Additional Information

Head and shoulders above all others, the best fig for Florida gardeners is 'Celeste'. It has small, purplish to bronze fruit (with a closed end) and ripens in July and August. 'Brown Turkey' is also popular, but its fruit have a medium-sized eye opening. 'Brown Turkey' ripens from July through fall.

In addition to the old standbys there are many new varieties worth growing. The beautiful 'Green Ischia' fig is a medium-sized green fig with pale-green skin and very attractive strawberry-colored flesh. This cultivar is a very flavorful, productive variety and, interestingly, birds don't attack because the green fruit blends in with the foliage. One of my personal favorites is the 'Jelly' fig; it's a medium-sized yellow fig with very tasty, very sweet, amber-colored flesh.

GRAPE

You may have heard the terms "scuppernong" or "muscadine" when talking about grapes in Florida. They are all the same thing but are described differently depending on where you live. The grapes grown in Florida are unlike the grapes you buy at the store. Instead of thin, sweet skin, muscadine grapes have seeds and tough, almost leathery, exteriors. The sweetness of these grapes is in the pulp. Florida-grown grapes can be eaten right off the vine, and the juice can make excellent wine.

▓ *Where to Plant*

Plant grapes in full sun in well-drained soil with a clay base and a pH of 6.0 to 6.5. Mucky soils or sugar-sandy soil without a clay base are not good locations for growing grapes.

▓ *How to Plant*

Plant individual plants 8 feet apart in rows that are at least 6 feet apart. Dig a hole twice as wide and as deep as the containerized root ball and backfill with native soil. Make certain that the top of the root ball is 1 to 2 inches above the native soil line to compensate for settling. It is recommended that grape rows be placed on a north-south axis to maximize the sunlight each plant receives.

▓ *Care and Maintenance*

Pruning grapes can seem a bit mysterious, but once you learn the basics it's very simple. Grapes produce fruit on new wood, so it's important that the plants produce new growth to get good fruit production. However, if there is too much new wood, the grapes will be small both in size and in quantity. First, you must create a trellis system for the grapes to grow upon. Place 8-foot posts every 10 to 12 feet, sinking 2 feet of the post in the ground. Run two wires from post to post at heights of 36 inches (3 feet) and 72 inches (6 feet). Site one plant every 8 feet and train one vine to grow straight up to the 72-inch wire. Initially, remove all other shoots. (Sometimes it's helpful to place a long, thin bamboo shoot between the wires and train the fast-growing shoot to it while it is growing.) Once this is done, cut the top off the vine to encourage the development of side shoots. As shoots begin to "break" along the stem, train two sprouts to grow right

and left along the wire at the 36 and 72-inch levels. It is on these side shoots that the grapes will develop. Continue to remove all other shoots along the vertical stem. Every four years or so it is important to remove the horizontal stems. These can or will be replaced by new vines from spurs that were left near the upright stem. In the first year apply ¼ pound of 8-8-8 fertilizer to each plant. Increase this amount each year until the fourth year, when you'll apply 4 pounds of 8-8-8.

Muscadine grape 'Fry'

■ *Additional Information*

Good varieties of purple grapes include 'Conquistador', 'Blue Lake', and 'Black Spanish'. Good green varieties include 'Stover', 'Blanc Du Bois', and 'Suwannee'. 'Daytona' is a good red grape suited for Florida gardens.

➤ *Where did the word "muscadine" come from?*
When early settlers arrived in the southeast United States they discovered a wild grape. They were also familiar with a European grape, the Muscat grape, used to make muscatel wine. As time went on they called the local wild grape a muscal grape because of its similar sweet, earthy fragrance. Eventually the word "muscal" became "muscadine."

➤ *When I was out in the garden I noticed my grapes were ready to pick and planned to do just that the next day. But, when I arrived that morning all the grapes had vanished! Where did they go?*
Raccoons have an uncanny ability to know when you are ready to pick fruit, and they usually beat you to it. Before the fruit ripens place bird netting, available at garden centers, over the vines to prevent Mr. Raccoon's midnight raid!

GUAVA

One of the many reasons I enjoy Florida is due to all the exotic fruits we can grow in our backyards. Growing and eating guava fresh from the garden is one of those rare pleasures in gardening—its musky, sweet taste is indescribable. While there are a few people who will rise in opposition to its unique flavor, after a little while even they develop a taste for this unique fruit. The shrub is a handsome specimen in the landscape with small (1-inch), fragrant white flowers, and many people place it in the garden regardless of its ability to produce fruit. The fruit's shape ranges from round to somewhat like a pear and in size from 1 to 40 ounces. When a guava is ripe, the peel changes color from green to yellow, and the flesh color can be white, yellow, pink, or red. Flavors range from sweet to highly acidic and from strong and sharp to mild and agreeable.

Guava

■ *Where to Plant*

Make no mistake—guavas like warm temperatures and do not tolerate freezes. Guava plants may be killed when temperatures are lower than 27 degrees Fahrenheit. Plant growth and fruit production stops when temperatures reach 60 degrees Fahrenheit. Plant guava in full sun in well-drained soil with a pH of 4.5 to 7.0. Guavas planted in soil with a pH above 7.0 will require annual applications of chelated iron and sulfur. Many varieties of guava can reach 12 feet tall and 14 feet wide so give them plenty of room to grow. Make certain that the planting site does not flood even after hard summer rains— guava trees will not tolerate wet feet for even a short time.

How to Plant

Guavas are often grown in plastic containers in the nursery and therefore can be planted any time. In sandy soils dig a hole twice as deep and wide as the root ball. Backfill with native soil so the top of the root ball is 1 to 2 inches higher than the surrounding soil level and continuously add water as you backfill to prevent air pockets. Leave a soil ring around the circumference of the root ball to act as a water reservoir. In muck soils (which are highly organic and wet), create a 24-inch-high and 8-foot-wide mound of good soil and plant the root ball as described. In rock or marl, dig a hole three times the depth and width of the root ball and backfill with good garden soil. Water a newly installed plant once a day for two weeks and taper off as the plant becomes established. Guavas require 1 to 1½ inches of water per week.

Care and Maintenance

Fertilize guavas with 1 pound of an 8-8-8-2 (NPKMg) mixture every two months for the first year, increasing that amount to 5 pounds per application four times per year after the fifth year. Once the trees have become established, foliar nutritional sprays containing boron, manganese, zinc, and copper should be applied four times per year.

Additional Information

Pink or red guava fruits are picked when the peel begins to turn light green or yellow. The fruits should be allowed to ripen without refrigeration until they're ready to eat. White guavas are picked before they are fully ripe when the skins are light-green before turning yellow. Good pink varieties for Florida include 'Homestead', 'Barbi Pink', 'Hong Kong Pink', and 'Patillo'. Green types include 'Webber', 'Crystal', 'Lotus', and 'Supreme'.

> *I bought an older house in Miami and it came with a 12-foot-tall guava plant in the backyard. It is covered with fruit, but I moved here from Ohio and I don't know how to eat them! Help me, please.*

Select guavas that are firm but "give" a little when you exert a slight pressure. Wash the fruit thoroughly and eat it just like you did the apples in Ohio!

JABOTICABA

If you are looking for an unusual specimen tree for the landscape that also produces edible fruit, jaboticaba may be the tree for you. Reaching a maximum height of 15 feet, this Brazilian native produces a unique, vase-shaped growth habit with handsome tan and cinnamon-brown flaking bark. It's the fruit, however, that really steals the show. About the size and shape of a large grape, the fruits follow brilliant white flowers that erupt from the main trunk and stems of the tree. The fruits are commonly dark purple or black (with some green-skinned varieties) and have a thick skin with a gelatinous interior and flavor similar to that of muscadine grapes. Because it is so slow growing, many homeowners have begun to use it as a tree between the sidewalk and the street.

◼ *Where to Plant*

The freeze tolerance of jaboticaba is highly variable; however, it is generally accepted that they should not be planted where freezing temperatures fall below 28 degrees Fahrenheit. Plant in full to part sun (although part sun will reduce the number of fruit) in well-drained, deep, sandy soil with a pH of 5.5 to 6.5. It is not tolerant of salt air and does not like soggy soils. Soils that are slightly alkaline should be heavily mulched and drenched semiannually with chelated iron.

◼ *How to Plant*

Jaboticaba trees are grown in plastic nursery containers and therefore can be planted any time. Dig a hole twice as wide and as deep as the nursery-grown root ball and place the top of the root ball 1 to 2 inches above the native soil line (to compensate for settling). As the hole is filled with the native soil, add water to remove any air pockets that could kill the plant. For those areas where holes are difficult to dig, create a mound 24 inches deep and 10 to 12 feet wide and plant as described.

◼ *Care and Maintenance*

Although studies on jaboticaba's nutritional needs are few, an application of a general 8-8-8-2 (NPKMg) fertilizer four times a year is a generally accepted practice. Pests are negligible; however, deer have been known to eat new foliage and squirrels and raccoons enjoy the fruit. Harvest the fruit when the color is a dark purple or black and is soft to the touch, like a grape. Pruning is rarely needed but they can be trimmed into a hedge without significant reduction in fruit production since the fruit grows directly on interior larger stems and on the trunk of the tree. Roots of the jaboticaba are quite shallow and as a result additional irrigation may be needed to supplement natural rainfall (a good layer of mulch 3 to 4 inches deep will help, too).

Jaboticaba

■ Additional Information

Good varieties for Florida include 'Paulista', a well-developed tree producing very large fruit with a sweet flavor; 'Rajada', an unusual green-skinned fruit with very good, sweet flavor; and 'Sabra', a thin-skinned, small fruit variety that is the most popular form in Brazil, which can produce up to four crops a year in South Florida.

➤ *I enjoy creating bonsai, and I was wondering if jaboticaba would make a good specimen.*
Yes, also known as the Brazilian tree grape, jaboticaba is an excellent choice for bonsai or espalier work. Jaboticaba has an unusually smooth bark similar to that of the crape myrtle. It is a delicately branched tree with an appealing irregular growth pattern and small, elegant, light-green leaves.

➤ *I really enjoy the flavor of jaboticaba. Is there anything else I can do with the fruit?*
Jaboticaba fruit can be boiled with water to cover them and then mashed. The resulting juice can be made into a tart jelly or served as fruit juice. It has been reported to be a very good thirst quencher.

JACKFRUIT

Jackfruit trees, which grow to 18 to 40 feet tall, produce very large fruit—up to 60 pounds—with a "warty" or bumpy appearance. There are two distinct parts to the cut fruit. The first part is a white pulpy material, often called the "rag," found inside the skin, and it is inedible. It is the bright orange, sweet pulp surrounding the seeds that is prized. Though it may take some work to get to,

Jackfruit

the flavor is well worth it. Jackfruit is a member of the Moracea family along with Ficus and mulberry, so be careful of the latex-like sap that may cause skin irritation.

■ *Where to Plant*

Jackfruit is suited for gardeners growing fruit in South Florida where frosts rarely occur, because it can be killed at temperatures below 28 degrees Fahrenheit and limb damage can occur even at 32 degrees Fahrenheit. Plant in full sun in areas where flooding is not a problem. Jackfruits are tolerant of a variety of soils ranging from sandy to rocky, including those soils having a high pH. Even though they can reach a height of 40 feet in South Florida, they tolerate moderate to heavy winds. Plant them at least 30 feet from houses and other trees for maximum fruit production.

■ *How to Plant*

Jackfruit trees are grown in plastic nursery containers and as a result can be planted any time. Regardless of your soil type, dig a hole twice as deep and as wide as the root ball. Place the root ball in the hole 1 inch higher than the native soil level and backfill with native soil. Stay away from areas that flood or are constantly wet. For those areas where holes are hard to dig, try creating a 24-inch-tall and 8-foot-wide mound of good soil.

■ Care and Maintenance

Jackfruit trees can get big—up to 40 feet tall. Pruning is an option, and the trees can be kept to a moderate height of 15 feet without a significant reduction in fruit production. During the first year apply 1 pound of an 8-8-8 plus micronutrients five times. After the first year, gradually increase the amount, but do not exceed 5 pounds per application five times per year. A spray containing boron and manganese should be applied four times per year. Soils with a very high pH should receive an application of chelated iron once annually. Jackfruit trees are virtually pest free, although scale insects can affect the leaves and stems. Control scale by using an insecticidal soap, which is available at most garden centers.

■ Additional Information

To harvest, use clippers or loppers to snip the fruit off the tree when it develops a pungent odor. Avoid contact with the sap because it can cause skin irritation and permanently stain clothes. The fruit will ripen four to seven days after harvesting. The orange pulp surrounding the seeds is the tasty part and can be retrieved by first cutting the fruit crosswise with a sharp knife that has been coated with cooking oil. Continue to cut the fruit crossways and extract the seeds. Varieties good for Florida gardens include 'Black Gold', 'Cheena', 'Chompa Gob', 'Honey Gold', and 'Lemon Gold'.

➤ *Other than its great taste, is jackfruit good for you?*
Jackfruit is high in vitamin C and potassium and contains lignins, isoflavones, and saponins, which are called phytonutrients; their health benefits are wide-ranging from anticancer to antihypertensive, anti-aging, antioxidant, and anti-ulcer. The jackfruit root is the basis for a remedy for skin diseases and asthma. An extract of the root is taken to cure fever.

➤ *Do you have a recipe for the tropical "egg roll" I ate as a child?*
Turon is a Philippine dessert roll made of bananas, jackfruit, and coconut. Cut a banana in half and cover with strips of jackfruit (minus the seeds). Place shredded coconut over all, and sprinkle with a little confectioner's sugar.

LONGAN

An attractive landscape tree, longan also produces large clusters of grape-sized, single-seeded fruit with a sweet and pleasant flavor. The leaves are evergreen and shiny, and the bark is dark brown, almost black. In their native China, longans can reach nearly 100 feet tall, although in South Florida heights of 30 to 40 feet are more common and in Central Florida, 15 feet is the norm. New leaf growth on longans is a beautiful wine-red color, and mature leaves are very glossy, making them a welcome addition to any home landscape.

Where to Plant

Longans don't like the cold, and a straight line from Tampa to Merritt Island is as far north as they will grow. Older, well-established trees can survive temperatures to 27 degrees Fahrenheit while younger trees might be killed at the same temperature. Plant longans 40 feet apart in full sun in soil that is well drained but not wet. Longans do not perform well in organically rich soils.

How to Plant

Longan trees are grown in plastic nursery containers and therefore can be planted any time. Dig a hole twice as wide and as deep as the nursery-grown root ball and place the top of the root ball 1 to 2 inches above the native soil line to compensate for settling. As the hole is filled with the native soil, add water to remove any air pockets that could kill the plant. For those areas where holes are difficult to dig, create a mound 24 inches deep and 10 to 12 feet wide and plant the root ball as described.

Care and Maintenance

To produce good-quality fruit, one-half of the light-yellow to light-brown flower spikes must be removed before or during flowering (from January to March). An application of a general 8-8-8-2 (NPKMg) fertilizer four times a year is a generally accepted practice. Make certain that longans receive adequate water during flowering and fruit production. Longans are very wind resistant.

■ Additional Information

One major handicap of growing longans is their irregular fruiting history. It is not uncommon for longans to produce heavily one year and then skip two to three years before producing again. The fruit ripen in August to September. There are no serious diseases or pests associated with longans, which makes them a great fruit tree for those homeowners wishing to become more "green" in their landscape management. The longan variety 'Kohala', introduced to Florida from Hawaii, is far superior in fruit quality and fruiting frequency to any cultivar presently grown or under evaluation to date in the

Longan

Sunshine State. The longan is generally eaten fresh, but it can also be canned, just like lychee or rambutans. It can also be used as an ingredient for drinks and liqueurs. Harvest longan fruits by cutting the entire fruit cluster using a sharp knife or hand pruners. Pulling individual fruits off the cluster will cause them to perish more quickly.

➤ *Many of my longans mature at the same time. Is there a good way to store the fruit for eating later?*
Longans should be selected when they are brown. Wrap the longans in a paper towel or thin tissue paper before storing them in a humid environment at a recommended temperature of 34 to 40 degrees Fahrenheit. This will help prevent the longan skin from deteriorating and help maintain its light-brown color.

➤ *I've heard that longan is good for you. How so?*
Longan can be made into a wonderful and delicious tonic used by the Chinese as a blood tonic, to nurture the heart, and to add luster and beauty to the skin. It is also thought to have a calming effect on men.

Loquat

LOQUAT

Even if the loquat didn't produce its marvelous, tart, yellow or orange fruit, gardeners throughout Florida would still use it as a landscape plant. Its bold, highly striated evergreen leaves coupled with a pleasing roundish habit make it a favorite throughout Florida. Several ornamental selections have appeared on the market in recent years, and there are well over 1,000 selections of loquat used for fruit production throughout the world. Generally loquats flower in the fall and produce fruit in the spring; however, in warmer tropical and subtropical areas of the state, it's not uncommon to harvest two or three crops per year. The fruit is ripe and ready to eat when it's slightly soft when squeezed between the thumb and forefinger.

▓ *Where to Plant*

Loquat can withstand temperature extremes as low as 15 degrees Fahrenheit without harm, and hot, humid temperatures don't seem to bother the plant (although extremely high temperatures can have an adverse effect on fruit production). Loquats produce fruit best when they're located in full sun. They are not finicky as to soil type; they grow and produce well in soils ranging from deep sand to gravely, rocky soils. They do not like wet or waterlogged soils. Loquats can reach 20 feet tall and 15 feet wide so select a planting location where they will get plenty of room.

■ *How to Plant*

Loquats are usually available from garden centers in plastic nursery containers and can be planted any time. Dig a hole twice as deep and as wide as the root ball, and place the top of the root ball 1 to 2 inches above the native soil line (to compensate for settling). When filling the planting hole, alternate water and native soil as the root ball is covered to diminish the possibility of air pockets in the root zone. For those areas where digging a hole might be too difficult, a mound of garden soil 24 inches tall and 8 to 10 feet wide can be used and the tree planted as described.

■ *Care and Maintenance*

Loquats do not require pruning except to remove an occasional dead limb after a storm passes through. One-year-old plants will need 1 pound of a general 8-8-8-2 (NPKMg) fertilizer four times per year spread evenly beneath the canopy. As the tree gets bigger the amount can be increased to 5 pounds per application four times per year. A micronutrient foliar spray containing boron, copper, molybdenum, and zinc can be applied four times per year. Loquats grown in alkaline soil will need to receive chelated iron as a soil drench twice per year.

■ *Additional Information*

Variety	Shape	Peel Color	Fruit Flavor
'Advance'	Pear	Yellow	Sweet-tart
'Champagne'	Pear	Pale yellow-pale orange	Sweet, spicy
'Emanuel'	Pear	Dark yellow-Orange	Sweet, good flavor
'Golitch'	Round	Orange	Sweet
'Juda'	Pear	Pale Orange	Sweet, mildly tart
'Judith'	Pear	Dark Yellow	Sweet
'Oliver'	Pear	Pale Orange	Very sweet
'Thales'	Pear	Dark Yellow-Orange	Sweet
'Thursby'	Pear	Dark Yellow-Orange	Sweet, good flavor
'Wolfe'	Pear	Light Yellow	Sweet, spicy, good flavor

LYCHEE

My first experience with lychee was in New York City's Chinatown. I was getting ready to get on a subway when I stopped to look at the various fruits for sale in one of the district's many outdoor fruit markets. There were several fruits I didn't recognize, and when I asked the vendor which I should try, he suggested the lychee. He told me the bright red, bumpy fruit the size of a large grape had to be peeled, and when I did just that it exposed a clear, gelatinous pulp with a single inedible seed. I popped the entire fruit into my mouth, and my lifelong love of fresh lychee began.

▦ *Where to Plant*

Lychee trees can grow to 40 feet tall so give them plenty of room. They grow best where temperatures never reach below 28 degrees Fahrenheit and where the winters are dry and cool enough to give the tree a rest. Hard frost will kill young trees, but more mature trees can withstand colder temperatures. Grow them in full sun and in soil with a pH of 6.0 to 7.0. Lychees have a high water requirement to produce superior fruit. The Chinese often grow lychee trees adjacent to ponds or streams to give the trees enough water. The trees enjoy well-composted, well-drained soil with high soil moisture but cannot withstand even short spells of standing water. If high water can be a problem in your area, plant the trees in raised mounds 10 feet wide by 2 feet deep made of good garden soil.

▦ *How to Plant*

Lychee trees are generally grown in 3- to 5-gallon containers and can be planted any time. Dig a hole twice the depth and width of the root ball, place the tree into the hole, and backfill with native soil. Make certain that the top of the root ball is 1 to 2 inches above the soil line in anticipation of the soil settling. More lychees have been killed by planting them too deeply than for any other reason. Make a soil ring utilizing the remaining backfill soil, and water every day for the first three weeks; taper off watering as the tree becomes established.

■ *Care and Maintenance*

Oddly enough, lychee trees respond negatively to high fertilizer regimens—too much nitrogen fertilizer reduces plant growth and inhibits the uptake of other nutrients. An annual fertilizer application of an 8-8-8-2 (NPKMg) is all that is needed. Mature trees can utilize 5 to 6 pounds of fertilizer annually. An annual application of dolomitic lime will also reduce fruit shedding and foliar chlorosis.

■ *Additional Information*

Lychees are harvested when they're fully bright red. The entire cluster is harvested, and the individual fruits are later clipped from the cluster. If lychees are picked individually, the top of the fruit with the stem will remain on the tree and the fruit will perish quickly. Lychee trees are not strong enough to support ladder picking (like citrus) and a long pole with sharp clippers is the tool of choice. Harvest every three to four days to prevent rotting of the picked fruit. Do not harvest immediately after a rain. Both 'Mauritius' and 'Brewster' are good varieties for Florida.

Lychee

➤ *As I was eating a fresh lychee the other day I wondered, could I grow a lychee from the large seeds I threw out?*
Yes, plants can be grown from fresh lychees, but not from canned lychees. Within five days of eating the pulp, plant the seed 1 inch deep in a 4-inch pot filled with good potting soil. The seed will germinate in ten to fourteen days. Place in bright light and keep the soil moist. When the tree reaches 18 inches, plant it into the garden.

Mango

MANGO

As with other handsome fruit trees, even if a mango tree didn't produce its juicy, delicious fruit, it would be planted as a beautiful landscape specimen. Its long and narrow evergreen leaves (sometimes up to 12 inches long) emerge in the springtime with a brilliant red color. The tree's shape is variable depending on the selection, but most are upright or rounded. A mango tree can live up to 100 years. The single fruits appear at the end of long stems and are best known for their juicy, musky, and peach-like flavor. The fruits can be kidney- or oval-shaped, and the ripe fruit exhibits colors ranging from green to melon to peach. Average weight is 1 to 1½ pounds, although the fruit of some varieties can grow to 5 pounds each. It is the flesh surrounding the very large, single seed for which the mango is best known. The tough skin contains a milky sap and should not be eaten. Mangoes are very popular in chutneys, fruit salads, and smoothies.

■ *Where to Plant*

Mangoes need a frost-free climate. Although mangoes can be seen growing in areas outside frost-free zones, this is due to specific microclimates that allow mangoes to survive. Young trees can be killed when temperatures drop below 30 degrees

Fahrenheit, but mature trees can survive fleeting temperatures as low as 25 degrees Fahrenheit. Flowers and small fruits may be damaged or killed if the temperature falls below 40 degrees Fahrenheit for a few hours. In Florida, mangoes can grow to 50 feet tall and require plenty of room. The roots of a mango are quite extensive, though they're not destructive, and they need plenty of room to grow. The mango must have warm, dry weather to set fruit. Mango trees tolerate a wide range of soil types, even lightly alkaline ones, but all soils must be well drained and free of standing water.

■ How to Plant

Mango trees are grown in plastic nursery containers and as a result can be planted any time. Select an area with deep soil to accommodate the mango's extensive root structure and dig a hole twice as wide and as deep as the root ball. Place the tree in the hole and backfill with native soil, keeping the top of the root ball 1 to 2 inches above the native soil line. Create a soil ring with the remaining soil and water the tree daily for two weeks; taper off watering as the plant becomes established.

■ Care and Maintenance

Mango trees require a regular application of 8-0-8-2 (NPKMg) fertilizer during the growing season. Begin the first application *after* the onset of the fruit, but do not fertilize after late summer. Young trees respond best to fish emulsion fertilizer and are otherwise very susceptible to synthetic fertilizers. Synthetic fertilizers can only be introduced after the tree has become well established. Occasionally, thrips, scale, and mealybugs can be noticeable pests, but they can be controlled with various horticultural oils and soaps.

■ Additional Information

Although mangoes will ripen on the tree, commercial fruit is considered mature when the shoulder of the fruit fills out and its color begins to change from green to yellow. Some people pick and enjoy the fruit while it's still green, using it in chutneys or even dousing it with hot sauce. Mangos are picked by hand or by using a long picking pole. Mature fruits ripen three to eight days after harvest. Good varieties for Florida include 'Floridan', 'Edward', 'Carrie', 'Van Dyke', 'Carrie Atkins', 'Parvin', 'Dunkin', and 'Keitt'.

PAPAYA

If eating tropical fruit is one of your favorite pastimes but growing them is not, papaya would be a good place to start. They are very easy to grow (there may not be an easier fruit) and provided the tall "trees" get plenty of water and occasional fertilizer, they will produce large, beautiful fruit frequently throughout the year. For North Florida homeowners, you may have to visit those counties farther south for a fresh taste, however. Individual plants can produce fruit for up to twenty years. Papayas are sometimes called the "cantaloupe tree of the tropics" because the taste is very similar and they are often served for breakfast.

■ *Where to Plant*

Plant papayas in full sun with average soil in locations where there is no danger of frost. Papayas show signs of cold stress at temperatures as low as 45 degrees Fahrenheit. Papayas can be grown to fruiting size in containers provided the container is large enough, at least 30 inches in diameter, and they get plenty of water and sun.

Papaya

◼ *How to Plant*

Papayas can be grown from seed (the sex of the parent will decide the sex of the seed) or planted as nursery-grown container plants. Select seed from known sexed plants, crack the hard seed covering, and dry in full sun. Seeds stored in the refrigerator can remain viable for many years. Plant three to four seeds 1 inch deep in sterile potting soil and wait for germination, generally in two to three weeks. Once the plants reach a height of 4 to 6 inches select the most robust specimen and eliminate the remainder by cutting them off at soil level with scissors or pruners. Place the single seedling into a 1- to 2-gallon container, place the container in full sun, and fertilize with a general liquid fertilizer every two weeks until the roots are well established but not root bound.

Plant homegrown or nursery-grown plants in average soil ranging from pH 5.5 to 8.0. Dig a hole twice as deep and as wide as the container-grown plant, and alternate backfilling with the native soil and water until the hole is filled and the top of the root ball is slightly higher than the native soil level. Papaya roots are particularly susceptible to nematodes so refrain from planting them in those garden areas where nematodes have been known to be a problem. Select nursery-grown plants that are 2 to 3 feet tall. Larger plants often have pot-bound root systems and can fall over even in the lightest wind. If they're given water and fertilizer, 2-foot-tall papayas will quickly grow to 8 feet and produce fruit eight to ten months after planting.

◼ *Care and Maintenance*

For obvious reasons, bisexual plants do not need other plants to produce fruit. If you have only female plants, ask a neighbor or fellow gardener for male seeds to grow a male plant to obtain well-formed fruit. Papayas are odd plants in that some plants will show various levels of being a male or female plant depending on temperature, day length, and the amount of available water in the soil. Some plants can produce more than one kind of flower at the same time and some plants produce flowers that are not one of the three basic forms, but have a mixture of male and female qualities.

Generally, female plants produce very large, oblong fruit of very high quality. Fruit from bisexual plants are small to medium in size with a small interior cavity. Male plants often produce elongated fruit of little or no quality.

Papayas are ready to pick when about one-third of the fruit is yellow.

Apply ¼ pound of a general 8-8-8-2 (NPKMg) fertilizer when the plants are young and increase to 1 to 2 pounds every two months as the plants get larger. A foliar or ground application including zinc and manganese should be applied at least twice per year.

■ Additional Information

Depending on the area of the Sunshine State where you live, bugs and diseases can either be serious or simply a nuisance. It seems the farther south you go, the more problems you may encounter. One important insect pest is the papaya fruit fly; you'll know it's present if you see yellow areas on the fruit itself and premature fruit drop. The easiest way to avoid the effects of this pest is simply to place a paper bag over the fruit and wait until the fruit matures. Papaya webworms look like a large spider web on an emerging stem or among the flowers. These can simply be removed with a hard stream of water. The papaya whitefly can cause premature fruit drop and often turns the very large leaves yellow. Whitefly of any kind is often an indicator of stress. Keep a watchful eye on water and fertilizer levels and whiteflies should not be a serious problem. The same is true for the papaya two-spotted mite. Stress is usually the culprit so keep the water and fertilizer levels up. Spider mites are indicated when the leaves turn yellow and there are "spider webs" on the bottom sides of the leaves and among the new leaf growth. A hard stream of water will help keep them under control.

A serious disease is the papaya ring spot disease. The leaves turn yellow, the veins become clear, and the fruit get little "C"-shaped spots. There isn't much you can do to prevent this disease except to remove any plant that exhibits these characteristics. If you are growing papayas from seed, try to get seed from the larger, oval-shaped fruit rather than the 'Solo' pear-shaped fruit, which seem to be susceptible. Powdery mildew can be a problem, but it's usually during the late spring to early summer months when nighttime temperatures range from 60 to 65 degrees Fahrenheit. Remove any yellowed leaves when possible and wait until nighttime temperatures get above 70 degrees Fahrenheit. The last disease to discuss is apical necrosis, which is identified by the drooping of new growth and a downward "cupping" of the leaves. There are no known cures for this one so remove the diseased plants and try a different location. Good varieties for Florida include 'Sunrise Solo', 'Red Lady', and 'Maradol'.

➤ *I know I can grow papayas from seeds, but can I take cuttings, too?* Papaya plants can also be grown from cuttings, which should be hardened off for a few days before being propped up with the tip touching moist, fertile soil until roots form. Semi-hardwood cuttings planted during the summer root rapidly and should fruit the following year.

PASSION FRUIT

Passion fruit are the edible podlike fruits of the passion flower vine. The fruit itself is either purple or yellow at maturity with a delightful juice inside and lots of seeds. There are two main types of passion fruit; both have evergreen leaves and both make nice vines to cover a pergola or fence. One passion flower is purple and is egg-sized with a rumpled skin. The other, the yellow passion flower, can have fruit the size of a large orange and that has a shiny, smooth exterior and a "pulpy" rind. The yellow form is the preferred variety for eating fresh off the vine. Its flavor has a musky, guava-like taste.

◼ *Where to Plant*

Passion flower vines can easily reach 40 feet long so give them plenty of room. They need full sun or the vines may grow but not produce flowers and fruit. Any average soil will do, but if compost-enriched soil is available you will have more fruit than you can eat. Passion flowers also enjoy a good layer of mulch to moderate variances in soil temperatures.

◼ *How to Plant*

Plant container-grown plants into the garden anytime. Dig a hole twice the height and depth of the root ball and place the root ball in the hole. Backfill, alternating the soil and water to eliminate air pockets. This vine likes to be planted a bit high, so plant the root ball about 1 inch higher than the native soil line.

◼ *Care and Maintenance*

Passion flower vines are virtually maintenance free provided they get plenty of sun and water. Most questions regarding their care revolve around too little sun, but the bottom line is they cannot get too much sun. The more sun, the better. Although they have little tendrils to attach themselves to things as they grow, it's a good idea to give them a helping hand while the vines are still young. Thread them in and out of a chainlink fence to help them get started or use Velcro designed for outdoor use to give them a leg up. If either is impractical, strings of 50-pound test fishing line attached to the top and bottom of the gazebo pergola make wonderful, and virtually invisible, supports on which to grow the vines. Make sure you

Passion fruit

use galvanized nails to prevent rust. Simply stretch the lines from nail to nail and train the vines around them.

◼ *Additional Information*

The passion flower vine is native to Brazil and Paraguay so don't plan on growing it as a landscape plant north of the Tampa/ Daytona Beach line. Given that they grow very fast and with little care, passion fruits are popular as a container-grown fruit-producing plant in colder areas of the state. Passion flowers are also important larval plants in a butterfly garden, attracting a variety of butterflies, including zebra longwing and gulf fritillary butterflies.

➤ *Why do my vines flower but don't set fruit?*
This could be due to several reasons. Overcast weather could account for poor fruit set, as could poor pollenization. Often, passion flower vines need a little boron to help them flower. An annual soil drench with a water-soluble fertilizer with minor elements should help.

➤ *Why do my passion fruits drop off the vine?*
Maintaining an irregular water regimen is probably the reason. The vines enjoy damp soil during their fruiting period. Keep up a regimen to fight spider mites, too, especially when the fruits are young. With a stiff stream of water, spray the undersides of the leaves to wash the mites away.

PEACH, NECTARINE & PLUM

Growing peaches, nectarines, and plums—commonly called "stone fruits"—in Florida has been possible only for those gardeners living in the northern areas of the state where winter temperatures can give the buds at least 400 to 500 hours of cold below 50 degrees Fahrenheit (referred to as "chilling hours"). New varieties released only a few years ago as part of an intensive breeding program at the University of Florida have enabled gardeners everywhere in the

Peach 'Florida Prince'

Sunshine State to grow high-quality, good-tasting stone fruits that require only 150 chilling hours. Given that most fruit types that have a hard, stone-like seed in the middle of the fruit have the same growing habits, I will refer to "peach" with the understanding that my advice pertains to peaches, nectarines, and plums unless otherwise noted.

◼ *Where to Plant*

Peaches need full sun and well-drained soil with a pH of 6.0 to 7.0. Planting them directly into alkaline or marl soils can be a problem leading to poor overall growth, leaf drop, and insect infestations. For that reason, in those areas of the state where the pH level is high, plant peaches in an elevated bed 2 feet tall and 10 to 12 feet wide made of good garden soil. A liberal sprinkling of granulated sulfur once a year in the spring will help lower the pH, as well. The trees can reach 12 to 14 feet tall and 12 feet wide.

■ *How to Plant*

Peaches are grown in 3- to 5-gallon plastic nursery containers and can be planted any time. Dig a hole twice the depth and width of the root ball, and place the root ball into the hole. Alternate adding water and the native soil into the hole to eliminate any air pockets. The top of the root ball should ultimately rest 1 to 2 inches above the soil line. Create a soil ring with the remaining soil, and water once a day for three weeks, tapering off watering as the tree becomes established.

■ *Care and Maintenance*

The secret to growing good stone fruit trees is proper pruning. The ultimate goal after several years of good growth is to have a peach or nectarine tree that is open in the middle (free of branches facing inward) with an upward growth pattern. It takes some discipline, but if good quality and quantity is your ultimate goal, some hard pruning at the beginning is essential. When the tree arrives from the nursery, it should be about 4 to 5 feet tall with several lateral branches. The first pruning cut should be a decisive cut 36 inches above the ground to remove the primary single, upright leader. This will encourage side branching, sometimes called scaffold branching. As the tree matures, continue to remove any sprouts in the center of the tree that will try to grow, and keep the center wide and open, removing all branches that begin to grow towards the center of the tree. New fruit will grow on one-year-old wood so annual pruning is necessary for good fruit production. Plums, however, grow best with a strong central leader. Rather than utilize the pruning technique described for peaches and nectarines, do not remove the central leader but instead encourage a central branch in the center of the tree.

■ *Additional Information*

Fruits ripen in early to mid-May. Varieties of low-chill peaches that are good for Florida's climate include 'Florida Prince', 'Florida Glo', and 'UF Beauty'. A good nectarine with both good fruit and ornamental landscape characteristics is 'Sunhome'; it has dark purple new growth. Good plum varieties for Florida include 'Gulfbeauty', 'Gulfblaze', 'Gulfruby', and 'Gulfrose'.

PEAR

Easy to grow and an enjoyable addition to any mid- to late summer fruit salad, pears should be in nearly every North Florida garden. Pears grown in the Sunshine State are smaller than those found in the local markets, but their flavor is just as good. Florida pears come in two main versions: soft and hard. Some varieties are good for canning only and some are equally good for fresh eating and canning. A pear tree's growth is quite handsome and would be a welcome addition to any landscape.

▓ *Where to Plant*

Pears prefer well-drained sandy loam soil but can grow in a variety of soil types with a pH of 6.0 to 6.5. Plant in full sun and avoid frost pockets; pears can be damaged by unseasonable frosts. Give them plenty of room in the landscape—pear trees can grow to 15 feet tall and 12 feet wide. Garden locations with good air circulation will lessen the occurrence of disease organisms and reduce cold damage. For varieties that require cross-pollination, plant no more than 30 feet apart. With a few exceptions, fruiting pear trees are best suited for North Florida gardens.

▓ *How to Plant*

Most pear varieties are grown as containerized nursery plants and can be planted any time. Dig a hole twice as wide and as deep as the root ball, and place the plant in the hole. Alternating soil and water, backfill the hole with the native soil making sure that the top of the root ball is 1 inch above the native soil line. Create a basin with the remaining soil, and water three times a week for the first month, tapering off watering as the plant becomes established. Place a 3-inch layer of mulch around the bottom of the pear tree in a 3-foot diameter to moderate soil temperatures.

▓ *Care and Maintenance*

Provided the trees were placed in locations conducive to good growth—good loamy soil, proper pH, and an area with good air circulation—pear trees are virtually trouble free. Established pear trees require 1 inch of water each week. Leaf spot diseases can be prevented by periodically spraying copper fungicides during the warm summer months. Other insects, including cotton cushion scale and mealybugs, can be a problem; applications of insecticidal soap or Neem oil will control them. As a preventative, spray the tree trunk, branches, and stems thoroughly with ultrafine horticultural oil in mid- to late winter to reduce summer infestations.

A balanced fertilizer (6-6-6, 8-8-8, or similar mixture) is recommended. About 1 pound for each year of the tree's age is usually sufficient until a maximum of 10 pounds is reached. This should be applied in two applications, during dormancy (January) and at the beginning of the rainy season (June). The fertilizer should be broadcast under the trees.

■ *Additional Information*

Good soft pear varieties for North Florida include 'Floridahome'; 'Baldwin' (eating and canning); 'Hood' (yellow fruit, good for fresh eating); and 'Tenns' (fresh eating). Hard varieties include 'Carnes' (fresh eating, also called "apple pear"); 'Orient' (very large, best for cooking); and the old-time favorite 'Pineapple' (best cooking pear, very prolific).

Pear

PECAN

Although pecans will grow from Pensacola to Miami, it's North Florida where most of the Florida-grown pecans can be found. There are more than 500 registered selections of pecans throughout the world, and each has its own special characteristics. The trees themselves can often reach 70 feet and the "old-timers" have been known to grow to 6 feet in diameter. Although Georgia grows the most in the United States, Florida often produces more than 10 million pounds a year. Fruit production is best in locations where the daytime temperatures are warm and the winter temperatures are moderately cool.

■ *Where to Plant*

Pecans need plenty of room to grow (at least 40 feet apart) and they need full sun. Plant them at least 30 feet away from any structure. Well-drained soil is a must, and good air circulation will reduce the incidence of diseases. Pecans enjoy growing in deep sand with a clay bottom so their roots can spread out to absorb available water and nutrients. A soil pH of 5.5 to 6.5 is best.

Pecan

◼ *How to Plant*

Unlike many plants, pecans prefer to be planted in the fall to allow good root development before the onset of cooler temperatures. Pecans can be planted either bare root or as container-grown plants. The planting hole should be twice the size of the containerized root ball if you are planting nursery-grown plants. Place the top of the root zone at the same level as the native soil and alternately backfill the hole with water and soil to eliminate the risk of air pockets. Create a shallow basin around the base of the tree to hold water, and water at least three times per week until the plant is established (usually about two months). Reduce the amount of water you apply until warm weather returns. A diluted solution of white latex paint can be applied to the trunk at least 4 feet high to reduce sunscald to the bark; only one application is usually necessary. Apply 1 pound of a general fertilizer (10-10-10-3 NPKMg) to the tree after planting.

◼ *Care and Maintenance*

Keep weeds away from the trunk to prevent competition for nutrients and water. Apply 1 pound of a general fertilizer (10-10-10-3 NPKMg) per 1 inch of trunk diameter in early March and again in June. Evenly spread the fertilizer over the root zone of the tree. Once the tree begins nut production (which varies by variety), increase the fertilizer amount to 2 to 4 pounds in February and June.

If planted as a "whip" (a short, single leader upright stem), pecan trees can be pruned by one-third and trained to have a symmetrical scaffolding of branches. If they have been trained appropriately in the nursery, containerized trees seldom need to be pruned. Mature trees are never pruned unless it's to remove dead or diseased branches or branches that cross over each other and cause wounds.

◼ *Additional Information*

Highly recommended varieties of pecans for Florida include 'Cape Fear', 'Moreland', and 'Elliott'. Other satisfactory varieties include 'Curtis', 'Sumner', 'Stuart', 'Choctaw', and 'Pawnee'.

PERSIMMON

An American native, persimmon trees have long been an important part of southern culture. Unfortunately, the flavor of the native fruits is far less appealing than the Asian selections, and it is the latter that are discussed here. The trees perform well in the landscape, and like Carambola trees, even if they didn't produce an edible fruit they would be a nice landscape plant. Improved taste has been the primary goal of persimmon hybridization research around the world, but improved hardiness and resistance to disease are also part of the equation. If you have never tried a persimmon fruit you are in for a real treat—provided you select one that is ripe. If you taste one that isn't quite ready, I'll guarantee it will take some serious persuasion to get you to try another!

◼ *Where to Plant*

Native persimmon trees can grow to 30 feet tall, although the Asian selections generally grow only 8 to 10 feet tall. Trees will grow in full sun or dappled, high-canopy shade. They tolerate a variety of well-drained soil types although they prefer a soil in the 6.0 to 7.0 pH range.

◼ *How to Plant*

Most persimmons are grown in 3- to 5-gallon plastic containers and can be planted any time. Dig a hole twice as wide and as deep as the root ball of the containerized plant and place the root ball in the hole, backfilling the hole with alternating amounts of soil and water. Asian persimmons are grafted, and the graft union (the swollen part of the tree trunk just above the container soil line) should be 1 to 1½ inches *below* the native soil line. Use the remaining soil to create a soil berm (ring) around the root ball to act as a water reservoir. Water the tree three times a week for the first month and reduce the amount of water as the tree becomes established.

◼ *Care and Maintenance*

Keep weeds and turf at least 3 feet away from the trunk of the newly planted tree to prevent competition for water and nutrients. Do not fertilize during the first year of growth.

Persimmon 'Great Wall'

Mature trees should receive 10 pounds per year of a general 10-10-10-3 (NPKMg) four times per year.

■ *Additional Information*

Persimmons are divided into astringent and non-astringent varieties. In Florida, astringent varieties are picked, peeled, skewered, and allowed to dry. The dried fruit is sweet and delicious. Non-astringent types are the commonly grown persimmon and account for most of the trees grown in Florida. These varieties can be picked when the fruit is hard or soft; they are eaten fresh and are often used in fruit salads with pears, raisins, citrus, and dates. Fruit size can range from 4 to 7 ounces, and fruit ripen in the fall.

Good varieties of astringent types for Florida include 'Saijo', 'Tenenashi', 'Sheng', 'Ormond', and 'Giombo'. Good non-astringent types include 'Izu', 'Hana Fuyu', 'Fuyu', and 'Suruga'.

PINEAPPLE

Besides growing and eating fresh bananas, being able to go into the garden and pick a fresh pineapple is one of my favorite Florida things to do. Fresh, sweet, and delicious, pineapple from the garden mixed in a fruit salad with fresh mango, papaya, and star fruit is one of life's rare pleasures.

Pineapple

■ *Where to Plant*

Plant pineapple anywhere in the garden where full sun is available and it is free of frost. Pineapples can grow in a wide variety of soils, from pure sand to alkaline marl, and make great container-grown plants. Full sun, water, and regular applications of fertilizers are all you need.

■ *How to Plant*

The easiest way to grow pineapple is simply to stroll on down to the local market and buy a pineapple. Cut off the spiky top 1 inch below the top (eat the bottom fleshy part as usual) and set the top aside to air dry for two to three days. Many gardeners in frost-free zones simply plant the top into the soil, but just to be safe it's recommended that they be planted in a container first and then into the garden. Begin with a 1-gallon container (plastic or clay, it doesn't make any difference) and fill it to within 2 inches from the top with good potting soil. Once the top is ready for planting, place it into the soil so that just the green spiky top is sticking out of the soil. Place the container in part sun and water daily. Once adequate roots have formed from the bottom of the spiky top (generally 60 days), plant directly into the garden in frost-free zones of the state. Avoid letting the plant be root bound; restricted root systems may not grow properly once they're planted in the ground. For those gardening where frost is commonplace, simply place the container in full sun during the warm months. When nighttime temperatures reach 55 degrees Fahrenheit, bring pineapple plants indoors until warm weather returns.

Care and Maintenance

Young plants should be fertilized with 1 to 2 ounces of 6-6-6-4 (NPKMg) every eight weeks, increasing the amount to 6 ounces as the plant grows after two years. Occasionally, root rot diseases occur on pineapples. These can be deterred by not overwatering the plant and by planting it in well-drained, sandy soil. Mealybugs often attack the plant where the spike meets the root top. An application made from Ivory soap (1 teaspoon to 1 quart of water) as a soil drench (don't get any in the spike) will do the trick. Should your pineapple grow large enough, a bamboo stake tied to the fruit stalk with stout garden twine will prevent the stalk from breaking. From the day you cut the store-bought pineapple to the time a new fruit is produced can take anywhere from two to three years. If the plant is large enough to produce a fruit but hasn't, simply place an apple in the top of the plant and cover the entire plant with a plastic trash bag overnight. Remove the bag the next morning. The plant will produce a fruit in about three months.

Additional Information

Raccoons and opossums have the uncanny ability to seek out and eat ripening fruit the night before you plan to harvest it. Often simply placing a paper bag over the top will work, but it's just as easy to harvest the fruit when the bottom starts to change from green to yellow. Once harvested, the fruit will ripen on the kitchen counter in a few days.

POMEGRANATE

If ever there was fruit that has taken over the grocery stores in every conceivable form it has to be pomegranate. It shows up in juice, jellies, wine, desserts, breads, yogurt, vitamins—you name it and there is something with pomegranate in it. And that's for good reasons, too. The fruits are rich in antioxidants (more than three times that of wine and green tea) and pomegranate juice contains about forty percent of the recommended daily allowance (RDA) of vitamin C. It also has vitamins A, E, and folic acid in good quantities. The fruits can be eaten fresh, and the juice can be extracted just like that of an orange. The orange-red flowers are quite attractive and look great in the garden. Pomegranate fruits range from 2 to 5 inches in diameter. In North and Central Florida, they mature from July to November, but may produce year-round in South Florida.

■ *Where to Plant*

Pomegranates are most often grown as shrubs from 6 to 10 feet tall, but they can be trained as a tree to reach 20 feet tall. They will even grow as far north as Washington, DC. They need full sun to produce an adequate number of fruit and grow well in deep, well-drained soil with a soil pH of 5.5 to 6.5, although they are able to grow in a wide variety of soils. They even tolerate minor, short-term flooding.

■ *How to Plant*

Pomegranates are usually grown in 3- to 5-gallon containers in the nursery and can be planted into the garden any time. Dig a hole twice as deep and as wide as the root ball and place the plant into the hole. Alternate adding soil and water until the hole is filled, making certain the top of the root ball is 1 inch higher than the native soil line to compensate for settling. With the leftover soil, create a saucer around the tree and fill the saucer three times a week with water for the first month after planting.

■ Care and Maintenance

One of the reasons pomegranates are so popular in the landscape is because they are so easy to grow. Fruits are borne on new growth so it's a good idea to lightly trim the end of the branches before July 1 to create buds for the next year's fruit. The showy shrubs enjoy regular (four times per year) applications of a general fertilizer (8-8-8-4, NPKMg) with micronutrients including, but not limited to, manganese, boron, zinc, and molybdenum. One cup of fertilizer for every year of a shrub's age, sprinkled widely over its root zone, works well. After the plant is two years old fertilize once in the fall and once in the spring and withhold winter, and summer applications. Too much plant food can cause the fruit to drop prematurely, so be careful with the "groceries."

Pomegranates are virtually pest free. Scale insects can be controlled with a dormant oil spray in winter and mealybugs can be sprayed with insecticidal soap.

■ Additional Information

'Al-sirin-nar', 'Azadi', 'Christina', and 'Vkusnyi' appear to perform well in Florida gardens.

Pomegranate

CHAPTER 7

THE FINAL REWARD: HARVESTING & STORING VEGETABLES & FRUITS

After planting the seeds, watering the plants, controlling the bugs, and pulling the weeds, you come to the final reward: harvesting. After all, picking the fruit and bringing it to the kitchen as fresh, safely grown food for the family is why you got into this project in the first place, right? Homegrown vegetables can taste much better than those usually available in markets, but to be at their best, they need to be harvested at the peak time.

Each vegetable has a window of opportunity for harvest. While some vegetables and fruits are quite forgiving and have a long harvest window, others can go from tender and tasty to tough and bitter virtually overnight. For instance, tomatoes can be left on the vine until they're fully ripened or picked when they're partially ripened. Other crops, such as winter squash and watermelon, are not ready until they are fully developed.

Fruits and vegetables should be picked at the proper time to assure the best quality and to have optimum vitamins and mineral content. Vegetables left in a garden and fruit left on a tree too long will often become fibrous and tough. In the case of vegetables, harvesting at the proper stage tends to keep the plants producing. Because vegetable and fruit growth depends on many factors, including precipitation, temperature, and soil fertility, their maturation can vary from year to year. The best way to determine when a vegetable or fruit is ready to harvest is based on the characteristics of the plant itself. These signs can often be subtle, and it takes practice to become familiar with them.

There are just a few things to remember after harvesting. The fruit, even though it has been removed from the plant, is still very dynamic and will continue to change until it is processed in some way or eaten. In some plants, peas and corn for instance, the sugars within the fruit that are inherent to its sweetness change very quickly to starches. Although it's still edible, it won't be as sweet if it's left lying around. For vegetables such as corn, for example, my grandmother used to tell us that the water should be boiling on the stove when the ears of corn are picked. If freezing fruits and vegetables is your plan, then prepare the containers by washing them ahead of time. The water to blanch the fruit should be boiling before harvesting. If, for some reason, processing must be delayed, cool the fruit and vegetables in ice water or crushed ice, and store in the refrigerator to preserve flavor and quality.

Storing vegetables and fruit is equally important. When possible, harvest during the cool part of the morning, and process or store the harvest as soon as possible. Leafy vegetables, such as mustard and lettuce, need high humidity to maintain their crispness (hence the overhead sprayers in the produce department at the store). Others, such as onions, should be stored where it's dry (less than 50 to 65 percent humidity).

Be careful when harvesting fruits and vegetables. A tiny scratch from a shovel or pruning shears can cause a fruit or vegetable to rot at a faster rate while it's in storage. It's a good idea when harvesting vegetables to use hand clippers to remove the fruit from the plant. Okra, for instance, not only is difficult to remove without a sharp cutting blade, but without it, the plant can be damaged, jeopardizing the plant's health and future fruit production. The same approach is true for digging root crops such as potatoes. A lifting fork works best for harvesting root crops and causes less damage than a shovel. Remember, too, do not harvest while the plants are wet. Diseases like to catch a ride when they can, so harvest after the plants have dried from the morning dew or any overhead irrigation. Be careful to avoid stepping on vines or breaking stems because that could create openings through which diseases can enter a plant. Size is important when picking fruits and vegetables. Cauliflower, for example, will become bitter and "grainy" if it's allowed to grow too large.

Vegetables

If you want the vegetables you have grown to arrive on your table at the peak of perfection, the following are a few suggestions and basic rules on how and when to harvest them.

Beans, bush and pole. Pick snap beans when the pods are young, succulent, and almost full size but before the seeds inside begin to bulge. Tips should be pliable. Beans should be crisp and snap easily. For shelling beans, let the bean pods mature on the vines, but be sure to harvest before they get so dry that the pod opens.

Beans, lima. Pick lima beans when the pods and seeds reach full size but before the pods turn yellow. The end of a pod should feel spongy, and the pods and seeds should be fresh and juicy. Open a few pods to check. Use only the seeds; the pods are tough and fibrous.

Beets. Beets can be eaten as greens when the leaves are 4 to 6 inches long. When they're grown for the root itself, harvest when the beets are 1½ to 2½ inches in diameter. If they're allowed to get much larger, they become pithy, especially in warm, dry weather. Remove all but about 1½ inches of tops on late crop beets. Wash and refrigerate immediately.

Broccoli. Gather broccoli when the center bud is compact but before the buds begin to separate or open into flowers. Cut the stems off 6 to 7 inches below the flower heads. If you give them a little fertilizer and water they will produce additional florets further down on the stem.

Harvest some leaves from the tops of beets early in the season, and then enjoy the beet roots at the end of the season.

It's helpful to use a small hand shovel or trowel to dig up carrots.

Broccoli's small, tender leaves are also nutritious. Store in the coldest section of the refrigerator.

Brussels Sprouts. Harvest when the sprouts (buds) along the stem become firm. Remove the buds from the bottom to top as the sprouts develop. As the newer sprouts develop along the stem remove the bottom leaves—this helps the sprouts grow faster. Before the onset of warm weather, pinch out the growing point at the top of a plant to get larger sprouts. Store in the coldest section of the refrigerator.

Cabbage. Harvest cabbages when the heads are solid and firm. The outer leaves should possess a uniform green or purple color (depending on type). Excessive water uptake by plant roots will cause the heads to split. To prevent mature heads from splitting, twist plants one-quarter turn to break several roots, or plunge the blade of a shovel into the ground along *one* side of the stem. Store cabbage in a crisper drawer and use within one to two weeks.

Carrot. Harvest carrots when they are small and succulent. Do not let them get over about 1 inch in diameter. Always pull the largest carrots in the row first. Remove the tops and wash them before transferring carrots to refrigerated storage.

Cauliflower. Cauliflower is ready to harvest when a head is firm or when the curds (which are immature flower heads) are full sized (6 to 8 inches) but still compact and smooth. It's too mature when the head is soft, discolored or when the lower leaves turn yellow.

Corn, Sweet. Corn silks darken and dry out as the ears mature. As the kernels fill out toward the top, the cob end becomes blunt instead of pointed. Pick sweet corn when it's in the "milk stage," when a milky juice exudes from kernels when they're crushed with a thumbnail. Sweet corn is very susceptible to rapid sugar-to-starch conversion and is at prime eating quality for only 72 hours after harvest. Cook, eat, or chill the ears as soon as possible after harvest. It's best to harvest early in the morning or during cool weather.

Cucumber. Pick cucumbers when they're 6 to 9 inches long and still bright green and firm. Overly mature fruits are filled with hard seeds and are bitter, dull in color or yellowed, and less crisp. Cucumbers intended for sweet pickles should be 1½ to 2½ inches long; and for dill pickles, 3 to 4 inches long. Cucumbers can be stored in the refrigerator about five days. Do not try to pickle the salad-type cucumbers.

Eggplant. Harvest eggplant when the fruits are shiny, nearly full size, and firm. Older fruits become dull, soft, and seedy. Store eggplants in a cool and humid location.

Greens (mustard, collard, turnip, kale, Swiss chard, beet). Break off the lower leaves when they are 6 to 10 inches long (12 to 18 inches long for mustard and collards) and before they start to yellow. Avoid wilted leaves. Wash well and chill immediately.

Kohlrabi. Harvest when the bulbs (which are really thickened stems) reach 2 to 3 inches in diameter. Store in refrigerator. If kohlrabi bulbs are allowed to get much larger than 2 to 3 inches, they become pithy, especially in warm, dry weather.

Lettuce. Harvest leaf varieties when the outer, older leaves are 4 to 6 inches long; harvest heading varieties when the heads are moderately firm. Older, outer leaves may be removed from plants of either leaf or head lettuce as soon as the leaves are 4 to 6 inches long. New leaves provide a continuous harvest of tender, tasty lettuce until hot weather brings on bitter flavor and seed stalks appear. Wash and store in the refrigerator.

Melon, Honeydew. Harvest honeydew when the fruit is yellowish to creamy white with a soft, velvety feel. The rind should be slightly soft at the blossom end and have a faint, pleasant aroma.

Whether an eggplant is white or a more traditional dark purple, harvest it when it is shiny and firm.

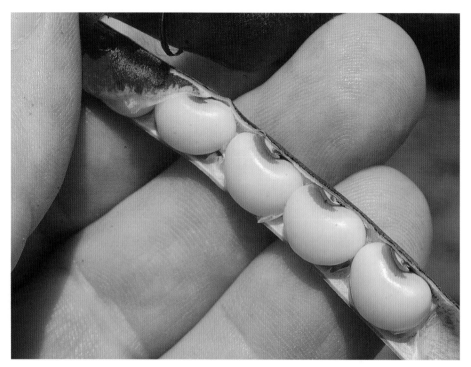

When peas have filled the pod, they can be harvested as dry beans.

Melon, Muskmelon. As they mature, the skin will remain green but will begin to show a netting pattern on the surface. Once the netting pattern becomes raised and turns a tan color, the fruit is ripe and can be harvested. If the melons are fully ripe, store them in the refrigerator. If they are not fully ripe, store them in a cool area.

Melon, Watermelon. When the stem that is attached to one end of the melon turns brown and curls, it is ready to be picked. It should also have a creamy or bright yellow bottom.

Okra. Okra pods are ready to harvest when they're 2 to 3 inches long, about four to six days after the flower wilts. Okra stops producing if the pods are not picked, so gather them every one to two days. Chill immediately.

Onion. Onion may be harvested any time after planting until maturity. Harvest when the tops fall over and begin to die. Dig the bulbs, brush off most of the dirt, and dry for several days. Cut off the tops and roots, and store in a cool, dry place. Harvest green onions when they are 6 to 8 inches tall.

Peas, English, Snow, and Sugar Snap. If you expect to shell the peas, harvest the pods when they are shiny green and fully developed; overly mature peas are of poor quality. For edible podded varieties (sugar snap), harvest when the pods are fully developed (about 3 inches) but before the seeds are more than one-half developed. Snow peas can be harvested at any time before they mature and get tough. Deterioration occurs rapidly at high temperatures. Wash and chill immediately.

Peas, Summer. Summer peas will be ready to harvest about 55 days after sowing the seeds. The young, immature pods can be eaten like green beans. For dry beans, harvest the pods when they are well filled and have changed to a light straw, silver, or purple color (depending on the cultivar). Ideally, shell and use the peas the day they are harvested. If the pods are going to be held for more than a day, they should be refrigerated until they can be shelled. Shelled peas may be stored in a covered bowl in the refrigerator for several days prior to cooking. For longer storage, freeze peas; the quality is excellent when they are thawed and cooked later.

Pepper. Harvest bell peppers when they are shiny green and the size of a baseball with full, well-formed lobes. Harvest banana and banana-like peppers at any stage. Harvest jalapeños when they are 2 to 2½ inches long. Although many people eat peppers while green, most peppers turn orange or red when mature. Store at 45 to 50 degrees Fahrenheit.

Potato, Irish and New. For Irish potatoes, a good tuber size is 2 to 3 inches in diameter, but individual preference is the rule here. You can harvest new potatoes at any size, but generally do not dig them before the tubers are 1¼ to 1½ inches in diameter. Let potatoes dry several hours

Harvest peppers with scissors, so you don't pull the plant out of the ground.

in the garden after digging them, but do not expose potatoes to sunlight for any length of time. Remove the soil but do not wash the potatoes before storage. Store in a cool, dry place.

Potato, Sweet. Sweet potatoes should be harvested when the vines begin to turn yellow in the fall. Lift the plant with a spading fork to avoid any bruises and broken roots. Remove any soil from the sweet potatoes, but do not wash them. Allow the tubers to dry (cure) in a warm, well-ventilated place for two to three weeks before eating. Store in a cool, dry place.

Pumpkin. Pick pumpkins when the fruit is full size, the rind is firm and glossy, and the bottom of the fruit (the portion touching the soil) is cream to orange colored. Store in a cool, dry area.

Radish. Pull most radishes when they are about 1 inch in diameter. Radishes become "hot" and tough when they're left in the garden soil too long. Wash and chill immediately.

Spinach. Spinach leaves are ready when they're 4 to 6 inches long. Pull out larger, whole plants or harvest older leaves to encourage new growth. Wash the leaves thoroughly and store in the refrigerator.

When harvesting spinach, cut the outer leaves first.

Squash, Summer. Harvest summer squash when it is 4 to 6 inches long for yellow crookneck squash, 6 to 8 inches for yellow straight neck, and 2 to 3 inches in diameter for white scallop. A glossy color indicates tenderness.

Squash, Winter. Harvest winter squash when the fruits are full size. The rind will be firm and glossy and the bottom of the fruit (the portion touching the soil) will be cream to orange colored. A thumbnail pressed into the skin will not leave a mark. A light frost will not damage mature fruit. However, squash, like cucumbers, are susceptible to chilling injury; do not store at cold temperatures for more than two to three days.

Tomato. Harvest tomatoes when they're fully colored but still firm. Harvest red tomatoes for eating fresh. For canning or juicing purposes, pick tomatoes that are fully colored. If fruit cracking at the top is a problem in hot weather, pick them when they are turning pink. These tomatoes will ripen in the shade indoors. Before a frost or the onset of hot weather (depending on the season grown), pick green tomatoes and store in a dark place, individually wrapped in newspaper, where they can ripen. Ripe tomatoes may be stored in the refrigerator briefly. Unripe tomatoes ripen in the dark, not in bright light.

If your tomatoes aren't quite ripe when a frost threatens, harvest them anyway. They will ripen in a dark area.

Turnip. Harvest turnips when the roots are 2 to 3 inches in diameter but before frost. When turnips are grown for their leaves, pick them when they're 4 to 6 inches long. Keep turnip greens chilled until used.

Fruits

If you want the fruit you have grown to arrive on your table at the peak of perfection, use the following suggestions and basic rules on how and when to harvest them.

Avocado. Oddly enough, avocado fruits do not ripen on the tree. Usually, the fruit is picked when it is of maximum size, but the timing of that can change from year to year depending on weather conditions. Harvest one large fruit and bring it indoors (do not refrigerate). If the fruit softens in four to eight days, the remaining fruits are ready, too. If, on the other hand, the fruit gets wrinkly or becomes rotten, those remaining on the tree are not ready either; try the same test in a week or two. That's the great thing about avocados; they don't all have to be picked at the same time.

Banana. The fruit at the top of the "hand" ripen first and the entire hand should be picked at that time. Hang in a cool, dark location, and pick individual bananas as they ripen. Be careful—banana sap will permanently stain clothes.

Blackberry. There are two methods to determine if blackberries are ready for harvest. First, look at the color; the berries should be deep purple or burgundy (almost, but not quite, black) and look plump. The second method is to pick a test blackberry. Grasp a berry between your thumb and finger and then gently twist. If the fruit comes off easily leaving the stalk behind, then it's ripe. Wash the berries and store them in the refrigerator.

Blueberry. Ripe blueberries can retain their freshness for as long as ten days on the bush. Multiple pickings are required to harvest blueberries because they do not ripen uniformly within clusters on the plants. Most

Blueberries will ripen several days apart, so they will require multiple days of harvesting.

of the common cultivars can be picked clean in two to three harvests, spaced seven to ten days apart. Use both hands to harvest by rolling the ripe fruit from a cluster into the palm of the opposite hand (do not squeeze the fruit). After a rain, wait until the bushes have dried before harvesting the berries. Handling fruit when it is wet will lead to a loss of the berries' surface wax, leading to an increase in decay. Gently wash berries and then refrigerate.

Carambola. Gently shake a carambola tree and harvest those that fall. Star fruit that is difficult to remove from a branch is not fully ripe. Star fruit trees can produce three to four crops per year.

Citrus. The best test to determine if a citrus fruit is ripe is to pick a sample fruit and taste. Readiness of fruit can change from year to year depending on a variety of climatic factors.

Fig. Figs must be allowed to ripen fully on the tree before they are picked. They will not ripen once picked. A ripe fig will be slightly soft and starting to bend at the neck. Harvest the fruit gently to avoid bruising. Fresh figs do not keep well and can be stored in the refrigerator only for two to three days.

Grape. Pick muscadine grapes by spreading a cloth beneath the vines and shaking the branches gently. Gather the ripe grapes that fall onto the cloth. Eat the grapes fresh or store unrefrigerated, but in a cool place, for up to one week.

Guava. The fruit of a guava bruises very easily and requires care when they are being picked. They are ready for harvest when they begin to turn soft and have a musky fragrance to them. To maintain quality, it is best to use the fruits soon after harvest. In addition to eating fresh guava, it can be puréed and chilled or frozen.

Be sure figs are completely ripe before harvesting them.

Jaboticaba. When the individual jaboticaba fruits become somewhat soft, select an individual fruit and taste it for sweetness. Fruits on the tree will remain edible for several days. However, jaboticabas, once harvested, ferment quickly at ordinary temperatures. Eat the fruit within hours of harvest or wash and store in the refrigerator.

Jackfruit. Pick jackfruit when the rind is soft, emitting an aromatic scent, and when the leaf nearest the stalk turns yellow. At this stage, the flesh of the fruit is yellow-orange, shiny, and juicy. When you cut the stem of the fruit with a sharp knife, be sure to wear gloves to protect your hands from the spines. When harvesting from tall trees, place the fruit in a sack to prevent it from falling to the ground. Tie a rope to the stalk, snap the fruit from the tree, and slowly lower the bundle to the ground. Harvesting should be done from midmorning to late afternoon to reduce the latex flow. Remove the leftover stem and unwanted water sprouts from the trunk after picking the fruit.

Longan. During late summer, longans are harvested and eaten fresh. The best practical test is to taste the fruit, which should be quite sweet.

It's best to cut the entire fruit stalk when harvesting longan.

Longans are best harvested with the entire fruit stalk, or they should at least retain a short piece of stem. Not only does plucking the fruit during harvest result in skin tears but fruit left on the fruit cluster lasts longer. When stored at room temperature, longans remain in good condition for several days. Because of their firmer rind, longan fruit is less perishable than the lychee. Preliminary tests in Florida indicate that longan fruit can be frozen and will not break down as quickly as the lychee does when it's thawed.

Loquat. Loquats can produce two to three crops of fruit a year depending on their location. When the fruit becomes plump and slightly soft, cut off the individual fruit with a knife or pruning shears for eating. Loquat fruit ripen at different times on the same plant, and it can take several weeks to complete the ripening of the entire plant. Refrigerated loquats can be stored for up to two weeks.

Harvest pears as they start to change to their final color.

Lychee. Unlike many fruits, lychees should remain on the tree to ripen. Fruit left on the tree too long, however, turns darker and loses its sheen. As with longans, it's important to clip the entire fruit stem cluster rather than select individual fruits. The fruit must be allowed to ripen fully on the tree. Lychees can be stored for up to five weeks in the refrigerator. They can also be frozen or dried. Lychees are highly perishable and will begin to deteriorate within three days at room temperature.

Mango. For the best flavor allow mangoes to ripen on the tree. The fruit will change to its characteristic color (depending on the variety) at the top of the fruit near the stem and will be soft to the touch. Mangoes should be removed from the tree with a sharp knife or hand pruners. When the first fruit shows color while it's on the tree, all of the fruit that size or larger may be removed; repeat when the remaining fruit changes colors. Do not store below 50 degrees Fahrenheit.

Papaya. Pick papaya when most of its skin is yellow-green. Papaya can be stored in the fridge for a few days once they're fully ripe.

Passion Fruit. Pick the fruit when they change color and shrivel just slightly, or wait till they fall off the vine. Homegrown fresh passion fruit will

Ripe peaches will easily pull off the branch.

keep for several weeks in the fridge, but fruit will gradually lose its sweetness.

Peach, Nectarine & Plum. Ripe fruit will be slightly soft to the touch and easily removed from the branch. Fruits will ripen at different times on the same tree, and it's important to check every other day to prevent an invasion of opossums and raccoons. Ripe peaches, nectarines, and plums can be stored in the refrigerator for up to two weeks.

Pear. When the fruit begins to change to its characteristic color (depending on the variety) a pear is ready to pick. Pears ripen well off the tree, and by harvesting at different times over several weeks the fruit can be enjoyed for up to one month. Pears can be refrigerated, but to slow the ripening process remove any apples from the same storage drawer. (Apples release ethylene gas, which promotes fruit ripening.)

Pecan. When mature nuts begin falling from a pecan tree in the autumn, that's the sign that the others in the tree are ready to be harvested, too. Gather the nuts by spreading a cloth beneath the tree and shaking the branches gently. Store the collected nuts loosely in cloth sacks in a cool, dry place after harvest. As the pecans cure, their flavor and quality will improve over time.

Persimmon. Persimmons are harvested when their color has fully developed (color varies depending on the variety) and they're somewhat soft to the touch. The fruit is removed from the tree by clipping or breaking the stems, leaving the lobes attached to the top of the fruit. Persimmons must be handled carefully to avoid damage. Rough handling causes bruising and skin discoloration.

Pineapple. Because pineapples ripen from the bottom, it's important to pick the fruit at the first signs of a color change. If you wait one more day, the raccoons and opossums will beat you to it. Pineapples ripen well at room temperatures so be sure to pick them early.

Strawberry. Strawberries should be picked when the berry is fully red (with no white spots) or with slightly green "shoulders." Diseased or damaged fruit should be removed at the same time usable berries are harvested to prevent further disease infestation.

Strawberries won't ripen once picked, so be sure to pick only those that are fully red.

CHAPTER 8

PESTS: BUGS, DISEASES & WEEDS

No discussion of gardening in Florida would be complete without talking about pests. Insects will do their best to eat vegetables down to a nub, diseases are always lurking around the corner, and weeds will do their best to choke out your fruit trees or vegetables and absorb every last bit of fertilizer you systematically applied last week. That's the bad news. The good news is that all of these things are manageable. Gardeners in North Florida have it a little easier than those in Central and South Florida. North Florida often gets cold temperatures down into the teens, and such weather will severely diminish the insect populations in the following growing season. Cold weather is a two-edged sword, however. As much as Central and South Florida gardeners would like fewer bugs and diseases, cold weather will freeze to the ground or even kill many tropical and subtropical plants, especially fruit trees. Sometimes we have to take the good with the bad and make the best of it. Living and gardening in Florida still beats pulling the snow boots out of the closet every November.

Squash vine borer

Bugs: Believe Every Word

Everything you have heard about bugs in Florida—living, breathing, biting bugs—is true. For every one you see there are twenty more hiding somewhere, just waiting to chew and suck the life out of the precious seedlings that you babied from seed or just spent your children's college fund to purchase. They are just waiting for you slip up, giving them an invitation to stop by.

Rather than think of ways to kill them, think instead of ways to prevent or deter them. Plants are living things much like people, and they act much the same way. If you don't get enough sleep, don't eat properly, and are under pressure from daily activities, then the chances are if you're exposed to a cold virus or a flu bug you will get it. On the other hand, if you eat properly, get plenty of sleep to help your body defend itself against

---

GROWING TIP

To repel cucumber beetles, squash bugs, and borers around squash, plant a few seeds of nasturtiums at the same time you plant the squash seeds.

---

infections, and relieve the anxiety in your life, there is a good chance that, even though you may be exposed to germs, you won't get a cold or come down with the flu.

Don't get me wrong—there are some plants (such as roses, orchids, and turf grasses) that, despite your best efforts, will suffer from bugs no matter how hard you try to prevent it. For the most part, however, healthy plants will not get bugs. Think about that Ficus tree in your home with its constant state of hosting mealybugs and spider mites. If that tree had good air circulation, proper sunlight (instead of being stuck in the corner), and proper water (instead of water every day or worse, once a month) it would not play the role of a B&B host to mealybugs or spider mites. With the proper growing conditions, it would have the ability to defend itself. Fruit trees and vegetables are the same way; give them well-drained soil, adequate water, good nutrition (regular, small applications of fertilizer), and enough sunlight (don't try to grow fruit trees and veggies in only five hours of full sun) and they will be healthy as can be. Last summer, the eggplant in my garden was covered in mealybugs. It was not the plant's fault. It was mine; there wasn't enough water, I forgot to fertilize the plants regularly, and I didn't pick the mature fruits when I was supposed to. As if that wasn't enough, I didn't weed for several weeks. There might as well have been a flashing "Welcome Mealybugs" sign.

Aphids

Think of it this way: bugs are not the problem, but rather a symptom of something that's gone wrong. Let's face it; given the arsenal of chemicals found in any garden center or home improvement store, bugs are easy to kill. But until the reasons why a plant is stressed are alleviated (water, sunlight, nutrition, and so forth), the bugs will continue to come back. Plants will tell you when they need help; just correct the problem and the bugs won't get a foothold. And who wants to blast their food with an arsenal of chemicals anyway?

A collar made of a cardboard paper towel roll cut into three lengths will frustrate cutworms. Cut the collar down the side and push it down into the ground 1 inch deep.

Now, there are some insects that will attack plants despite your best efforts. Take the army-worm, for instance. They are about 1½ inches long when they're mature, and they hide in the soil during the day. At night, they crawl out and mow down newly emerged vegetable seedlings. It's as if a miniature Paul Bunyan visited during the night. In this case you can't kill them but you can prevent them from doing damage. In anticipation of their arrival, place a paper towel or toilet paper roll around each tender stem and push it into the soil to prevent the caterpillar from reaching the plant.

The best thing to do is to get started on the right foot. At the garden center, select healthy plants free of bugs. Keep the garden free of weeds; weeds can act as incubators for bugs waiting for your plants to show signs of stress. Select plants that are genetically resistant to pests. Tomatoes, for instance, that have the letters "VFN" after their name on the plant label will be stronger than those without this designation. The letters indicate that the specific variety has been bred to be resistant to certain pests (in this case, Verticillium wilt, Fusarium wilt, and nematodes). Finally, time the planting to its proper season. Vegetables placed out too soon in spring may be stressed by too much cold and could succumb to insect pressures soon after.

Biological Controls

If we're given a choice, our natural tendency is not to use chemicals. After all, one of the reasons we grow our own food is to know that they haven't been sprayed and they are completely safe to eat. That's where biological controls—the use of living organisms to combat pests—come into play.

First, let me stress there are "good" bugs and "bad" bugs. (Maybe we should call the good ones something other than "bugs.") The good

Ladybugs will attack and eat aphids, which is good for your garden.

bugs can be killed by the same chemicals that are used to kill the bad bugs. When plants are stress free, the good bugs will stop by periodically to eat whatever bad bugs are around. Once the buffet is over, they move on. If the use of chemicals is stopped, then the good guys can move in and out without danger. Note: even "organic" sprays such as rotenone, *B.t.*, and pyrethrins kill good bugs, and they should only be used when absolutely necessary.

If you want the good bugs to stick around, you need to make your garden appealing to them. Many beneficial insects are attracted to plants other than vegetables. Including nectar plants in the vegetable garden means beneficial insects will stay around longer. (See the table of beneficial nectar plants on page 233.)

Insects can get diseases, too, and one in particular is called *B.t.*.; it is perfectly safe for humans but deadly to any caterpillar that ultimately turns into a butterfly or moth. Note I said *any* caterpillar. After a caterpillar eats any part of the plant that has been sprayed with *B.t.*, it dies from a bacterial infection. In addition to being nontoxic to people, *B.t.* is not toxic to animals and can be used safely around pets. Just beware that *B.t.* is nondiscriminatory and will kill *all* caterpillars that eat it. Be careful when you use *B.t.* in your yard and garden. If you spray it specifically on a plant that needs it, you will probably not cause harm to butterflies found elsewhere in the yard.

Plants Fighting Plants: Pesticides Derived From Plants

There are many useful insecticides that are derived from plants themselves. Pyrethrins (not be confused with synthetic pyrethroids) are derived from the flowers and seed heads of the pyrethrum daisy. Pyrethrin insecticides work by direct contact with an insect, so it is essential that the chemicals have direct contact with the pest. Apply pyrethrins when the temperatures

Try to control the potato beetle with natural insecticides such as Neem.

are at the lowest of the day, and spray at two-hour intervals. Once the spray has been applied wait two hours (to give the insect time to come out of hiding) and spray again for the best control.

Rotenone is another good natural-control material, though it is tougher to find on the shelves. It is derived from the root of a tree (*Lonchocarpus*) found in South America. It is a broad-spectrum, slow-acting material that paralyzes insects. It works very well on the flea beetle, potato beetle, aphid, cucumber beetle, spider mite, whitefly, and many chewing insects.

Of all the insecticides derived from plants, Neem is the newest member in the arsenal. This broad-spectrum insecticide comes from the seeds of the Neem tree, which is native to India. Depending on the insect, Neem can act as a repellent, a growth inhibitor, or it can even paralyze some bugs. It controls a wide range of insects, including, but not limited to, the Colorado potato beetle, aphid, flea beetle, whitefly, two-spotted spider mite, striped cucumber beetle, and even some nematodes.

Spinosad is a relatively new insect killer that was discovered from soil in an abandoned rum distillery in 1982. Spinosad can be used on vegetables and fruit trees to control caterpillars, thrips, leaf miners, borers, fruit flies, spider mites, aphids, and more. Spinosad is relatively fast acting (one to two days) and will not persist in the environment. It is classified as an organic substance by the USDA National Organic Standards Board. Spinosad loses its toxicity after 8 to 24 hours and so it may be necessary to reapply a few days later. It is toxic to bees when wet, but relatively safe for them once it dries. Therefore, it should be used when pollinators are not actively foraging.

Chemical Controls

Despite our best efforts, there may come a time when biological and manual pest controls don't work. Let's face it, given that we live in Florida Bug Central, sometimes the bugs invade in such force that we have to use the method of last resort—chemical controls. When that happens we must select chemicals that don't harm insects other than those we are trying to control. Also, we must only use those that won't have a long-lasting effect, won't build up in the environment, and will stay out of the food chain.

One chemical control is horticultural oils; they work by covering an insect pest with a fine film of highly refined oil, which suffocates it. Oils have to be used carefully in Florida; generally they are used only when the daytime temperatures are below 85 degrees Fahrenheit. Otherwise, the oils cover up the breathing apparatus on the undersides of leaves and the leaves can suffocate, causing leaf burn or total leaf drop. Horticultural oils are generally used in winter, just before the new growth begins to emerge on trees and shrubs. When applied properly and in adequate volume, horticultural oils flow into every nook and cranny of the bark where eggs of insects and spider mites overwinter. Volck oil is an example of highly refined horticultural oil.

If you must spray chemicals, use a sprayer that will target just the problem area.

Insecticidal soaps work very well to control a wide range of insects. Both commercial forms of horticultural soaps and concoctions made from Ivory soap are equally toxic to pests. Both utilize the salts of fatty acids to interfere with an insect's growth cycle or to paralyze them on contact. Beetles are less susceptible to insecticidal soaps, meaning they can be used when ladybugs are present (although the soap is lethal to ladybug larvae). Be careful using these around beans, Chinese cabbage, young peas, and cucumbers; these vegetables can be harmed by insecticidal soaps.

Most chemicals need to be applied using some sort of equipment. If your garden isn't too large, use premixed chemicals that come in a one-quart spray bottle. Dusts such as Dipel or rotenone often come in shaker cans and additional tools aren't needed. It's when you need to spray to the top of a fruit tree or spray many plants that some sort of equipment is needed. The most common is a hose end sprayer. The best type is the kind to which a chemical is added to the spray bottle beneath the hose connection. With this type, the dial at the top allows you to spray the chemical at the recommended dilution rate on the label. Here's how to do it: Pour the concentrate into the sprayer bottle, set the dial to the proper amount, and spray as directed. These sprayers usually have a fine spray for spraying at close range for foliage and a removable tip that allows you to spray to the top of small trees. The fine tip can also be rotated to let you direct the spray beneath leaf surfaces where bugs often hide. Leftover concentrate can be put

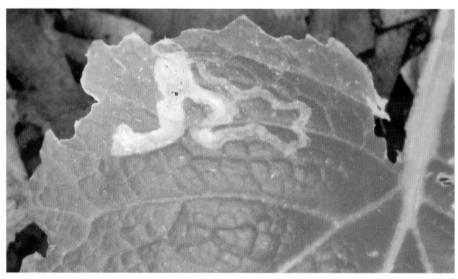

Leaf miners are worms of tiny flies that leave white lines in the leaves as they eat leaf tissue between the upper and lower leaf surface. Chemical control is not available. However, leaf miners rarely have a negative impact on the overall quality or quantity of the fruit produced. If the white lines are bothersome, the infested leaves can be cut off and thrown away (and not in the compost pile).

GROWING TIP

To deter aphids on squash (which can lead to mosaic on the leaves), place aluminum foil over the mulch underneath the leaves. The aphids don't like the shiny reflection and will go elsewhere to eat.

---

back into the chemical bottle. Hose end sprayers are used when spraying large areas. One primary disadvantage of hose end sprayers is that some of the chemical may drift onto other plants simply due to the sheer volume of water being applied.

If you need more specific application of a chemical, a pump sprayer may be the best method. The inexpensive one-quart sprayer works well if you only have a few plants. But if you have more plants, then larger sized sprayers come with 1- to 3-gallon-sized steel or plastic bottles with a pump handle at the top and a spray wand. Here's how it works: Water is added to the bottle, and the chemical is added to the water. The pump handle, which screws into the top of the bottle, is pumped up and down to create pressure. The spray wand handle has a trigger, and when the trigger is pulled the chemical is dispersed. The spray wand tip can be adjusted to provide a fine or coarse spray depending on your objective. Fine sprays use less chemical but the chemical also has the tendency to drift. A coarse spray uses more chemical mix but because the droplets are larger, they tend to stay where you want them to without drifting. Try to buy one with a plastic bottle rather than a steel bottle; no matter how carefully you rinse, eventually the steel bottle will rust. There is nothing more aggravating than trying to remove rust particles from a sprayer tip when you are trying to work.

Other Controls

When our children were little we would give them a nickel for every tomato hornworm they could find. (Some met their demise under the wheels of the Big Wheel.) Handpicking insects from plants is the easiest, and perhaps the most therapeutic, method to rid the garden of insect pests. When webworms make their nests in fruit trees, simply saw the tip of the branch off with the "tent" and throw it in the trash. Slugs are another satisfying victim. Slugs eat virtually everything, but they can be trapped by placing a 1 × 6 board on the ground of a slug-infested zone and leaving it overnight. Slugs come out only at night, and before daytime comes around they will hide under the board. They can then be removed from underneath the board and thrown away. (Keep reading for more about slugs.)

When a plant produces new growth, the tender shoots are prime targets for the piercing mouthparts of aphids. Rather than spraying some sort of chemical, a sturdy stream of water is the best solution. The aphids will fall to ground and not return. Likewise, a hard stream of water applied to the undersides of leaves infested with spider mites in three- or four-day intervals will do a good job, too.

A variety of barriers will lessen if not eliminate pests. A synthetic row cover will keep birds away from vegetables and berries. Fine netting placed over vining berries and fruit-laden trees will protect the fruit from harm. A collar made from a paper towel roll and slipped over a young seedling will prevent cutworm damage. Dusts that dehydrate harmful insects will protect plants, too. Although somewhat limiting around vegetables because it disappears after irrigation or rain, diatomaceous earth added to a little liquid soap and spread around the trunk of a fruit tree will discourage pests from climbing the tree trunk.

In addition to insects, slugs are tough and sneaky pests that eat both leaves and fruit. There are a number of chemicals available to kill them, but the best deterrent is a slug trap. Slugs love beer of any kind, and if they happen upon a small container of beer during the night, well, they can't help themselves. Provided the trap is readily accessible (a pot pie tin works well and the tin has to be flush with the soil level) they mosey on in and drown. In the morning, check the trap for dead slugs. It won't take long to rid the garden of the nasty critters. Commercially available traps with covers that prevent the dilution of the beer from irrigation water work very well and may be worth the investment (see www.kinsmancompany.com).

GROWING TIP

If you're not a beer drinker, then dissolve 1 teaspoon of dried yeast in three tablespoons of water and place in the slug trap instead of beer. It will kill the slugs, all the same.

NECTAR PLANTS THAT ATTRACT BENEFICIAL INSECTS

Plant	Beneficial Insect
African Blue Basil	Honeybees
Agastache	Honeybees
Aster	Honeybees, green bees
Catnip	Honeybees, parasitic wasps
Cilantro	Honeybees
Cosmos	Honeybees
Dill	Aphid predators
Fennel	Hover flies
Goldenrod	Honeybees, spiders, aphid predators
Lavender	Honeybees
Marigold	Hover flies
Penta	Honeybees
Rudbeckia	Honeybees, spiders, aphid predators
Sage	Honeybees, lace bugs
Salvia	Dragonflies
Thyme	Honeybees

Salvia will attract dragonflies, which eat insects.

VEGETABLE INSECT PEST CHART

Vegetable	Insect Pest Name	Control Method(s)	Additional Information
Bean	Aphid	Neem, insecticidal soap, malathion	Wash insects off with a strong stream of water.
	Corn ear worm	Carbaryl, spinosad, *B.T.* Neem	
	Mexican bean beetle, bean leaf beetle, flea beetle, cucumber beetle	Carbaryl, Neem	Crops mulched with straw or other organic materials appear to suffer less damage.
	Potato leaf hopper, stink bug	Malathion	
	Spider mite	Neem, malathion, insecticidal soap	Wash mites off the bottoms of leaves with a strong stream of water; keep plants well watered.
	Whitefly	Insecticidal soap	
Beet	Flea beetle, blister beetle	Carbaryl	Time the last spray 14 days before eating if the tops are used; 3 days, if roots are used. Crops mulched with straw or other organic materials appear to suffer less damage.
Broccoli, Brussels sprouts, Cauliflower	Aphid, flea beetle	Malathion, insecticidal soap	
	Cabbage looper, imported cabbageworm	*B.T.* , spinosad, esfenvalerate	
	Harlequin bug	Malathion	
Cabbage	Aphid	Malathion, insecticidal soap, Neem, rotenone, spinosad, *B.T.*	
	Cabbage looper, imported cabbageworm, cutworm	*B.T.* , carbaryl, spinosad, esfenvalerate, lambda-cyhalothrin	Purchase only clean transplants. Control weeds in nearby fields that act as an overwintering site for the imported cabbageworm. After harvesting early-season crops, till crop debris into the soil to destroy larvae and pupae that could lead to higher populations on later crops.
	Flea beetle, blister beetle	Carbaryl, malathion, rotenone, spinosad, Neem, capsaicin	Crops mulched with straw or other organic materials appear to suffer less damage.
	Harlequin bug	Malathion, lambda-cyhalothrin	

B.T. = Bacillus thuringiensis

VEGETABLE INSECT PEST CHART

Vegetable	Insect Pest Name	Control Methods	Additional Information
Cantaloupe	Aphid, thrips	Malathion, insecticidal soap	
	Cucumber beetle (striped and spotted), squash bug, squash vine borer	Esfenvalerate	Reflective mulches may help to repel aphids while also providing horticultural benefits. Use varieties that are less attractive to beetles or less susceptible to bacterial wilt. Crop rotation and sanitation are important. Avoid leaving cucurbit crop debris available for overwintering sites.
	Spider mites	Neem, insecticidal soap	
Carrot	Armyworm, leafminer, leafhopper	*B.T.*, carbaryl, cyfluthrin	Bt will not control leafhoppers.
Collards	Aphid, flea beetle	Malathion, insecticidal soap	
	Cabbage looper, imported cabbageworm, cutworm	*B.T.*, spinosad	
	Harlequin bug	Malathion	
Corn, sweet	Aphid	Insecticidal soap	Avoid rotenone, pyrethrum, or other broad-spectrum insecticides in corn. If an aphid outbreak occurs, insecticidal soaps can be used.
	Corn earworm, flea beetle	Esfenvalerate	
	Corn earworm, European corn borer, fall armyworm	*B.T.*, cyfluthrin, esfenvalerate, lambda-cyhalothrin, permethrin, spinosad	Control weeds in nearby fields that act as an overwintering site for the imported cabbageworm. After harvesting early-season crops, till crop debris into the soil to destroy larvae and pupae that could lead to higher populations on later crops.
Cucumber	Cucumber beetle (striped and spotted), squash bug	Esfenvalerate	Reflective mulches may help to repel insects while also providing horticultural benefits. Use varieties that are less attractive to beetles or less susceptible to bacterial wilt. Crop rotation and sanitation are important. Avoid leaving cucurbit crop debris available for overwintering sites.
	Spider mites	Insecticidal soap	
	Whitefly	Insecticidal soap	

B.T. = Bacillus thuringiensis

VEGETABLE INSECT PEST CHART

Vegetable	Insect Pest Name	Control Method(s)	Additional Information
Eggplant	Aphid	Malathion, insecticidal soap	
	Colorado potato beetle, hornworm, corn earworm	*B.T.* , carbaryl, spinosad, Neem	Crop rotation out of susceptible crops is the first line of defense. Mulch crops with straw or hay before adults arrive.
	Flea beetle, blister beetle	Carbaryl, malathion	
	Lace bug, spider mite, white fly	Malathion, insecticidal soap	
Endive	Aphid	Malathion, insecticidal soap	
	Cabbage looper, corn earworm	*B.T.* , spinosad	Purchase only clean transplants. Control weeds in nearby fields that act as an overwintering site for the imported cabbageworm. After harvesting early-season crops, till crop debris into the soil to destroy larvae and pupae that could lead to higher populations on later crops.
Garlic	Onion maggot		Spread liberal amounts of wood ash in furrows prior to planting.
	Onion thrips		Keep areas surrounding garden free of weeds. Release lady beetles.
Lettuce	Aphid	Malathion, insecticidal soap	
	Cabbage looper, corn earworm	*B.T.* , spinosad	Purchase only clean transplants. Control weeds in nearby fields that act as an overwintering site for the imported cabbageworm. After harvesting early-season crops, till crop debris into the soil to destroy larvae and pupae that could lead to higher populations on later crops.
	Leafhopper	Malathion	
Mustard Greens	Aphid, flea beetle	Malathion, insecticidal soap	
	Cabbage looper, imported cabbageworm	*B.T.* , spinosad	Purchase only clean transplants. Control weeds in nearby fields that act as an overwintering site for the imported cabbageworm. After harvesting early-season crops, till crop debris into the soil to destroy larvae and pupae that could lead to higher populations on later crops.

B.T. = Bacillus thuringiensis

VEGETABLE INSECT PEST CHART

Vegetable	Insect Pest Name	Control Method(s)	Additional Information
Okra	Corn earworm, European corn borer, flea beetle, stink bug	Carbaryl	Purchase only clean transplants. Control weeds in nearby fields that act as an overwintering site for the imported cabbageworm. After harvesting early-season crops, till crop debris into the soil to destroy larvae and pupae that could lead to higher populations on later crops.
	Stink bug	Malathion	
Onion	Onion maggot		Spread liberal amounts of wood ash in furrows prior to planting.
	Onion thrips		Keep areas surrounding garden free of weeds. Release lady beetles.
Peas	Aphid	Insecticidal soap	
	Cowpea curculio	Endosulfan	
Pepper	Aphid	Esfenvalerate, malathion, insecticidal soap	
	European corn borer, flea beetle, tomato fruitworm, hornworm, stink bug	Carbaryl, cyfluthrin, esfenvalerate, permethrin, spinosad	Purchase only clean transplants. Control weeds in nearby fields that act as an overwintering site for the imported cabbageworm. After harvesting early-season crops, till crop debris into the soil to destroy larvae and pupae that could lead to higher populations on later crops. Crops mulched with straw or other organic materials appear to suffer less damage.
Potato	Aphid	Malathion	
	European corn borer	Carbaryl, esfenvalerate	Purchase only certified seed potatoes. Control weeds in nearby fields that act as an overwintering site for the imported cabbageworm. After harvesting early-season crops, till crop debris into the soil to destroy larvae and pupae that could lead to higher populations on later crops.
	Potato leafhopper, potato flea beetle, Colorado potato beetle, blister beetle, stink bug	Carbaryl, Neem	Crops mulched with straw or other organic materials appear to suffer less damage. Crop rotation out of susceptible crops is the first line of defense. Mulch crops with straw or hay before adults arrive.
	Potato tuberworm	*B.T.*, carbaryl, esfenvalerate	

B.T. = Bacillus thuringiensis

VEGETABLE INSECT PEST CHART

Vegetable	Insect Pest Name	Control Method(s)	Additional Information
Pumpkin	Aphid	Insecticidal soap	
	Cucumber beetle (striped and spotted), flea beetle, leafhopper	Insecticidal soap, Esfenvalerate	Crops mulched with straw or other organic materials appear to suffer less damage. Reflective mulches may help to repel aphids while also providing horticultural benefits.
	Squash bug	Malathion	
	Squash vine borer		Winter squash and zucchini are particularly susceptible. Butternut squash (*C. moschata*) is resistant. Soon after crop harvest, plow the vine debris deeply to bury over larvae. Rotate fields.
Radish	Flea beetle, imported cabbageworm	Cyfluthrin	
Rutabaga	Aphid, flea beetle	Insecticidal soap	Crops mulched with straw or other organic materials appear to suffer less damage.
	Cabbage looper, imported cabbageworm	*B.T.* , spinosad	
	Harlequin bug	Malathion	
Spinach	Aphids, leafminer	Insecticidal soap	
	Corn earworm, loopers	*B.T.* , spinosad	
Squash, Summer	Aphid	Insecticidal soap	
	Cucumber beetle (striped and spotted), flea beetle, leafhopper	Insecticidal soap, Esfenvalerate	Crops mulched with straw or other organic materials appear to suffer less damage. Reflective mulches may help to repel aphids while also providing horticultural benefits.
	Squash bug	Malathion	
	Squash vine borer		Winter squash, pumpkin, and zucchini are particularly susceptible. Butternut squash (*C. moschata*) is resistant. Soon after crop harvest, plow the vine debris deeply to bury over larvae. Rotate fields.
Tomato	Aphid	Malathion, insecticidal soap	
	Cutworm	Esfenvalerate	
	Flea beetle, Colorado potato beetle	Carbaryl, spinosad	Crops mulched with straw or other organic materials appear to suffer less damage. Crop rotation out of susceptible crops is the first line of defense. Mulch crops with straw or hay before adults arrive.

B.T. = Bacillus thuringiensis

VEGETABLE INSECT PEST CHART

Vegetable	Insect Pest Name	Control Method(s)	Additional Information
Tomato (cont.)	Spider mites	Insecticidal soap, malathion	
	Stink bug	Cyfluthrin, lambda-cyhalothrin, malathion, permethrin	
	Thrips	Insecticidal soap	
	Tomato fruitworm, cabbage looper, tobacco hornworm	*B.T.* , carbaryl, cyfluthrin, esfenvalerate, lambda-cyhalothrin, permethrin, spinosad	Purchase only clean transplants. Control weeds in nearby fields that act as an overwintering site for the imported cabbageworm. After harvesting early-season crops, till crop debris into the soil to destroy larvae and pupae that could lead to higher populations on later crops.
	Whitefly	Malathion, pyrethrum, insecticidal soap	
Turnip	Aphid, flea beetle	Insecticidal soap	Crops mulched with straw or other organic materials appear to suffer less damage.
	Cabbage looper, imported cabbageworm	*B.T.* , spinosad	
	Harlequin bug	Malathion	
Watermelon	Aphid	Insecticidal soap	Reflective mulches may help to repel aphids while also providing horticultural benefits.
	Cucumber beetle (spotted and striped)	Esfenvalerate, malathion, insecticidal soap	Reflective mulches may help to repel aphids while also providing horticultural benefits. Use varieties that are less attractive to beetles or less susceptible to bacterial wilt. Crop rotation and sanitation are important. Avoid leaving cucurbit crop debris available for overwintering sites.
	Spider mites	Insecticidal soap	
	Thrips	Carbaryl, malathion, insecticidal soap	

B.T. = Bacillus thuringiensis

Disclaimer: Mention or exclusion of any product is not intended to discriminate for or against any products. No endorsement is intended for the products mentioned, nor is criticism meant for products not mentioned. Please read labels before purchasing and then read them before using to ensure that target sites are properly listed.

FRUIT INSECT PEST CHART

Fruit	Insect Pest Name	Control Method(s)
Avocado	Lace bug	Citrus oil, insecticidal soap
Banana	Nematodes	Maintain a high level of organic matter in the soil.
Blackberry	Aphids	Carbaryl, pyrethrin, rotenone
	Crown borers	Carbaryl
	Flea beetles	Rotenone
	Leaf hoppers	Malathion, pyrethrin
	Leafminers	Rotenone
	Leaf rollers	Carbaryl
	Mites	Malathion, pyrethrin
	Red spider mites	Insecticidal soap
	Thrips	Pyrethrin, malathion
Blueberry	Ants	Spinosad
	Blueberry maggot	Carbaryl, malathion
	Oblique-banded leaf roller	*B.t.*
Carambola	Aphids	Horticultural oil
	Mites	Horticultural oil, spinosad
	Scale	Horticultural oil
Citrus	Flower thrips	Spinosad
	Orangedog	*B.t.*, carbaryl
	Plant bugs	Malathion
	Rust mites, broad mites	Sulfur
	Scale	Horticultural oil
Fig	None of note	
Grape	Aphids	Neem oil
	Grape leaf folder	*B.t.*, carbaryl
	Grape leaf roller	*B.t.*, carbaryl, pyrethrin
	Grape leaf skeletonizer	*B.t.*, carbaryl
	Leaf hopper	Malathion
	Mites	Neem oil, spinosad
	Red spider mite	Sulfur
	Spider mites	Neem oil
Jaboticaba	None of note	
Jackfruit	Borers	Remove dead branches, where they lay eggs.
	Mealy bugs	Neem oil, horticultural oil
	Scale	Horticultural oil

B.T. = Bacillus thuringiensis

FRUIT INSECT PEST CHART

Fruit	Insect Pest Name	Control Method(s)
Longan	Scale	Insecticidal soap, horticultural oil
	Webworms	*B.t.*
Loquat	Caterpillars	*B.t.*
Lychee	Scale	Insecticidal soap, horticultural oil
	Webworms	*B.t.*
Mango	Caterpillars	*B.t.*
	Thrips	Imidacloprid
	Whitefly	Imidacloprid
Nectarine	Mealy bugs	Horticultural oil, insecticidal soap
Papaya	Caterpillars	*B.t.*
	Scale	Malathion, horticultural oil
	Thrips	Malathion, horticultural oil
Passion Fruit	None of note	
Peach	Scale	Horticultural oil, insecticidal soap
Pear	Scale	Insecticidal soap, horticultural oil, Neem oil
Pecan	Aphids	Insecticidal soap, horticultural oil
	Casebearers	Carbaryl, imidacloprid
	Hickory leaf stem gall	Carbaryl, imidacloprid
	Pecan weevil	Carbaryl, imidacloprid
Persimmon	Aphids	Insecticidal soap
	Caterpillars	*B.t.*
	Mites	Rotenone, pyrethrin, spinosad
	Scale	Insecticidal soap
	Thrips	Rotenone, pyrethrin
Pineapple	None of note	
Plum	Borers	Carbaryl, lorsban endosulfan, thiodan
	Caterpillars	*B.t.*
	Plum curculio	Imidan
	Scale	Imidan, horticultural oil, insecticidal soap
Pomegranate	None of note	
Strawberry	Two-spotted spider mite	Spinosad
	Caterpillars	*B.t.*

B.T. = Bacillus thuringiensis

Disclaimer: Mention or exclusion of any product is not intended to discriminate for or against any products. No endorsement is intended for the products mentioned, nor is criticism meant for products not mentioned. Please read labels before purchasing and then read them before using to ensure that target sites are properly listed.

Diseases

Most plant diseases, like animal diseases, are caused by microscopic bacteria and viruses. They are everywhere, and the goal of the gardener is prevent their spread and keep them from becoming more active. Diseases are spread a number of ways. Some are transmitted by insects carrying disease organisms around on their bodies or by gardeners handling plants and working in the garden when the plants are wet. Some diseases attack the stem, harming a plant's vascular system. Others affect the leaves and even the roots.

Have you heard this expression: "An ounce of prevention is worth a pound of cure?" I have rarely seen a healthy vegetable or fruit tree attacked by disease. Plants, like people, have the ability to fend off diseases if they are supplied adequate sunshine, water, and nutrition. There are a number of things you can do to prevent diseases in vegetables and fruit trees, such as:

- Do a little research to find those selections of vegetables and fruit trees that have a proven track record of disease resistance in your area.
- Control the insect population. Insects carry diseases around with them and infest plants as they travel.
- Good air circulation can help prevent many diseases. Planting plants close together will certainly maximize the yield but at the expense of the plant's health.
- Fruit trees and vegetables need at least 8 hours of full sun. Anything less and a plant will be stressed, making it a prime candidate for disease infestation.
- Make certain the soil is well drained. If the spot where you planted the garden is soggy, move the garden to a different spot or create a raised bed to provide good drainage.
- Touch the plants as little as possible. It's not just the bugs that carry diseases with them; gardeners carry plant diseases around with them, too. The more you handle the plants, the greater the chances that you will infect them with something. Never, ever till, harvest, or pull weeds when plants are wet. Your hands and clothing may become infected, and wet plants are more susceptible to diseases than dry plants.
- Water plants only when they have a chance to dry off quickly. Watering in the late afternoon or at night creates perfect conditions for pathogens to grow.

- Keep plants well fed. The amounts of fertilizer and the timing of the applications are described in the individual plant profiles.
- Crop rotation will help prevent the buildup of disease-causing organisms in the soil. Some disease-causing organisms affect one vegetable or group of vegetables, but they may not affect another. Even several vegetables of the same family, such as squash, cucumber, and cantaloupe, may be affected by the same disease. Therefore, it is not a good practice to grow plants in the same family in the same place in the garden year after year. The table shown here gives crop groupings for rotation to control soil-borne diseases.

Group 1	Group 2	Group 3
Cantaloupe	Brussels sprouts	Beet
Cucumber	Collards	Carrot
Honeydew melon	Cabbage	Garlic
Pumpkin	Cauliflower	Onion
Squash	Lettuce	Shallot
Watermelon	Mustard	Sweet potato
	Radish	
	Rutabaga	
	Spinach	
	Swiss chard	
	Turnip	

Group 4	Group 5	Group 6
Sweet corn	Bean	Eggplant
	Cowpea	Okra
	Pea	Pepper
		Tomato

VEGETABLE DISEASE CHART

Vegetable	Disease Name	Description	Control(s)	Additional Information
Bean, Snap	Anthracnose	Brown spots on leaves with pink ooze	*B.s.*, Daconil, copper sulfate	Destroy infected plants. Do not plant beans in the same location for three years. Spray at weekly intervals, and do not work in garden while it's wet.
	Bacterial blight	Water-soaked spots on leaves and pods with red margin	*B.s.*, fixed copper	Same as Anthracnose.
	Gray mold (Botrytis)	Gray, fuzzy mold on leaves and pods	*B.s.*, Daconil	Begin spraying at 25 to 50 percent bloom in wet weather.
	Mosaic virus	Leaves yellow; leaves cupped		Remove diseased plants and replant elsewhere.
	Powdery mildew	White, powdery mold on leaves	*B.s.*, sulfur	Plant in the garden after nighttime temperatures remain above 70°F. Water when plants have a chance to dry off before nighttime.
	Rust	Reddish brown pustules on leaves	*B.s.*, Daconil	Do not work among plants when they are wet.
Beet	Downy mildew	Various leaf spots	*B.s.*, fixed copper	Spray every 7 days.
	Rust	Orange pustules	*B.s.*, sulfur	
Broccoli	*See* Cabbage			
Brussels sprouts	*See* Cabbage			
Cabbage, Rutabaga	Alternaria leaf spot	Target spots in older leaves	Daconil, maneb	Begin spraying when the disease is first seen and continue every 10 days until it's under control.
	Bacterial soft rot	Soft, watery rot occurs, favored by hot, wet conditions; begins in center of broccoli or cabbage head	*B.s.*	Only water the soil (when possible); otherwise, prevent overwatering from overhead irrigation. Remove the central head to encourage side shoots from below.
	Downy mildew	Yellowing on upper leaf surface, downy growth on lower leaf surface	*B.s.*, Daconil, maneb	
Cantaloupe	Alternaria leaf spot	Tan spots on leaves	Daconil, maneb, Mancozeb	Begin spraying when the disease is first seen, and continue at 7- to 10-day intervals until it's under control.
	Anthracnose	Sunken spots on fruit and tan spots on leaves	*B.s.*, Daconil, maneb, mancozeb	Begin spraying when the disease is first seen, and continue at 7- to 10-day intervals until it's under control.

B.s. = Bacillus subtillis

VEGETABLE DISEASE CHART

Vegetable	Disease Name	Description	Control(s)	Additional Information
Cantaloupe (cont.)	Bacterial wilt	Runners suddenly wilt and die	*B.s.*, rotenone	Apply insecticide at regular intervals to control cucumber beetles that spread disease.
	Downy mildew	Yellow, irregular spots on leaves	*B.s.*, Daconil, maneb, mancozeb	Begin spraying when the disease is first seen, and continue at 7- to 10-day intervals until it's under control.
	Powdery mildew	White, powdery mold on leaves	*B.s.*, sulfur	Apply at 10- to 14-day intervals. Do not apply when temperatures exceed 90°F.
Carrot	Alternaria blight	Numerous dark-brown spots on leaves	Daconil	Apply at 7- to 10-day intervals until it's under control.
	Cercospera leaf spot	Numerous black-to-brown spots on leaves	Daconil	
	Southern blight	White mycelial at plant top, eventual death of plant	Fixed copper, maneb	Do not plant carrots in the same location every season.
Cauliflower	*See* Cabbage			
Collards, Kale, Mustard, Turnip	Alternaria leaf spot	Brown target spots on leaves	Fixed copper, maneb	Maintain thinned plant stand. Avoid low-lying or poorly drained soils. Avoid the hot part of the growing season. Use maneb for kale only. Begin spraying when the disease is first noticed, and repeat at 7- to 10-day intervals. Use a spreader-sticker for better fungicide coverage.
	Anthracnose	Small spots with dark-brown margins	*B.s.*, fixed copper, maneb	
	Cercospera leaf spot	Tan spots with yellow halos on leaves	Fixed copper, maneb	
	Downy mildew	Yellow spots on upper surfaces of leaves with white, downy growth on the undersides	*B.s.*, fixed copper, maneb	
Corn, sweet	Blights	Spots on leaves and drying or blighting of leaves	*B.s.*, Daconil, mancozeb	Apply at 7-day intervals when the disease is first seen.
	Maize dwarf mosaic	Alternating light and dark streaks on leaves; plants are stunted		Plant early in the season where Johnson grass is not growing. 'Silver Queen' is tolerant of this disease.
	Rust	Bronze elongated spots	*B.s.*, Daconil, mancozeb	Apply at 7-day intervals when the disease is first seen.
Cucumber	Bacterial wilt	Runners turn brown and entire plant eventually dies.	*B.s.*, rotenone	Apply an insecticide to control the cucumber beetle, which transmits the bacterium.
	Downy mildew	Yellow, irregular spots on leaves	*B.s.*, Daconil, maneb, mancozeb	Apply at 7-day intervals when the disease is first seen.

B.s. = *Bacillus subtillis*

VEGETABLE DISEASE CHART

Vegetable	Disease Name	Description	Control(s)	Additional Information
Cucumber (cont.)	Gummy stem blight	Dark brown spots on leaves, oozing cracks on stems	Daconil, maneb, mancozeb	Apply at 7-day intervals when the disease is first seen.
	Powdery mildew	White powdery mold on upper leaf surfaces	*B.s.*, sulfur	Apply at 7- to 10-day intervals. Do not apply when temperatures are above 90°F.
	Scab	Sunken spots on fruit	*B.s.*, Daconil	Plant resistant varieties. Apply at the first sign of the disease in 7- to 10-day intervals.
Eggplant	Leaf spots and fruit rots	Spots develop on fruits and leaves	*B.s.*, Daconil	Apply at 7- to 10-day intervals when the disease is first seen.
Kale	*See* Collards			
Lettuce, Endive	Bottom rot	Sunken, reddish-brown spots on leaves that are touching the soil		Apply straw to keep leaves off soil. Thin plants to recommended spacing to increase air circulation.
	Fusarium wilt	Seedlings wilt and die; mature plants exhibit tipburn, a yellowing of leaves; infected plants may be stunted		Remove diseased plants. Do not replant lettuce in the same location for at least two years.
	Leaf drop	Soft, watery decay of plant tissue		Avoid excess irrigation.
Mustard	*See* Collards			
Okra	Verticillium wilt	Yellow leaves; inside stem is discolored brown		Rotate crops every year.
Onion, Leek, Garlic	Downy mildew	Pale-green or purple spots on leaves	*B.s.*, Daconil, chlorothalonil, maneb, mancozeb	Apply when the disease first appears, and repeat at 7- to 10-day intervals. Do not apply mancozeb or maneb to exposed bulbs. Do not apply chlorothalonil within 7 days of harvest on dry-bulb onions or within 14 days on green onions, leeks, or shallots. Do not apply chlorothalonil to sweet Spanish onions.
	Leaf blast (Botrytis)	White to tan streaks on leaves; leaves eventually die	*B.s.*, Daconil, maneb, mancozeb	Same as Downy Mildew.
	Purple blotch (Alternaria)	Purple target spots on leaves	Daconil, maneb, mancozeb	Same as Downy Mildew.
Peas, Southern	Cercospera leaf spot	Light- to dark-brown leaf spots on leaves	Daconil	Apply at pre-bloom and at 7-day intervals.
	Mosaic virus	Alternating light- and dark-green areas on leaves		Plant resistant varieties.
	Powdery mildew	White, powdery mold on upper leaf surfaces	Sulfur	Apply at 7- to 10-day intervals when the disease is first seen.

B.s. = Bacillus subtillis

VEGETABLE DISEASE CHART

Vegetable	Disease Name	Description	Control(s)	Additional Information
Peas, Southern (cont.)	Rust	Brown to rust-colored spots on leaves that rub off on fingers		
Pepper	Anthracnose	Sunken spots on ripening fruit	Fixed copper, maneb	Apply at 7- to 10-day intervals when the disease is first seen.
	Bacterial leaf spot	Black, angular spots appear on leaves and fruits; plants drop affected leaves	Fixed copper, maneb	Buy disease-free plants. Fixed copper will prevent spread of the disease.
	Blossom end rot	Tan, sunken areas on the bottoms and sides of fruit		Maintain adequate and consistent soil moisture.
	Cercospera leaf spot	Circular spots with gray centers on leaves	Fixed copper, maneb	Apply at 7- to 10- day intervals when the disease is first seen.
	Phytophthora	Rapid wilt and death of plant in wet areas		Plant in a drier location or plant in raised beds.
	Sunscald	White, sunken areas on fruit		Healthy plants rarely get sunscald. When bacterial blight occurs and the leaves drop as a result, the fruits often get sunscald.
Potato	Ring rot	Brown discoloration of vascular tissue of tuber		Use disease-free seed potatoes and practice crop rotation.
	Scab	Brown, scruffy areas on tuber		Use disease-free seed, and rotate crops.
	Seed piece decay	Seed piece decays after planting	Maneb, mancozeb	Dust seed pieces with potato dust. Plant two to three days later. Allow scabs to dry before planting. Do not use treated seed pieces for food.
	Virus diseases	Curled, discolored leaves; plants may be stunted		Use disease-free seed potatoes and practice crop rotation.
Pumpkin	Downy mildew	Yellow, irregular spots on leaves		Begin spraying when the disease is first seen.
	Gummy stem blight	Cracked, oozing stems and black, circular spots on fruit	Daconil, maneb	Begin spraying when the disease is first seen.
	Michrodochium blight	White streaks on stems		Begin spraying when the disease is first seen.
	Mosaic virus	Discolored green patterns on fruit		Control is difficult. Control aphids that spread disease, use reflective mulches, and control weeds that harbor insects that carry the disease.
	Scab	Sunken or raised spots on fruit		Begin spraying when the disease is first seen. Use higher rates for scab control.

B.s. = *Bacillus subtillis*

VEGETABLE DISEASE CHART

Vegetable	Disease Name	Description	Control(s)	Additional Information
Rutabaga	*See* Cabbage			
Spinach	Downy mildew (blue mold)	Yellow spots on leaf surfaces; gray downy mildew on undersides	*B.s.*, basic copper sulphate	Start fungicide applications after the first sign of the disease and apply at 7- to 10-day intervals.
	White rust	Yellow spots on upper leaf surfaces and white mildew on the undersides	*B.s.*, basic copper sulfate	Start fungicide applications after the first sign of the disease and apply at 7- to 10-day intervals.
Squash	Blossom blight	Blossom rots and sticks to the end of young fruit; the ends of fruit often turn black		Provide good air circulation.
	Downy mildew	Yellow, irregular spots on leaves	*B.s.*, Daconil, maneb, mancozeb	Begin spraying at the first sign of disease. See label directions for spray intervals.
	Mosaic virus	Greening of fruit; leaves mottled and stunted		Difficult to control. Try controlling aphids that spread the disease, and use reflective mulches.
	Powdery mildew	White powdery mold on upper leaf surface	*B.s.*, sulfur, Daconil	Begin spray regimen at the first sign of disease. Do not apply sulfur when temperatures exceed 90°F.
	Scab	Sunken or raised spots on fruits	*B.s.*, Daconil	Begin spraying at the first sign of disease. See label directions for spray intervals.
Sweet Potato	Black rot	Sunken black spots on surface that extends into the flesh of the root		Use certified seed, and practice crop rotation.
	Cork	Small, black, corky spot in the flesh of the potato		Use certified seed.
	Scurf	Brownish-black discoloration on the surface of roots		Use certified seed.
	Soil rot	Circular sunken areas on the root; feeder roots are black		Maintain soil pH of 5.8 to 6.4 or less in infected areas.
	Stem rot	Leaves are yellow; stunted interior of plant is brown		Select disease-free seed.
Tomato	Anthracnose	Circular sunken spots on ripe fruit	*B.s.*, Daconil, maneb, mancozeb	Begin preventative spraying as soon as the plants are established in the garden. Spray at 10- to 14-day intervals.
	Bacterial spot	Small raised spots on fruit; water-soaked spots on foliage	*B.s.*, fixed copper, maneb, mancozeb	
	Blossom end rot	Sunken black area at bottoms of fruit		Maintain consistent, adequate soil moisture.

B.s. = Bacillus subtillis

VEGETABLE DISEASE CHART

Vegetable	Disease Name	Description	Control(s)	Additional Information
Tomato (cont.)	Buckeye fruit rot	Large, circular spots on fruit, especially on the lower clusters		Stake plants to keep fruit off soil.
	Early blight	Brown target spots on leaves	*B.s.*, Daconil, maneb, mancozeb	Begin preventative spraying as soon as the plants are established. Spray at 10- to 14-day intervals.
	Fusarium wilt	Yellowing and wilting of leaves; brown discoloration of inside of stems		Use resistant varieties.
	Gray mold (Botrytis)	Leaves turn brown from the tip back	*B.s.*, Daconil	Begin fungicide applications at the first sign of the disease.
	Late blight	Irregular water-soaked spots on leaves, especially in wet weather	Daconil, maneb, mancozeb	Begin preventative spraying as soon as the plants are established in the garden. Spray at 10- to 14-day intervals.
	Leaf mold	Yellow spots on upper surface; olive-green mold beneath	Daconil	Begin spraying with fungicides at the first sign of the disease.
	Pythium stem rot	Dark water rot of lower stem		Remove diseased plants.
	Septoria leaf spot	Small, circular leaf spots with gray borders	*B.s.*, Daconil, maneb, mancozeb	Begin preventative spraying as soon as the plants are established in the garden. Spray at 10- to 14-day intervals.
	Verticillium wilt	Yellowing of leaves; brown discoloration inside stems		Use resistant varieties and practice crop rotation.
Turnip	*See* Collards			
Watermelon	Alternaria leaf spot	Brown target spots on leaves	Daconil, maneb, mancozeb	Begin spraying at the first sign of the disease. See label for frequency of spray.
	Anthracnose	Brown, irregular spots on leaves; sunken spots on fruit	*B.s.*, Daconil, maneb, mancozeb	Begin spraying at the first sign of the disease. See label for frequency of spray.
	Cercospera leaf spot	Tiny, dark-brown spots	Daconil, maneb, mancozeb	Begin spraying at the first sign of the disease. See label for frequency of spray.
	Downy mildew	Yellow, irregular spots on leaves	*B.s.*, Daconil, maneb, mancozeb	Begin spraying at the first sign of the disease. See label for frequency of spray.
	Fusarium wilt	Yellowing and wilting of leaves; brown discoloration inside vine stems		Grow resistant varieties. Practice crop rotation.
	Gummy stem blight	Irregular spots; cracked stems that ooze	Daconil, maneb, mancozeb	Daconil
	Scab	Small, raised warts on fruit	*B.s.*, Daconil	Begin spraying at the first sign of the disease. See label directions for spray interval.

B.s. = *Bacillus subtillis*

FRUIT DISEASE CHART

Fruit	Disease	Control Method(s)	Additional Information
Avocado	Algal leaf spot	Copper sulfate	If timely applications of fungicides are made to control other common diseases, powdery mildew rarely exceeds threshold levels in the home garden
	Anthracnose		Good anthracnose control depends on good control of Cercospora spot and avoiding cuts and bruises to the fruit
	Cercospora spot	*B.s.*, copper sulfate	Effectively control by timely applications of fungicide
	Powdery mildew	*B.s.*, copper sulfate	If timely applications of fungicides are made to control other common diseases, powdery mildew rarely exceeds threshold levels in the home garden
	Scab	*B.s.*, copper sulfate	One spray should be applied at bud swell; the second during late bloom; and the third three weeks later
Banana	Black sigatoka		If 50 percent of leaf is diseased, remove entire leaf
	Panama disease		'Gros Michel', 'Apple', 'Oro Noco' are susceptible; replace with resistant cultivars 'Goldfinger' (FHIA 01), 'Mona Lisa' (FHIA 02), FHIA 18
Blackberry	Anthracnose	*B.s.*, fixed coppers	Plant certified, disease-free stock; prune old cane stubs after planting; prune old canes as close to the ground as soon after harvest as possible; thin weak canes; eliminate weeds to provide good air movement; avoid overhead irrigation or limit the time plants are wet from irrigation
	Crown gall		Use certified nursery stock; inspect planting stock and do not plant new canes that show signs on canes, crowns, or roots; remove infected plants
	Leaf spot	*B.s.*, fixed copper	Remove old fruiting canes after harvest; control weeds
	Orange rust	*B.s.*	Scout for the disease during summer and quickly remove and destroy infected plants; establish new plantings from a clean source
	Rosette		Use certified nursery stock; plant disease-resistant varieties
Blueberry	Botrytis	*B.s.*	Less serious on rabbiteye varieties; flowers and flower buds should be kept as dry as possible; overhead irrigation should be avoided during bud swell and bloom; keep plants well pruned to improve air circulation
	Mummy berry		Rake the soil or mulch layer beneath the plants as leaf buds swell; pick off and remove infected berries from the patch before harvest; pick up and throw away infected berries that fall to the ground
	Phytothphora root rot	*B.s.*	Lasting control is accomplished by improving drainage
	Stem blight		Prune infected wood; remove flower buds and fruit from young plants; prune mature bushes to thin crop loads; minimize drought

B.s. = Bacillus subtillis

FRUIT DISEASE CHART

Fruit	Disease	Control Method(s)	Additional Information
Carambola			No diseases that require control measures
Citrus	Citrus scab	Copper	Lemons, Murcotts, Mineola tangelos, Temple and Page oranges are susceptible; apply copper sprays 2 to 3 weeks after petal fall, and again 2 to 3 weeks later; install drip irrigation to avoid overhead irrigation that spreads the disease
	Foot rot		Remove mulch from around the base of the tree; remove low-hanging branches to improve air circulation
	Greasy spot		Remove old and diseased leaves beneath tree
	Melanose	Copper	Remove small dead twigs; avoid overhead irrigation
Fig	Rust	*B.s.*, copper	Apply copper in May and June
Grape	Angular leaf spot	*B.s.*, mancozeb	
	Bitter and black rot	Manzate, maneb	Remove old fruits and leaves
	Black rot	Manzate, maneb	
	Powdery mildew	*B.s.*, sulfur	
Jaboticaba			No serious diseases that affect fruit quality
Jackfruit	Anthracnose	*B.s.*, mancozeb	Prune/remove damaged limbs
	Phomopsis fruit rot		Careful handling will prevent this disease
	Phytothphora	*B.s.*	Do not plant in flood-prone sites; control weeds and cover soil with mulch; remove damaged stems
	Pink disease	Mancozeb	Remove damaged stems; encourage good air circulation
	Root rots		Avoid flooding
Longan	Algal spot	*B.s.*, copper	
	Anthracnose	*B.s.*, copper	
	Pink limb blight		Prune exposed wood
	Stem canker		Remove damaged wood
Loquat			No serious diseases
Lychee	Algal spot	Copper	
	Anthracnose	*B.s.*, copper	
	Pink limb blight		Prune exposed wood
	Stem canker		Remove damaged wood
Mango	Anthracnose	*B.s.*, copper sprays	Begin sprays when new growth flushes and continue until flowers open; begin again until fruits form
	Soft nose		Reduce nitrogen fertilizer applications
	Sunscald		Fruits burn in high temperatures; no cures

B.s. = Bacillus subtillis

FRUIT DISEASE CHART

Fruit	Disease	Control Method(s)	Additional Information
Papaya	Anthracnose	*B.s.*, copper	Begin copper applications at fruit set
	Corynespora leaf spot	Copper	No effective controls
	Necrosis		Remove affected plants; isolate papaya from other plants
	Phytothphora	*B.s.*, copper	
	Ring spot		No effective controls
Passion Fruit	Bitter rot	Copper	Pick up and remove infected fruit
	Brown spot		
	Grease spot		Remove diseased leaves beneath vines
	Septoria blotch		
	Sclerotinia	*B.s.*	Pick up and remove infected fruit; cut out infected shoots below the lesion and destroy
Peach, Nectarine, Plum	Bacterial spot	*B.s.*	Not controlled by sprays; use resistant varieties; maintain good fertilizer program
	Brown rot		Prune dead wood; remove brown rot and mummies
	Rust	*B.s.*, copper	Not usually a problem
	Scab	*B.s.*, sulfur	Spray 4 to 6 weeks after full bloom
Pear	Black rot	Pyraclostrobin	Remove damaged/dead limbs
	Bot rot/white rot	Pyraclostrobin	Fruit should be picked up and removed from the orchard; cut out infected shoots below the lesion and destroy
	Cercospora spot		Remove infected fallen leaves
	Fireblight	*B.s.*, copper	Remove cankers during dormant period; prune active sores 8 inches below damage; disinfect pruners between cuts
	Flyspeck	Manzate, mancozeb	
Pecan	Scab	*B.s.*	Pecans have several diseases but these rarely affect fruit production in home gardens; once trees are more than 15 ft. tall, chemical control is impractical; plant resistant varieties
Persimmon	Alternaria, anthracnose	*B.s.*, copper	Apply fungicide cover spray during full bloom and again in 3 to 4 weeks
	Cercospora spot	Copper	Apply a fungicide cover spray during full bloom and again in 3 to 4 weeks
Pineapple	Phytothphora, pythium	*B.s.*	Avoid overly wet soil; provide adequate drainage
Pomegranate	Leaf blotch	Copper	

B.s. = *Bacillus subtillis*

FRUIT DISEASE CHART

Fruit	Disease	Control Method(s)	Additional Information
Strawberry	Alternaria rot		Remove overripe berries
	Angular leaf spot	Copper	Plant certified, disease-free plants
	Anthracnose	*B.s.*	Use pathogen-free plants; varieties 'Carmine' and 'Sweet Charlie' are resistant; 'Strawberry Festival', 'Camarosa', and 'Treasure' are susceptible
	Botrytis (gray mold)	*B.s.*	Remove infected fruit and plant debris
	Leaf scorch		Reduce prolonged overhead irrigation
	Leaf spot	*B.s.*	Plant disease-free plants
	Phytothphora crown rot	*B.s.*	Plant disease-free plants
	Powdery mildew	*B.s.*	Use disease-resistant varieties; 'Strawberry Festival', 'Camarosa', and 'Winter Dawn' are quite susceptible

B.s. = Bacillus subtillis

INDEX

MEET ROBERT BOWDEN

 Robert Bowden is the Executive Director of the renowned Leu Gardens in Orlando, Florida. He served in the same capacity at the Atlanta Botanical Gardens and as Director of Horticulture at the Missouri Botanical Garden. A prolific media presence, Bowden's photographs and fun-filled essays have appeared in *The New York Times* and in such magazines as *Garden Design*, *Traditional Home*, and *Southern Accents*. Bowden appears regularly on a variety of nationally syndicated television shows including Discovery Channel's *Home Matters*, *Rebecca's Garden*, HGTV's *Way To Grow!*, and *Victory Garden*. Robert travels extensively in the United States and the Caribbean talking about vegetables, perennials, tropical and sub-tropical plants, flowering vines, trees, and shrubs.

When he's not on the road, speaking to groups, taking photographs, writing books, or serving as the "answer man" for all kinds of gardening, Robert can be found in his own garden in Longwood, Florida.